HEADING

SOUTH,

LOOKING

NORTH

HEADING SOUTH, LOOKING NORTH

A BILINGUAL JOURNEY

Ariel Dorfman

Hodder & Stoughton

Grateful acknowledgement is made for permission to reprint the following: Excerpts from "Mr. Tambourine Man" with permission of Special Rider Music. Copyright © 1964, 1965 by Warner Bros. Inc. Renewed 1992 by Special Rider Music. Written by Bob Dylan.

First published by Farrar, Straus and Giroux in 1998
First published in the UK in 1998 by Hodder and Stoughton
A division of Hodder Headline PLC

10 9 8 7 6 5 4 3 2 1

A CIP catalogue record for this title is available from the British Library.

ISBN 0 340 71300 3

Printed and bound in Great Britain by Mackays of Chatham PLC, Chatham, Kent

Hodder and Stoughton
A division of Hodder Headline PLC
338 Euston Road
London NW1 3BH

Angélica: this book is for you.

It's my story, the story of my many exiles and my three countries and the two languages that raged for my throat during years and that now share me, the English and the Spanish that I have finally come to love almost as much as I love you.

Thank you for being there, close by, while I lived this story, while I forced myself to write and rewrite it, first in one language and then in the other.

Sin ti, no hubiera sobrevivido.

Without you, I wouldn't have survived.

PART ONE

NORTH
AND
SOUTH

ONE

A Chapter Dealing with the
Discovery of Death
at an Early Age

I should not be here to tell this story.

It's that simple: there is a day in my past, a day many years ago in Santiago de Chile, when I should have died and did not.

That's where I always thought this story would start, at that moment when history turned me, against my will, into the man who could someday sit down and write these words, who now writes them. I always thought this story was meant to start on that morning when the Armed Forces of my country rise against our President, Salvador Allende, on the 11th of September of 1973, to be exact, and the death I have been fearing since I was a child enters my life and, instead of taking it, leaves me to survive: I am left here on this side of reality to remember what ends forever that day in me and in the world, still wondering why I was spared.

And yet I cannot bring myself to begin there, that day I should have died.

There is one last night of reprieve, that is when I really need this story to start: the night of September 10, the night before the coup. By tomorrow at this time Allende will be dead and I will be in hiding, by tomorrow I will have had to accept a future in which I am alive and far too many others will have been killed in my place. But not yet. Tonight I can tell myself, against the overwhelming evidence screaming at me from inside and outside, that there will be no military takeover, that Chile is different from other Latin American countries, all the comforting myths about our democracy and stability and reasonableness.

Perhaps I am right. Perhaps I should not be poisoning my last moments of peace. From the next room, my six-year-old son, Rodrigo, is calling. Angélica has already tucked him in. Now he clamors for his bedtime story. Perhaps I am right to crush the sudden sick thought that snakes up from my stomach. This is the last time I will ever see him, the last story I will ever tell him, *la última vez*. Perhaps I am right to turn a final blind eye to reality.

It is not the first time I will try to cheat death, pretend it does not exist.

As far back as I can remember, there it was. I see myself then, awake in my bed for hours thinking about death, my eyes wide open in the dark of our apartment in New York, a child lost and found in the first exile of his life, terrified, trying to convince death to let him go. If I had known that many years later death would indeed let me go and that what I did or did not do, thought or did not think, would have no effect on whether or not I survived . . . But back then in 1947 I didn't even know that it is dying we should fear and not death. Oh yes, there were monsters out there, under the bed, inside the soft light breathing from the hall, dripping in the bathroom, always scrambling away as I turned my head, just out of sight, behind me, ready to pounce, and yet, even so, that's not what really threatened me, the monsters. I was five years old, perhaps less, and I absurdly assumed that the pain they would inflict on my body when I died would somehow be swift, somehow be merciful. No, what I could not bear was the aftermath of death itself, its loneliness, that I would have to be alone forever and ever.

"But will you be there?" I asked my mother, clinging to her, trying to blackmail her into never leaving. "Will you be close by, when I'm dead?" And she would answer something that was only partly a lie: Yes, she would be there. And afterwards, when the lights had been dimmed and she was gone and I thought about my death and the very thinking dragged me deeper into the pit of its terror, death was precisely the moment when I would not be there to think it, when I would be abandoned by myself, by the one person I could always count on never to turn off the light and walk away down the hall to another bedroom. That's what I will do to you, death said, you'll be so alone that not even you will be able to accompany yourself, and there is nothing you can do to avoid it. Just as I was spiraling myself into madness, my mother's words would swim back to me; she had promised to be there in the midst of that nothingness, and if she was there others might also find a way, and that's how I could commence the slow ascent back to the surface of sanity, conjecture death as a vast empty space filled with horizontal bodies in coffins, none of them able to touch each other but secure in the knowledge that the other silent bodies were there, millions of us, each with our own stories, our own beginnings, our own endings, a brotherhood of the dead defeating my isolation, the first time I conceived humanity as something wondrous and healing, a hint that if it could not escape death, a community might at least provide consolation against its outrage. And because my parents had told me that God did not exist, I prayed to that humanity every childhood night, asking it to allow me to awaken every hundred years to take a quick look around: the afterlife as a screen watched by a silent eye, eternity as one movie every century, the dead as intermittent voyeurs of the living.

That is how I managed to soften myself into sleep in the United

States in those days before I found out that another language can keep us company as if it were a twin. Later, as an adult—in fact, now—I discovered a more ingenious way of draining the slime that thoughts of my mortality secrete into my mind. Now if I can't fall asleep at night, I'll banish the saw-buzz of language, say, English, that's keeping me awake, and switch to my other language, Spanish, and lazily watch it erase the residues of dread from me as if I were a blackboard.

But that was later, that is now. My first insomnia struck at a child who had condemned himself to being monolingual in English, who had repudiated the Spanish he had been born into, that boy I used to be who could not conjure up another tongue to save his soul. All I could do to swindle death at that very early age in the City of New York was to make up stories in the night, colonize the emptiness with multiplications of myself, hoping somebody out there would hear me, accompany me, keep me alive after I had died.

What that child could not conceive, of course, is that his adult self would, in fact, survive his own death several times over, that a quarter of a century into the future this day in September of 1973 was awaiting me—and that the language in which I would try to make sense of the series of connected miracles that spared me would be Spanish and not English. By then, by the time I was an adult of thirty-one, I had renounced and denounced the language of my childhood America as imperial and Northern and alien to me, I had fiercely and publicly reverted to my original native Spanish and pro-claimed that I would speak it forever, live forever in Chile. Forever. A word that I naïvely cast to the winds at the time, a word that this wanderer in love with the transitory that I now have become knows he should be wary of. I hadn't learned yet that when other, more powerful people control the currents of your life, very few things are forever.

It is that sort of lesson I will have to learn as of tomorrow, when death catches up with me and makes me face the fact that my imag-ination can no longer protect me or my country.

I am now going to postpone that moment for one last time, crossing to Rodrigo's room to offer myself and him a final delusion of our immortality. But before I console my son with a story, just as I consoled myself as a child long ago, I will make a call. That call. If I had understood then its true significance, how it was warning me of what was about to befall me, befall all of us. But I would not have heeded it, did not know what to look for.

It is a call to La Moneda, the Presidential Palace, where I have been working for the last two months as a cultural and media advisor to Fernando Flores, Allende's Chief of Staff. Today, so many years later, as I write this, it seems obvious that to accept a minor post of dubious utility in a foundering government was an act of folly. But that is not what I felt then. Then I saw it as my duty.

As a child I had imagined a fictional community as the best answer to death and loneliness—and it was that persistent hunger for a real community that had now led me here, to this revolution, to this place in history. Needing to prove my loyalty to a country I had chosen and a cause I had adopted as my own and that could only materialize if everybody who believed in it, myself included, was ready to give up their life. And I had therefore purposefully, recklessly, joyfully sought out the most dangerous spot in the whole country to spend the last days of the Chilean revolution—the spot I am neurotically calling right now, even now on my night off duty, to find out if my services are required. They are not. Claudio Gimeno, a friend since my freshman year in college, answers. He's in a good mood, I can conjure up the shy grin of his buckteeth, his wide black eyes, his sallow, angular face.

In the years to come, he will be there, in a vision. Each time I imagine my death, I will invariably picture myself in a chair, hands tied behind my back. I am blindfolded—and yet, in that picture, I am also, impossibly, watching myself, and a man in uniform approaches and he has something, a stick, a pair of electrodes, a long needle, something blurred and piercing in his right hand. In that vision which still assaults me unexpectedly at any time, anywhere, the body about to be hurt beyond repair is the body of Claudio Gimeno. He is naked in that chair. That is his body, but it is my face he wears. My face, because I had been assigned that *turno*, that stint, I was the one who should have been at La Moneda standing guard the night of September 10, I was the one who should have received the news that the Navy has just disembarked in Valparaiso, it should have been my hand that puts the receiver down and then with a heavy heart dialed the President and informed him that the coup has begun. It is Claudio who will receive that information in the next hours, merely because last week I had wondered, rather offhandedly, "*Oye,* Claudio, hey, would you mind coming to La Moneda next Monday, yes, September 10, it's the night I've been assigned, and I'll take your shift on Sunday, September 9, what do you say?" And without giving it a second thought, Claudio had agreed.

So now I am here at home and he is at La Moneda and we are talking on the phone. No premonition of how chance is playing with us startles our conversation. On the contrary. Claudio tells me that things are looking up, there may be a way out of the crisis that is fracturing the country and has paralyzed it, a democratic and sovereign way of avoiding what seems an imminent civil war. Allende will announce tomorrow that he will submit his differences with the opposition to a plebiscite and will resign if the people reject his proposals. I'm as relieved as Claudio. Neither of us recognizes this peaceful resolution of the political impasse for what it is: a mirage, an outcome that Allende's enemies, moving in for the kill, will never allow.

We are, nevertheless, in a position to understand that, in a sense, the military takeover has already happened.

Just one week ago, Claudio and I, along with another aide, had been ushered into a musty secluded room in the Presidential Palace by Fernando Flores. The Minister wanted us to listen to an old Mapuche Indian woman who had come to Santiago from the south of the country to denounce her husband's torture and death. She was one of hundreds of thousands of peasants who had, for the first time in their lives, been made owners of their land by Allende's government. A group of Air Force officers had raided the family's communal farm in search of weapons and, when none was found, proceeded to tie the woman's husband to the blades of a helicopter. While the old man went slowly round and round for hours, the men in uniform had smoked cigarettes, taunted him, sardonically suggesting that he ask his President for help now, as the old man died they had forced him to call on his fucking pagan gods for help now, *sus putos dioses paganos.*

She had come to denounce this situation to the President. But the President could do nothing. We could do nothing. It was as if power had already been transferred to the miltary.

The old woman had looked at me, straight in the eye. *"A lo largo de mi vida,"* she had said to me. "In my life, white people have done many things to us, but never before something like this. They kept on telling my man that now they're going to take away our land." She paused. Then added: "They made me watch what they were doing."

I had looked away. I could not bear what she was seeing, the future she was able to anticipate because the past had already taught her what to expect. I had wanted so ardently to become a *chileno*, to belong; and what that meant, ultimately, was that what they had done to her and people like her for centuries they could now do to me. Maybe, in a flash, I had seen myself in her, I had imagined my body reduced to the defenselessness of that old woman, a foreigner in her own land; maybe, but I could not stand her visionary dress rehearsal of the violence that is about to invade the country, so that when Claudio, a week later, tells me everything is going to be all right, I am ready to believe in a miracle.

Not that we've got that much time to talk tonight. Claudio has work to do and I have a vociferous son demanding a story. When we say goodbye, nothing whispers that this is the last time we will ever speak to each other.

I hang up.

And go to comfort Rodrigo in the next room, off to tell my son that death does not exist, that I will be there with him, we can both delude solitude side by side one last time.

I do not inform him, of course, that real monsters are out there and that what they can enact on your body may be worse than death. That it is dying we should fear, the pain before and not the emptiness afterwards. That exile is staring us in the face, that soon he and I and his mother are going to leave this place where we gave birth to him and not return until many, too many, years have passed. I do not inform him that death and the fear of death inevitably lead to exile.

There will be time, tomorrow and the many days that will follow tomorrow, to discover this together.

For now, I say nothing of this to my son. Not a word.

What else can I do?

I turn out the lights and tell my son a fairy tale.

TWO

A Chapter Dealing with the Discovery of Life and Language at an Early Age

I was falling.

It was May 6, 1942, and the city was Buenos Aires and I had only just been born a few seconds ago and I was already in danger.

I did not need to be told. I knew it before I knew anything else. But my mother warned me anyway that I was falling, the first words I ever heard in my life, even if I could not have registered them in my brain, the first words my mother remembers being pronounced in my presence. Strange and foreboding that of all the many words attending the scattered chaos and delirium of my birth, the only shrapnels of sense my mother snatched from extinction and later froze into family legend should have been that warning.

It was not intended as a metaphysical statement. My mother had been dosed with a snap of gas to ease her pain as she labored, and when her newborn baby had been placed on a nearby table to be cleaned, she thought in her daze that it was slanted and the boy was about to roll off, and that was when she cried out. *"Doctor,"* she called, and my uncomprehending ears must have absorbed the meaningless sound. *"Doctor, se cae el niño, se cae el niño,"* she told the doctor that I was falling, the boy was about to fall.

She was wrong about my body and right about my mind, my life, my soul. I was falling, like every child who was ever born, I was falling into solitude and nothingness, headlong and headfirst, and my mother, by her very words, by the mere act of formulating her fear in a human language, inadvertently stopped my descent by introducing me to Spanish, by sending Spanish out to catch me, cradle me, pull me back from the abyss.

I was a baby: a pad upon which any stranger could scrawl a signature. A passive little bastard, shipwrecked, no ticket back, not even sure that a smile, a scream, my only weapons, could help me to surface. And then Spanish slid to the rescue, in my mother's first cry, and soon in her murmurs and lullabies and in my father's deep voice of protection and in his jokes and in the hum of love that would soon envelop me from an extended family. Maybe that was my first exile: I had not asked to be born, had not chosen anything, not my face, not the face of my parents, not this extreme sensitivity that has always boiled out of me, not the early rash on my skin, not my remote asthma, not my nearby country, not my unpronounceable name. But Spanish was there at the beginning of my body or perhaps where my body ended and the world began, coaxing that body into life as only a lover can, convincing me slowly, sound by sound, that life was worth living, that together we could tame the fiends of the outer bounds and bend them to our will. That everything can be named and therefore, in theory, at least in desire, the world belongs to us. That if we cannot own the world, nobody can stop us from imagining everything in it, everything it can be, everything it ever was.

It promised, my Spanish, that it would take care of me.

And for a while it delivered on its promise.

It did not tell me that at the very moment it was promising the world to me, that world was being disputed by others, by men in shadows who had other plans for me, new banishments planned for me, men who were just as desperate not to fall as I had been at birth, desperate to rise, rise to power.

Nor did Spanish report that on its boundaries other languages roamed, waiting for me, greedy languages, eager to penetrate my territory and establish a foothold, ready to take over at the slightest hint of weakness. It did not whisper a word to me of its own imperial history, how it had subjugated and absorbed so many people born into other linguistic systems, first during the centuries of its triumphant ascendancy in the Iberian peninsula and then in the Americas after the so-called Discovery, converting natives and later domesticating slaves, merely because the men who happened to carry Spanish in their cortex were more ruthless and cunning and technologically practical than the men who carried Catalán or Basque or Aymará or Quechua or Swahili inside them. It did not hint that English was to the North, smiling to itself, certain that it would father the mind that is writing these words even now, that I would have to surrender to its charms eventually, it did not suggest that English was ready to do to me what Spanish itself had done to others so many times during its evolution, what it had done, in fact, to my own parents: wrenched them from the arms of their original language.

And yet I am being unfair to Spanish—and also, therefore, to English. Languages do not only expand through conquest: they also grow by offering a safe haven to those who come to them in danger, those who are falling from some place far less safe than a mother's womb, those who, like my own parents, were forced to flee their native land.

After all, I would not be alive today if Spanish had not generously offered my parents a way of connecting with each other. I was conceived in Spanish, literally imagined into being by that language, flirted, courted, coupled into existence by my parents in a Spanish that had not been there at their birth.

Spanish was able to catch me as I fell because it had many years before caught my mother and my father just as gently and with many of the same promises.

Both my parents had come to their new language from Eastern Europe in the early years of the twentieth century, the children of Jewish émigrés to Argentina—but that is as far as the parallel goes, because the process of their seduction by Spanish could not have been more different.

And therein lies a story. More than one.

I'll start with my mother. Hers is the more traditional, almost archetypical, migratory experience.

Fanny Zelicovich Vaisman was born in 1909 in Kishinev. Her birthplace, like her life itself, was subject to the arbitrary fluctuations of history: at that time, Kishinev belonged to Greater Russia, but from 1918 was incorporated into Romania and then in 1940 into the Soviet Union—only to become, after the breakup of that country, the capital of the republic of Moldavia. If my mother had stayed there, she would have been able to change nationalities four times without moving from the street on which she had seen the first light of this world. Though if she had remained there she would probably not have lived long enough to make all those changes in citizenship.

Her maternal grandfather, a cattle dealer, was murdered in the pogrom of 1903. Many years later, I heard the story from my mother's uncle Karl, in Los Angeles, of all places. It was 1969 and he must have been well over eighty years old but he cried like a child as he told us, tears streaming down his face, speaking in broken English and lapsing into Yiddish and being semi-translated by my mother into Spanish so Angélica and I would understand, his pain imploding like a storm into the mix of languages, unrelieved by the passing of time: how his mother had hid with him and his sisters and brothers in a church, how they had listened for hours while the Cossacks raged outside—those screams in Russian, those cries for help in Yiddish, the horses, the horses, my great-uncle Karl whispered—and how he had emerged who knows how many centuries later and found his father dead, his father's throat slit, how he had held his father in his arms.

It was that experience, it seems, that had led the family, after aeons of persecution, to finally emigrate. Australia was considered, and the United States, but Argentina was selected: Baron Maurice de Hirsch's Jewish Colonization Association had helped to open the pampas to Jews anxious to own land and cultivate the prairies. Two brothers of my grandmother Clara set out, and when they wrote back that the streets of Buenos Aires were paved with gold, the rest of the family started making plans to leave as well. Only Clara's mother was unable to emigrate: her youngest daughter would not have passed the tests of the health authorities in Argentina, apparently because she had had meningitis, which had left her seriously retarded. Which meant that both of them, mother and daughter, lived their lives out in Kishinev until they were killed by the Nazis. According to my mother, the old woman went out into the streets the day the blackshirts drove into town and insulted them and was shot on the spot; and though I would love this story to be true, love to have a great-grandmother who did not let herself be carted off to a concentration camp and forced her foes to kill her on the same streets where her husband had been slaughtered, I have often wondered if this version is a fantasy devised more to inspire the living than to honor the dead.

What is certain is that my mother was saved from such a fate by departing with her parents. At the age of three months, she found herself on a boat from Hamburg bound for an Argentina that, devoid as it might be of pogroms, nevertheless had enough Nazis and Nazi-lovers to force her, thirty-six years later, into her next exile. The ambivalent attitude of the host country toward the Jews was presaged in two run-ins my mother had with the Spanish language at an early age.

When she was six years old, my mother recalls, she had been sent to her first school. In the afternoons, private piano lessons were offered and my grandmother Clara insisted that her child take these, perhaps as a way of proving how genteel and civilized the family had become. On one of the first afternoons, my mother was by herself in the music room waiting for the teacher, when the door slammed shut. From the other side, a mocking chorus of Argentine children started shouting at her in Spanish. She tried to open the door but they were holding it tight. *"No podés,"* they taunted her. You can't open the door, because you're a Jew, *"porque sos judía."* Definitely not the first words she ever heard in Spanish, but the first words she ever remembers having heard, the words that have remained in her memory like a scar. You talk funny, they said to her. You talk funny because you're a Jew.

She probably did talk funny. Yiddish had been the only language her family spoke in Argentina for years. It is true that my mom's father, Zeide, forced himself to learn some rudimentary Spanish: a week after arriving in Argentina, he was peddling blankets house-to-house in Buenos Aires, starting with the Jewish community, and was soon knocking at the doors of Spanish-speaking goyim as well, prospering enough to eventually start a small shop. But his wife, at least during those first years, was inclined to stay away from the new life, from the new language: almost as if Clara feared, clutching her baby daughter to her, that out there the Cossacks were still lurking, ready to attack.

Instead of the dreaded Cossacks, another military man passed briefly through the family's life and inadvertently convinced my Baba Clara, several years before those anti-Semitic school brats refused my mother entry into the community, that Argentina was truly willing to welcome the immigrants.

One day, an Argentine colonel emerged from his brother's residence, next door to the Zelicovich house. He stepped into the torrid heat of the Buenos Aires summer and there, on the sidewalk, he saw his little niece playing with a pretty, blond-haired, foreign-looking girl—my mother, who was probably three years old, maybe four, who had by then picked up a smattering of Spanish from the neighborhood kids. The colonel advanced, reached out with one hand toward his Argentine niece and with the other did not take out a gun and shoot my mother but clasped her small hand and trundled both of them off to the corner for some ice cream. An irrelevant incident, but not to Baba Clara: my mother's mother, upon seeing the colonel go off with the children so amiably and then return with prodigal ice-cream cones, was amazed beyond belief. She said she lifted her hands to heaven to thank the Lord. An Army officer, any member of any Army, was a devil, a potential Jew-killer: that such a man should invite a child from the Tribe of Israel to share sweets with his niece was as miraculous as the Czar quoting the Torah.

My mother does not remember the colonel or the little friend or the ice cream. What she has consigned to memory is the reaction of her mother. What she remembers is her mother's voice that very night, recounting in Yiddish the marvels of Argentina and its love of the Jews to her skeptical sister Rosa. Or was it on a later occasion? Because Clara repeated the same story over and over again through the years. Paradoxical that it should have been in Yiddish, because the story registers and foretells the defeat of Yiddish, how kindness forced it to retreat, her offspring's first tentative, independent steps into a world where Yiddish was not necessary. A world that would demand of my mother, as it demands of all immigrant children, that she abandon the language of her ancestors if she wanted to pass through that door those children would soon be trying to slam shut. I believe this story has abided in the family memory so many years because it is foundational: the prophetic story of how my mother would leave home and assimilate, escaping from that ghost language of the past into the Spanish-echoing streets.

Streets where my father, many years down the road, was waiting for her.

By then, fortunately for me, they both spoke Spanish. I can almost hear him now convincing her to marry him in the one language they both shared, I try to eavesdrop so many years later on the mirror of their lovemaking, listening to how they conceived me, how their language coupled me out of nothingness, made me out of the nakedness of night, *la desnudez de la noche.*

My father's trail to the wonders of the sleek Spanish he murmured in her ears had not been as direct and simple as my mother's. Rather than the normal relay race of one language replacing the other, it had been a more convoluted bilingual journey that he had taken.

To begin with, he had emigrated not once but twice to Argentina; though perhaps more crucial was that he came from a family sophisticated in the arts of language, a sophistication that would end up saving his life several times over.

Adolfo was born in 1907 in Odessa, now Ukraine, then Greater Russia, to a well-to-do Jewish family that had been in the region for at least a century and probably longer. As well as Russian, his father, David Dorfman, spoke English and French fluently, as did his mother, Raissa Libovich, who also happened to be conversant in German after three years of studying in Vienna. All those languages, but no Yiddish: they considered themselves assimilated, cosmopolitan, definitively European. If David and Raissa ended up in Argentina, it was not due to any pogrom. In fact, the 1903 pogrom where my mother's grandfather died had been beaten back in Odessa by the Jewish riffraff and gangsters immortalized later in Isaac Babel's writings. Their expatriation derived from a more trite and middle-class problem: in 1909, at about the time my mother was being born across the Black Sea, David Dorfman's soap factory had gone bankrupt and he had been forced to flee abroad to escape his creditors. Of that venture, only a seal, used to stamp certain particularly fragrant epitomes of soap, remains in my father's possession: "Cairo Aromas," it grandly proclaims in Russian. But my grandfather, rather than heading for the mythical Cairo of the seal, set off for the more distant and promising Buenos Aires of history. And one year later his wife and three-year-old Adolfo followed him.

Some years later—it was 1914 by then and the child was six—Raissa and her son were headed back to Russia, purportedly on a visit to the family, though persistent rumors mention another woman, whom David might have been scandalously visiting. Whether or not the gossip is true, what is certain is that my grandmother and my father picked the worst time to go back: they were caught in the eruption of the First World War and then in the Russian Revolution. The reasons for their staying on have always been nebulous. "We were going to beat those Prussians in a matter of months, it was going to be a picnic," my baba Pizzi told me half a century later, when she and the world knew that it had been anything but a picnic. "And," she added, "you always think it's about to end and then it doesn't and you wait a bit more and you've invested so much hope in believing that it'll all finish tomorrow that you don't want to give up that easily." Pizzi would tell me this in English on my visits to Buenos Aires, before I myself would experience what it is to believe that something terrible will end soon, before my own exile would teach me that we spend a good part of our lives believing things will get better because there is no way we can imagine them, wish to imagine them, getting worse. My exile—when I fled Buenos Aires after fleeing Chile; my exile—when the phone rang in Amsterdam with the news that Pizzi had died and I learned that banishment does not take from you only the living but takes their death from you as well. Pizzi had died and I had not been there, I would never sit by her side again and ask her about the past, the steps of Odessa and the *Potemkin*, the Russian secret police raiding the house, never again be able to ask her about the day my father had brought my mother home to be introduced as his future wife, never again discuss with my favorite grandparent the difficulties of being a woman journalist in Buenos Aires, never again hear her painstakingly translate into English for my benefit the stories for children she wrote for the Argentine Sunday papers and had herself translated from Russian into Spanish, as she had translated *Anna Karenina* for the first time into Spanish, never again hear from her lips the tales of how they had survived the hardships of the war, how she had spent those years alone with her son, preparing to return to the land where her husband awaited them.

And then the Revolution had come. Like so many Jews at the

time, she fervently supported it. But how to make a living with everything in turmoil? While her son went to school with the bullets flying and the walls splattered with red slogans and the city changing hands overnight—she kept a home for him, and food on the table, and managed to put him through school, and it was all due to her languages; that's what kept them alive. And she was so proficient at them that she started working with Litvinov and ended up serving the most prominent Bolshevik Jew of them all, Trotsky, acting as one of his interpreters at the peace talks with the Germans at Brest Litovsk, where the fate of the Soviet Union was decided. She remembered how he had paced up and down on the train as it sped through the Ukraine to the meeting: how much to give up, how much to concede, how much to pay for peace and the time to build a new Army, a new society?

And while she was translating German into Russian in order to survive, her husband, half the world away, was patiently translating from Russian into Spanish in order to bring her and the boy safely to Argentina. When the Revolution broke out, it became almost impossible to get people safely out of the newly formed Soviet Union, but my grandfather had hit on a plan: there was a flood of immigrants streaming into Argentina and the police needed people who could interpret for them and help streamline the process, and David found a job with them, hoping that his new post would strengthen his assertion that his faraway wife and son were de facto Argentine citizens and should be helped to exit from Ukraine. Incredibly, he managed to convince some official in the Argentine government to intervene, and more incredibly, somebody in the frenzied Soviet Foreign Minstry listened, and that is how Raissa and Adolfo managed to take the last ship—at least so goes the family legend—to leave Odessa at the end of 1920. My father remembers a stowaway: the Red Army soldiers coming on board and the young man's fearful eyes when he was discovered, the stubble on his face, the look of someone who knew he would die—and then they hauled him away, dragged him back to that glorious Odessa of my father's youth, that Odessa now of danger and death.

It's hard to be sure, but there's a good chance, my father says, that he and his mother would not have outlived the terrible year of 1921. The civil war, the famine, the plague, decimated Odessa and so many other cities in the country: most of Raissa's family, left behind, died. And among the dead was Ilyusha, Adolfo's older cousin. To the fatherless boy, Ilyusha had been a protector, an angel, a brother for seven lonely years. That cousin of his had let my father tag along as he plunged into the turmoil and romance of the Revolution. My father's participation had not gone beyond carrying a mysterious black bag that Ilyusha always wanted near him, a bag that contained nothing more dangerous, it seems, than poems and pamphlets, but it was the first social activism of my father's life and he was never to forget it. Ilyusha's memory was to haunt him through the turbulent twenties and into the thirties as Argentina itself began to head for what seemed a revolution of its own.

Spanish received my father with open arms, a smoother welcome than my mother's. Either because he had already had previous experience with the language as a child or because his parents were polylingual themselves, he was soon speaking and writing Spanish brilliantly, so well that, soon after graduating from the university, the Russian émigré Dorfman wrote and had published the first history of Argentine industry, becoming his country's leading expert on the subject. More books, many articles and essays followed, all of them focusing on Argentina and its tomorrow, all of them in Spanish: apparently an absolute commitment to his new land and language.

My father was bilingual and remains so to this day. That he kept his Russian intact can be attributed to his having spent his formative years in Odessa, to the fact that Russian contained within its words the full force of its nationhood and literature and vast expanses— unlike the language that my mother discarded, a Yiddish that occupied no territory, possessed no name on the map of nations, had never been officially promoted by a state. But my father's retention of Russian may signal something else: a doubleness that did not plague my mother. She rid herself of Yiddish as a way of breaking with the past, bonding forever with the Argentina that had taken her by the hand the day when she was three and offered her an ice cream in Spanish. She could easily segregate her first, her original, language, relegate it to the nostalgia of yesteryear, a gateway to a land that no longer existed except in the shards of hazy family anecdotes. Her monolingualism was a way of stating that Yiddish had become irrelevant to the present, to her present.

My father could never have said that of Russian. The language of his youth, the language his parents spoke with him at home, was to embody, for many in my father's generation—in Argentina and all over the world—the language in which the future was being built: the first socialist revolution in history, the first socialist state, the first place on the planet where men would not exploit men. Always vaguely leftist and rebellious, by the early 1930s my father had joined the Communist Party and embraced Marxism. Like many men and women his age, he saw no alternative to what he was sure were the death throes of capitalism reeling from the Depression. It is one of the ironies of history that those ardent internationalists who were so suspicious of nations and chauvinism and proclaimed that only the brotherhood of the proletariat of all countries would free mankind should have ended up subjecting their lives, ideas, and desires to the policies and dictates of one country, the Soviet Union. They perceived no contradiction: to defend real socialism in the one territory where it had taken power would mean sustaining a state that, by its shining example—and later by armed force—would help bring freedom and equality and justice to every corner of the globe.

And the Moscow trials? And Stalin's purges? And the famine and destruction of the peasantry? And the Kronstadt massacre? And the gathering bureaucratic power of a new elite speaking in the name of the vast masses?

Few Communists at the time protested or even seemed to care. My father was no exception. Though I have wondered whether my father's love affair with the Soviet Union was not also buttressed and even hardened by his romance with Russian, the circumstance that the language that had caught him as he fell into the abyss of birth happened to be the very language that he believed was destined to redeem the whole of fallen humanity. The language of his dead cousin, the language of the streets of Odessa, the language of the Revolution: my father's past was not something to be thrown away, as my mother threw away her Yiddish. It could coexist with his Argentine present and inseminate it and bring together the two sides and periods of his life, Russia and Latin America, to create a nation-less future, socialism in Argentina.

But there is, in fact, no need for this sort of pop psychology, no need to resort to linguistic explanations for my father's blind adoration of the Soviet Union. History was furnishing reasons enough: the consolidation of Mussolini and the rise of Hitler and then the Civil War in Spain convinced innumerable revolutionaries to swallow their doubts (if they had any) and embrace the one power ready to stand up to the Nazis. And even after my father was expelled from the Party at the end of the 1930s—but not, I am sad to report, because of ideological or political differences, but due to a slight divergence about some abstruse question of internal democracy—even then, even after the Hitler-Stalin Pact of 1939, he adhered steadfastly to Marxist philosophy and politics.

Up to the point that when I was born in 1942 my father gave me a name I would disclaim when I was nine years old, for reasons that will be revealed: the flaming moniker of Vladimiro. In honor of Vladimir Ilyich Lenin and the Bolshevik Revolution, which, my father felt, was fast approaching the pampas.

What was really approaching those pampas was Fascism—at least, a deformed and mild criollo version of it. A year after my birth, in June 1943, the military headed by General Ramírez toppled the conservative government of Ramón Castillo. It was a pro-Axis coup and behind it was the enigmatic figure of then Colonel Juan Domingo Perón.

My father would soon run afoul of these men. When the new military government took over the Universidad de la Plata, where my father taught, he resigned indignantly, sending them a letter of protest, à la Emile Zola. A copy, unfortunately, does not exist: but I have been told that in it my father insulted the military, their repressiveness, ignorance, clericalism, extreme nationalism, and, above all their infatuation with Franco, Hitler, and Mussolini. The authorities reacted by expelling him from his position (a first in the history of Argentina) and then decided to put him on trial, demanding that his citizenship be revoked. I have taken out the old boxes in my parents' Buenos Aires apartment and leafed through the yellowed pro-government tabloids of the day, and there they are, the headlines calling for the "dirty Jew-dog Dorfman" to be shipped back to Russia, "where he belonged."

History does repeat itself, first as tragedy and then as farce: almost half a century later, ultra-conservative anti-Semitic right-wingers in the United States would suggest that I do the same thing, following me around with signs screeching VLADIMIRO ZELICOVICH (*sic*) GO HOME TO RUSSIA whenever I gave a lecture about Chile at a university, waving copies of a twenty-minute speech Jesse Helms had delivered against me on the Senate floor, brimming with information provided to him by the Chilean Secret Police. But those people in America in the 1980s couldn't do anything to me. The men who threatened my father in Argentina in 1943 were somewhat more powerful.

Again, my father was falling.

But this time it wouldn't be Russian that would catch him, save him. Or the Russians, for that matter. It would be their arch-rivals.

Before he could be jailed, my father skipped the country on an already granted Guggenheim Fellowship. My anti-imperialist father fled in December of 1943, to the United States, the most powerful capitalist country in the world, protected by a foundation built with money that had come out of one of the world's largest consortiums. Money that had come from tin mines in Bolivia and nitrate in Chile and rubber plantations in the Congo and diamonds in Africa saved my Leninist dad.

But the Americans were preparing Normandy and Stalingrad was raging and Auschwitz was burning Jews and homosexuals and Gypsies and Roosevelt had created the New Deal and anyway, even if my father had not been able to offer himself all these expediently progressive reasons for journeying to the center of the empire, there was a more practical one: he had to escape. And America was the only place he could go.

And therefore the place where, over a year later, in February of 1945, the rest of the family joined him.

First, we hopped across Latin America, Santiago and Lima and Cali and Barranquilla, and then finally Miami, each flight delayed for a day or two because of the war, as if Spanish was saying goodbye to me very slowly, as if it were reluctant to let me depart on what would end up being a bilingual journey. Though what may have been most significant about that initial trip North was that the first night of my first exile was spent in the neighboring country just across the Andes, the place that still symbolizes the South for me, there, in that city of Santiago de Chile which was to become my home so many years later. *Wondrous* may be a better word than *significant*: that my first night in that city should have been in a hotel, the Carrera, facing the Presidential Palace of La Moneda, where I was to spend so many nights in the last days of the Allende revolution, looking out onto the plaza, catching a glimpse of men behind the windows of that hotel looking back at me, perhaps from the very room where I had slept as an infant. A mysterious symmetry which would have been even more amazing if I had died at La Moneda—because, in that case, my first childhood voyage to Santiago could have been construed as truly premonitory, that two-and-a-half-year-old child visiting the site of the murder that awaited him twenty-eight years in the future.

If the gods existed and if they were inclined to literary pastimes, they would have organized precisely that sort of ending for their enjoyment, they would have taken my life and harvested one hell of a metaphor. Fortunately, in this case at least, nobody powerful enough to intervene was playing a sick practical joke on me.

Instead, I was the one playing jokes—on my mother and older sister, who spent most of the one afternoon they had for sightseeing shut up in that hotel room searching for the baby shoes, my only pair, that I had mischievously hidden in a pillowcase. With such skill and malevolence, according to my mother, that we almost missed the chance to tour the city before it grew dark. I like to think that the boy I used to be knew what he was doing, that he was in fact trying to intercept my innocent eyes from seeing Santiago for the first innocent time, from crossing the path of Angélica, the woman of my life, who was that same afternoon breathing those very molecules of air under those same mountains. I like to think he recognized Santiago, he had heard the city or its future calling quietly to him to wait, to hold himself in reserve, to hide the shoes. Or maybe it was the city that recognized him.

New York, however, did not recognize me at all. Or maybe sickness is a form of making love, tact, contact, the winter of New York seeping into the lungs of the child still immersed in mind, if not body, in the sultry heat of the Buenos Aires summer, New York blasting that child inside his simulacrum of a snowsuit, inside the garments that had been hastily sewn together by his mother in the remote southern tip of the hemisphere to simulate a snowsuit, New York claiming that child, telling him that things were not going to be easy, no hiding shoes in this city, no guided tours: in this city we play for keeps, kid.

Our family descended from the train onto the platform in Grand Central Station, and there was no one there to greet us but the cold. We had crossed the South of the United States during the night. I have no memory, again, of that trip, except that years later, when I read Thomas Wolfe and his long, shattering train ride to the home toward which the angel was fruitlessly looking, the home he said you could never return to, I felt a shudder of acknowledgment—I had been on that train, I had crossed that U.S. South leaving my own Latino South. So I do not remember the moment when I stepped for the first time in my life onto the concrete of the North, there in New York, holding my mother's hand.

My father was not there waiting for us.

He appeared fifteen minutes later, explained that he had made a mistake or the train had arrived at a different platform, but my mother felt something else was wrong, she felt the mix-up was ominous, because my dad was distant, unfamiliar, his eyes avoiding hers. What my father could not bring himself to tell her was that just before our arrival, at around the time I was hiding my shoes in a Chilean pillow, he had been conscripted into the U.S. Army, and unless he could get a deferment or change his 4A classification, he would be off to the European Front and my mother, who didn't know a word of English, would be stranded in a foreign city with two small children, forced to live on a fifty-dollar-a-month GI salary. Four days later, still without telling his wife the truth, my father departed early from the hotel where we were lodged and reported for duty in downtown Manhattan, fully expecting to return in uniform to break the news to my mother; the uniform would tell the news he dared not utter himself. He showered with dozens of other conscripts, he slipped into the Army clothes and then, at the very last moment, was informed that he had been reclassified because the sort of work he was doing at the newly established office of Inter-American Affairs had been deemed "essential." David Rockefeller, who had created that office in the State Department to fight the advance of fascism in Latin America had intervened. Again, the tricks and treats of history: a Republican saved my philo-Communist father from being sent to war against the allies of the fascists he had just escaped from back home. The point is that my father was able to make a cheerful trip back uptown and tell my mother the reason why he had seemed so remote since our arrival, assure her there was nothing to worry about, from now on happy days would be here again.

But they wouldn't, at least not for me, at least not immediately.

The first order of business was to move out of our prohibitively expensive hotel, not easy in a New York where no new housing had been built since the start of the war. A savvy Uruguayan friend suggested my parents read the obituaries in the newspapers and nab a vacated apartment. Implausibly, that stratagem worked. They rented what in the folklore of the family would always be called *la casa del muerto*, the Dead Man's House. It was, according to my mother, the most depressing, run-down joint she had ever inhabited: a two-room dump, airless under a weak dim bulb hanging like a noose from the ceiling, with small slits of windows gaping onto a gray desolate inner courtyard, three beds in each room, as if several people had died there, not just one.

That was the place, the house of death. That's where I caught pneumonia one Saturday night in February of 1945, when my parents had gone out by themselves for the first time since we had arrived in the States—and I carefully use that verb, to catch, aware of its wild ambiguity, still unsure, even now, if that sickness invaded me or if I was the one who invited it in. But more of that later. To save his life, that boy was interned in a hospital, isolated in a ward where nobody spoke a word of Spanish. For three weeks, he saw his parents only on visiting days and then only from behind a glass partition.

My parents have told me the story so often that sometimes I have the illusion that I am the one remembering, but that hope quickly fades, as when you arrive at a movie theater late and never discover what really happened, are forever at the mercy of those who have witnessed the beginning: *te internaron en ese hospital*, my mother says slowly, picking out the words as if for the first time, *no nos acordamos del nombre*, there is a large glass wall, it is a cold bare white hospital ward, my parents have told me that every time they came to see me, tears streamed down my face, that I tried to touch them, I watch myself watching my parents so near and so far away behind the glass, mouthing words in Spanish I can't hear. Then my mother and my father are gone and I turn and I am alone and my lungs hurt and I realize then, as I realize now, that I am very fragile, that life can snap like a twig. I realize this in Spanish and I look up and the only adults I see are nurses and doctors. They speak to me in a language I don't know. A language that I will later learn is called English. In what language do I respond? In what language can I respond?

Three weeks later, when my parents came to collect their son, now sound in body but in all probability slightly insane in mind, I disconcerted them by refusing to answer their Spanish questions, by speaking only English. "I don't understand," my mother says that I said—and from that moment onward I stubbornly, steadfastly, adamantly refused to speak a word in the tongue I had been born into.

I did not speak another word of Spanish for ten years.

THREE

A Chapter Dealing with the
Discovery of Death in the
Early Morning of
September 11, 1973, in
Santiago de Chile

If it had not been for Susana la Semilla, a cartoon character I invented, I would not have survived the coup against Allende.

At least, that is the story I like to tell. Partly because it's bizarrely true, but above all, I think, because this less solemn version of my survival gives me the illusion that I somehow created the conditions whereby I thwarted death, that I had a hand in it. When oblivion breathes down your neck, takes you for a ride to the outskirts of emptiness and then yanks you back to the shores of reality trembling and intact, you need to find a reason, you need to find a meaning. Why me? Why was I spared? Questions that burn through the lives of survivors, questions we ask ourselves because the people who might hold the answer are all dead. So we answer as best we can, we try to find one thread in the absurd chain of circumstances which leads to our deliverance and say: Here! This is it! This is of my making!

And for many years my answer, to myself and anyone who made the inquiry, was Susana la Semilla, the smiling character I had concocted as my contribution to forestalling the coup, my secret weapon against the CIA.

An admittedly puny weapon against the gigantic conspiracy financed by Nixon, Kissinger, and ITT to "destabilize" the government the people of Chile had freely elected in 1970. This aggression was eventually to be exhaustively documented in 1975 by a Senate Investigating Committee headed by Frank Church, but by 1973 it was already being openly discussed in newspapers in Chile and abroad. What had begun as a covert operation was, by then, not a secret at all. In fact, as the end approached, many of those benefiting from American meddling and money were, instead of hiding the intervention, flaunting it.

I myself witnessed such a display when, around ten days before the coup, I trekked, with a group of Unidad Popular militants, into some hills twenty miles to the north of Santiago. There, under the Andean cordillera, on an isolated knoll that our group leader had supposedly explored and deemed sufficiently remote, we were supposed to receive our first lesson in handling firearms, part of a clumsily improvised training program meant to prepare us for what seemed an imminent civil war.

Not only too little (we had one pitiable gun among the seven of us), but too late as well.

Looking back, I realize that those of us who supported Allende were always a step behind our adversaries in our willingness to use violence. While we subscribed to the idea of a peaceful, democratic revolution, without bloodshed, while we danced along the avenues, they were taking lessons in martial arts. I can remember my surprise when, in 1971, a year after Allende was inaugurated President, right-wing thugs made their appearance on the streets of Santiago, in military formation, swinging chains and lashing out with *linchacos*, as if they had come out of some perverse Bruce Lee film. We responded belatedly by starting to take karate lessons ourselves—I would sweat and strain with a group of friends at six in the morning, ready to take back our city. But by the time we were grunting and kicking and chopping away, our civilian enemies had graduated to firearms and were shooting at us, while the more adventurous among them blew up high-tension towers, sabotaged government television stations, and assassinated Allende's aides. And now here we were, holding a real gun in our hands for the first time, whereas they had already enlisted the Armed Forces; they would soon have tanks and planes and battalions at their command.

But we didn't know that then, and if we had, we still would have had no alternative but to "train" and pray that some sympathetic god would grant us the time to really learn: we pointed the solitary lonely-hearts gun by turns at a tin can on a nearby rock and hit the rock more times than we did the can and soon exhausted the two rounds of ammunition which was all we had been able to negotiate on the black market and the seven of us were left with a smoking gun and no bullets and a battered rock and more courage than confidence on that beautiful sunny afternoon under those mountains. And time on our hands. So we sauntered down to the other side of the hill to scout the area, almost like children on a holiday instead of would-be guerrillas, and discovered that the slope where we had been practicing was, in fact, not as secluded as our group leader had irresponsibly suggested.

In a nearby clearing, behind some scraggly trees, some fifteen to twenty truck drivers were roasting meat over a colossal fire, drinking away, laughing their heads off, while a smaller gaggle of women seasoned a prodigious salad. A dozen trucks were parked below on the road itself, blocking it: these men, with thousands of other drivers, were staging a transportation strike that had paralyzed Chile in the last few weeks by cutting off many of the main highways, inter-rupting the country's economic lifeblood in the hope that the chaos and confusion would pressure the Armed Forces into intervening to restore order.

The truck drivers recognized us at once. They had probably heard the shots. But even if they hadn't, it would have been enough to see us materialize out of the hills, like seven amateur Che Guevaras, to realize immediately that we were their enemies, that we would gladly have torched their trucks and sent them all to hell. They, on the other hand, didn't send us to hell, not at all: they were going to win, they were already winning, they were the owners of a future that they could envisage even if we couldn't, and they felt, therefore, as people often do when they have the upper hand, charitable and deadly calm. Maybe that's why their leader, without standing, mo-tioned us, with a Neanderthal joint of meat in his hand, to come closer, to join in the banquet. It was remarkable to see that much food; by then the strike itself, plus economic sabotage, a financial blockade by Washington, and quite a bit of government incompe-tence, had made provisions scarce.

We came closer, though we did not want to share the meal. I guess we were superstitious: never accept food from someone you might have to kill. We stood there, watching them eat and drink and be merry, mesmerized by their presence. And then their leader put an oversized hand into his pocket and took out a wad of bills— American dollar bills—as if he were a gangster in a movie, and waved them at us knowingly and counted them in our presence and made a signal and the other truck drivers took out their greenbacks as well. I realized that we were the audience for their triumph, that they wanted us to understand how things stood, how incredibly screwed we were, they were showing us, right then, a day that was not far off, when we would be hunted and they would be back on the road. Above all, they wanted their women to see our humiliation. Chile had become a country where we, who defended the legitimate gov-ernment elected by the people, had to hide our training, while these men, who were being paid by a foreign power to overthrow that government, had no need to hide their financing. And adding to the personal irony of the situation was something that neither the truck drivers nor their women nor my companions knew, because I had done my best to conceal it: that of all those present that day, I was the most "American," the only one who could have spoken in their own language to the CIA operatives who had provided that money and planned the whole damn thing; I would have understood their jokes, their references to Dagwood and Blondie.

But I had renounced my United States identity, I wanted nothing more to do with that country of my childhood. Chile was my land, it belonged to me, I thought, more than to those drivers willing to sell it off to the highest bidder. They could display their dollars all they wanted, because very soon I would be promenading my own weapon against them in every home in the country: Susana la Semilla, my cartoon character.

I had, in fact, conceived her as an answer to their transportation strike or, to be more precise, as a way of dealing with the most devastating of its many side effects: those thousands of trucks blocking the roads had left thousands of tons of fertilizer rotting in the ports, endangering next year's harvest. Because of my post at La Moneda, I had been asked by Jaime Tohá, the Minister of Agriculture, to contrive an angle for an advertising campaign that would put the blame on our anti-patriotic adversaries.

I had come up with more than an angle. I had come up with a love story, an epic, a saga. I conjured up sexy, luscious, loquacious Susana, Susan the Seed, a sort of Chilean version of Chiquita Banana, pining away in the lonely countryside, eager to bear fruit and be a mother. Her aspirations to multiply were, however, being frustrated by the fact that her faraway lover, Federico el Fertilizante, Fred the Fertilizer, is being held captive in a faraway port.

And I had proceeded to write the story of how Federico escapes his captors and goes on the road and foils the saboteurs and finally joins Susana and makes her germinate. I had scripted twenty-five one-minute TV spots to be aired week after week, starting in September of 1973 and culiminating in an orgasmic finale, my two lovers coupling under the stars of March 1974. Now I realize that this socialist soap opera was my utopian version of a future where the people defeated hunger: the shining anticipation of a victory of love over terror that was about to be resoundingly denied by history.

But in order to give birth to Susana, to move my harvest of visions from my own private page onto the screens of millions of my compatriots, I had to persuade one man to sign on: Augusto Olivares, the congenial director of National Television—and I was supposed to make the pitch on . . . "Let's say Tuesday, September 11," he had suggested to me nonchalantly when I had told him in early September that it was urgent that we get together. He had smiled at me through his bushy, overgrown mustache, looking somewhat like a walrus, perhaps thinking that I was a bit loony, but then—so was he. Discussing seeds and fertilizers when the ship was about to sink. "Let's say—ten-thirty. I've got an opening around ten-thirty in the morning. Not at La Moneda. At my office. Okay?"

Of all the days he might have chosen, he unwittingly chose the day when the coup against Allende was to be launched, and of all the times, he chose, again without the slightest prescience, the time of the day that would keep me away from La Moneda in the morning, which allowed me to oversleep, to be wakened late on the morning of September 11 by the drone of military planes flying low over our house, buzzing the neighborhood.

It was only then that I found out that the coup was under way. When I switched on the radio and the station was playing a military march and I changed stations and that one was also playing a march, and on and on, flipping the dial, and I heard the first proclamation of the Military Junta that had taken over Chile, and at the end of the proclamation the name of General Augusto Pinochet Ugarte, who was supposed to be heading the forces loyal to the democratically elected government, and I knew that the revolution had failed, that's when I knew, that exact moment, that death had finally caught up with me, that all my fears from childhood were about to mate-rialize savagely in real life. And a few minutes later, with Angélica's hand in my trembling hand, I listened to Allende's *últimas palabras* from the Presidential Palace, his farewell speech in which he told his people that he would not resign, that he would die defending de-mocracy, die so others might live. Later I'd find out that next to him as he spoke was his old friend Augusto Olivares, readying himself for death at the President's side. Augusto never heard how Susana la Semilla was supposed to save his life, how in my delirium I had her symbolically saving the nation. He never knew that, implausibly, the only life my cartoon character ended up saving was mine.

But is that true? I have told the story so many times that I may have ended up believing it, comforting myself with the notion that somehow I had evaded my own death through the efforts of my own invention, that some fiction I had saved from nothingness saved me from that same nothingness, from becoming fictional. It's symmet-rical and a bit cute and makes a great story. But is it true?

As far as it goes, yes: it was enough for Claudio Gimeno to have said no, for Olivares to have said another day, for Susana not to have said anything, to have been silent and not inspired me—one slight variation and I would be dead, I would have made it to La Moneda the night of the coup or the dawn of the coup or the early morning of the coup.

Essential as they were, however, none of these happenstances really guaranteed my survival. Dozens of other activists who were close to Allende or worked at the Presidential Palace did no guard duty on September 10, and many of them had, like me, activities planned elsewhere that morning, appointments far from Allende's side—and that did not save them from being killed at La Moneda. They ended up there because they were called sometime during the night: there's an emergency, they were told, the coup has started, they were told, they were told to report immediately. Their names were on a list, I had held that list in my hands on the nights when I myself was sleeping at La Moneda, I had read my own name and phone number on that list just two nights ago, I was one of those who were supposed to be summoned in case of an emergency.

But nobody gave me a call.

Why? Had it been just one more crazy coincidence? One more chaotic incident in a chaotic day, a misunderstanding that had, once again, favored me instead of somebody else? Is that all? Is that it? No more than a series of arbitrary intercessions had spared me? Could the difference between living and dying really just grind down to this: destiny or fate or sheer dumb wonderful idiotic luck or whatever you want to call it? And life is just one more accident in an accidental universe? And we are no more than insects played with by a demented, impenetrable, faceless force that offers no reasons because there are none?

Or is there an explanation? Is there a meaning in all this, a message being sent, something I was being taught? Agnostic that I am now, agnostic that I was then, how to make sense of this sudden reprieve: I had deliberately placed myself in harm's way, almost challenging violence to come and ravish me, and that violence, when it had exploded in all its fury, had ignored me. How to avoid wondering, with humility, perhaps with terror, that there might have been a design, a deeper miraculous meaning to my deliverance from death? How to avoid the temptation of a mystical interpretation, that some sort of power was trying to rescue me, redeem me, forbidding death to come closer, saying to that reckless man: No you don't—you're needed elsewhere. Your time hasn't come yet.

This religious reading of my survival alternately fascinates and disgusts me. What sort of joy can I derive from imagining a God who condemns so many innocents to death and saves me? What sort of comfort is there in assigning responsibility to some equally precarious higher entity for what happened? Isn't randomness preferable, less cruel, than a supposedly superior consciousness playing haphazardly with our lives? And yet let me confess that for many years I could not rid myself of the suspicion that some benevolent deity had intervened on my behalf. Some benevolent deity had decided to counter the malevolent gods of the Central Intelligence Agency, the demons of the Chilean Armed Forces, the men in the shadows who were determining my death.

It turned out that there was a benevolent deity, a secret hand, a message: but luckily for my stubborn atheistic convictions, it was not the hand of a God but that of a real human being of flesh and blood. By the time he gave me the message, many years later, I had more or less figured it out for myself, had confronted the loneliness of survival and had puzzled out on my own why I had been blessed by the random insane finger of the universe.

The man to whom I owed my life was Fernando Flores, the very Minister who had originally given me the job at La Moneda. He was the one who, in the hours before dawn on that September 11, had decided to cross me off the list of people to be called. When the news of the uprising was confirmed, his bodyguard reached for the phone, started to dial—and Flores interrupted him, asked him for the list and read it carefully, taking his time. When he came to me, he took out his pen and carefully eliminated my name.

I was to hear this story a long time later, when we both met in exile, when I visited him in the United States, I think it was in early 1978. During the previous years, he had been in prison. The military had arrested him in mid-morning the day of the coup, when he left the Presidential Palace to negotiate a truce with the seditious troops on Allende's behalf. They ignored his white flag and packed him off to the brutal Military Academy for a few days, after which he was dispatched, along with other surviving Ministers of the former government, to a prison camp on Dawson Island, off Tierra del Fuego, one of the most barren, forsaken sites on the planet, and later was detained for several more years in a scattering of other concentration camps, awaiting a trial that never came. So it was only after he had been deported that he was able to tell me how he had intervened to save my life.

Why? I asked him. Why had he done it?

He paused, he turned inward as if consulting some person he had once been, he thought a bit and then said, in the same offhand way in which he probably had crossed my name off the list: "Well, somebody had to live to tell the story."

During the Allende years, from 1970 to 1973, I had constructed my identity as primarily political: fused with Chile and its cause and its people through the revolution that would, we thought, liberate the country. And so, as the end approached, I had accepted working with Flores at La Moneda because that is where I felt I belonged if the revolution failed, because I could not imagine myself surviving that failure, because it was a way of confirming who I was and who I wanted to be. Flores, in that desolate September dawn when it became clear that we had lost, saw things differently. Maybe he already knew that the tasks of defeat are not the tasks of victory. Maybe he knew that some of us would die, some of us would be jailed, some of us would turn traitor; and if that was going to happen, a witness would be needed who could escape the conflagration and tell the world the story. He thought I was that person, and at the last moment he had used his power over life and death to correct what he considered had been his error in offering me the job, what he considered my error in accepting it.

It is a comforting idea, that I was spared because I was to be the storyteller. It does not explain why a friend switched places with me, why a TV executive asked me to come to see him at the one time that would save me, why Susana la Semilla came to me as if in a childhood dream to insist there was salvation. It does not explain, in fact, any of the fortuitous coincidences that pulled me back into life as I was hurtling toward self-destruction. It does not explain why so many of my brothers and sisters, just as talented, as much in love with life, had to die. It does not assuage the mystery that still gropes and crawls in the center of my existence, does not entirely beat back the fear that life is blind and hazardous and that we stumble in the tender darkness and try to fool ourselves into believing there is a pattern to all this.

But what Flores decided that day, without consulting me, merely because he thought he had to put history right and not let it take its mad course—what he decided for me that day, that does make sense. Principally because of what happened later: who I became. It makes sense of what I forged with the life that had been given to me, loaned to me, chosen for me by chance or providence or whatever you want to call it the day I should have died.

If it is not true that this was why I was saved, I have tried to make it true.

In every story I tell.

Haunted by the certainty that I have been keeping a promise to the dead.

FOUR

A Chapter Dealing with the
Discovery of Life and
Language in the Year 1945 in
the United States of America

P lease understand: it is not the quick and complete surrender to English that surprises me today. In that nameless hospital in Manhattan the new language coming at me from all directions had, after all, been transformed into the sudden vocabulary of food and affection, warmth and punishment, the doorway into the hearts of the people who held me hostage. That painful experience only accelerated a learning process that lay in store for me anyway, like any child of immigrants, like my parents before me, like my own sons in their own uprooted lives when it would become their turn to change countries the way others, perhaps most of those who read these words, change brands of cereal.

All through history, people have been switching languages as a way of surviving. They are invaded, they are conquered, they are enslaved, their homes are smashed, their small or vast kingdoms turned to ruin: and inside the seeds of violence, almost like a gentle brother on another horse, barely a bit behind the fist holding the sword, is the verb. A captive always ends up being a captive of somebody else's words.

But if you look more closely at those countless victims who were forced, in far more traumatic circumstances than mine, to learn the language of those who held power over them, you will remark how many of them decided to become bilingual. Some of them succeeded and others were only able to secretly blend the forbidden and hidden language into the new and dominant one, infiltrate its rhythms, its grammar, its sounds, make it more familiar. But most of them, I am sure, tried to keep their first language alive, warm, close by. While they could, for as long as they could, those converts comforted themselves in their misery with the promise that the past was not entirely dead, that it would someday resurrect. They dared risk being double, the anxiety, the richness, the madness of being double.

It was a risk I was not willing to take there, at my beginning.

Instead, I instinctively chose, the first time I was truly alone with myself and took control of the one thing that was entirely my own in the world, my language, I instinctively chose to refuse the multiple, complex, in-between person I would someday become, this man who is shared by two equal languages and who has come to believe that to tolerate differences and indeed embody them personally and collectively might be our only salvation as a species. I refused to take a shortcut to the hybrid condition I have now embraced.

Why? Why is it that at some point, one day, one hour, one minute, during the infinity of those three weeks in that hospital, the boy I once inhabited found himself crossing a line of apparently no return and decided to suffocate the person he had been, to kill the language in which he had built the house of his identity?

I don't remember.

No matter how hard I try, I am unable to return to the mind of that boy forgotten in the first of his many exiles.

We all desire to find out how we began, force the legs of memory open. That obsession: go back as far as you can to your origins, try to be there before you are submitted to any look, any name, the shade of a vocabulary. Be there to watch yourself being watched into existence. But the species has decreed by law that we will be present at, but never be able to remember, the two most important events of our life: when we are born and when we die. And why should I be any different? But I was, I presumptuously thought I was. I thought I could bypass that law, access what had been my second birth, the moment when I had mothered and fathered myself. I had been present then, both of me—the Spanish child I had been and the English child I had become. I had witnessed that event in two languages and one of them would have to reveal what had happened, would open the door so I could spy on the moment when I had created myself, made myself into the person who can write these words in either language fifty years later.

And so, during the far too many years it has taken to write this text, I puzzled that event, interrogated it like a dead prisoner, rolled it around and around in my mind like a talisman or a curse. But the stone of my past became smoother and more enigmatic the more I fingered it. The harder I tried to access those children who occupied my body, see through their dual eyes what they saw, the further I drifted from what they witnessed that day. One of them, the child inside who speaks Spanish, will not respond, because I left him to die in the dark, atrophied the language with which he might have transmitted these memories to me; and the other child, the one who speaks English, he was present of course, but he was swept that moment from the fierce abscess of his mind, preferring to pretend that his start with me was painless and splendid and immaculate, that when he caught me as I fell I had no previous language.

I am left to ponder and milk that foundational moment of my life for meaning, forced to drag from the cracked black mirror of my past the story of how I invented myself that day.

I had behaved, I had obediently learned all the ropes, imitated all the right gestures, made sounds into syllables. I had baby-talked my way into the language that Borges, a few blocks from me in Buenos Aires, was using, almost like a dagger, to explore what it means to an Argentinian at the edge of the earth desiring to be someone else— and just as I was getting over the trauma of my first banishment from the womb, just as I was surfacing into articulation, here I was, subjected to another journey, another expulsion, another hospital, another doctor, here we go again, falling again, a repeat performance, entangled again in designs drawn up by people I could not control. With only my mother tongue to stave off the mouth of despair, to remind me who I was, the tongue my mother had bequeathed me with the promise never to desert me and speak me out of any pain, the tongue of my mother that now proved useless, as absent as my mother herself. And my father.

He had also abandoned me, I thought. For the second time. One day, barely a year after my birth, he had simply disappeared from our Argentine home, turned into a photograph next to my parents' bed, a blurred and vague phantom whose absence I probably lamented and simultaneously celebrated. I was left alone with my mother's overwhelming love: an Oedipal fantasy come true without any need of bloodshed, no soiled sense of guilt. Until abruptly, a year and a half later, in a foreign land where everything was cold and unknown, the photo materialized into a real body and those large male hands picked me up at the railway station in New York. I cannot really have recognized the man who had been my father and who had come back to protect me from loneliness but also to threaten me with it. Did I desire to keep my mother all to myself again? Did I fear he could read my guilty thoughts, magically be able to punish me? Did I punish myself before he could? Did I let myself grow sick to protest my exile, recuperate my mother, force her to tend me as she had done in Buenos Aires when my rash kept me awake all night, her hands holding mine lovingly all night? Did I let pneumonia into my lungs the first night they went out in almost two years and left me with a baby-sitter? And when I found myself alone again, this time without my mother or father, this time with no one between me and death, alone with the child and the language that child spoke, did I lash out at that Spanish language to deflect the impossibility of lashing out at my Spanish-speaking parents? Did I subscribe to a pact with my English self? Was that the price he had demanded for coming to the rescue that day I had found myself wordless in a roomful of alien adult voices with the power of life and death over me? The price that had to be paid for his protection: to sew up the abortive mouth of my Spanish self, to starve the little shit, brick by brick, like Fortunato being buried alive in "The Cask of Amontillado," brick by brick walling off my mother tongue from all contact with the world? To make love while he died?

I resist the interpretation that it all boils down to a trauma, that I can't access that moment because I am both abuser and victim, Cain and Abel rolled into one, Oedipus gouging out the eyes of his languages and his memory to atone for a sin he did not commit, he could not possibly have had the knowledge of committing. It can't all be in the psychology, the mythology, the archetypes, the twisted contortions of the personality. History also intervened.

Outside the hospital, ready to heal and possess my soul, was the most powerful nation in the world: the United States of America was waiting for me as I toddled out of that building, a two-and-a-half-year-old Argentine child babbling away in English to his Spanish-speaking parents, clutching his mother's hand, his father's hand, either in anguish or with the cheerful confidence that he had paid his dues, that they would never disappear again.

But they did. A few months later, they did disappear. And America was there this time, inside the English language, behind the English language, ready to work its enchantment.

Again, it wasn't my parents' fault. There was another sickness.

This time, my mother's: ever since that tense welcome at the railway station the day of our arrival, she had been sinking into a depression which the House of Death and the winter of New York and the near-death of her son did nothing to allay. But what she especially remembers from those grim months is how voiceless and vulnerable she felt. Every morning she would trudge through the alien snow to the butcher shop and there she'd watch the American ladies reap the choicest morsels of beef, watch them cracking jokes with the butcher and his assistant, inquiring about each other's families or the latest news from the front, my mother outside the circle of that vocabulary, excluded from that community, and when her turn finally came, she would stutter and stumble and collapse her way into negotiating a nice piece of meat for her carnivorous Argentine family and the impatient man in the smeared white apron on the other side of the gleaming counter would invariably hand her a hunk of nerves and fat and blood unfit for a dog—take it or leave it, lady—and she had to take it, day after day after day, swallow that and other humiliations, regressing to that moment as a girl when she had been told she could not open a door because she was foreign and Jewish and different, again feeling herself shunned, a stranger in Babylon.

But not every gringo was slamming the door shut on her: through all those difficult times, she felt protected, she would say later, by one American, a man who, though crippled and in a wheelchair, would somehow, she was sure, miraculously find the way to make things right for her and a fearful world: Franklin Delano Roosevelt. And when the President she adored died on April 12, 1945, my mother's grief sent her over the edge. Her depression turned into a mental and emotional breakdown. That death became emblematic of something deeper, something darker, in her life, some loss, in herself and in the life of the planet, which knew no relief, had no answer. The Nazis were retreating in Europe, the Japanese would soon surrender, the war was coming to an end, but my mother felt as if Roosevelt's death were wresting a father from her, as if what was about to end was not the war but the world, as if nothing would ever be sane again. And maybe she was right, maybe she sensed what Auschwitz was closing, what Hiroshima was about to open. She could not deal with what the orphaned world was sending her way.

There was no other solution. My father reluctantly placed his wife in an institution and, unable to care for us and keep his job, found a foster home just outside New York where my sister and I could be lodged along with other kids who had trouble in their families. I have the vaguest recollection of that place: summertime, swings, lemonade, perhaps those are my hands in my memory catching a firefly. But all this may be drifting back from some later zone in time. Nothing in my later development would signal any sort of abuse, the slightest hint that I may have been horribly unhappy. On the contrary. According to my father, who visited us frequently, I was much loved, ebullient and energetic as ever. I adapted and smiled and put on the best face I could, what else was I to do? I beguiled my caretakers, did everything I could to please them, deepened what must have been a preexisting inclination to be malleable and sunny, learned that if you are somebody's prisoner you can always try to turn the tables and imprison your warden in the net of your charm, amuse yourself into survival.

In English, of course.

So that by the time my mother was well enough to resume a normal life and my parents came to gather their two kids and move with us to a delightful apartment on Morningside Drive—on November 1, 1945, the Day of the Dead, the day after Halloween, what other day would have served the purposes of this tale?—by the time my Spanish-speaking parents were finally able to do battle for the Latino soul of their son, they discovered that they had lost me to the charisma of America, that what had begun in that hospital as a childish linguistic tantrum had, in the foster home, hardened into something more culturally permanent and drastic: the question of language had become ensnared in the question of nationality, and therefore of identity.

It is true that, even if I had possessed a language and an identity of my own to interpose between my self and America when it came calling, it still would have been hard to resist its allure. All over the world, people in those years were dazzled by the American dream of life. Why should I, living there, have bucked that trend?

And yet I cannot dismiss the idea that my life did not have to turn out the way it did. I tell myself that if it had not been for those two accidents, my sickness and my mother's, I would most certainly have evolved into a bilingual child, might have spent those ten years in the North at least partly anchored in the South, preparing myself for a return to a legendary Latin America that I would never have lost contact with. So that when the time came for history to play more games with me, when yet again forces I did not control sent me hurtling southward in 1954, I could have seen that experience as a homecoming for a bilingual Latino and not an exile for a mono-lingual would-be American.

But that's not how it turned out.

Without their language as an ally inside me, my parents didn't stand a chance against the country that, during their six-month ab-sence, had welcomed me from sea to shining sea. With all its vi-brancy, its optimism, the buoyant certainty of its people who thought they were the greatest ever to breed on the face of the earth.

And I thought so, too.

Listen to me in the car as we drive home, listen to me in the following days: I was coming around the mountain when she comes, I was coming from Alabama with a banjo on my knee, I was rowing the boat ashore, I was working on the railroad all the live-long day, even if sometimes I felt like a motherless child, still, Zip-A-Dee-Doo-Dah I had the whole world in my hands, my soul was marching on and it was marching on to the green green grass of home.

Home. That's where I was, where I had chosen to be: I was swing-ing low sweet chariot, come to carry me home, I was home, home on the range, I was in the land of the free and the home of the brave, this land was my land and it was made for you and me, but especially, I felt, it had been made for me.

The friendly story the United States told me about myself could not have been more suited to the needs of a child who wanted to remake himself, free himself from who he had been. It was the story that America had told itself, had already used to convert to nation-hood the teeming millions that had come to its shores in hopes of a better life, the story that had treated those huddled masses of foreign adults from underdeveloped lands as if they were children and needed to grow up. It was the story of modernization and virtue and zest, the get-up-and-go story that the United States was preparing to sell to a shocked world, a world terrified of its own powers of destruction, a world split apart like the atom, a world in dire need of a global system of values and standards and unity—the mythical American success story about to be exported, with its products and its dreams, to every corner of the globe by the "sleeping giant" (Ad-miral Yamamoto's fateful words after Pearl Harbor) that had awak-ened from the Second World War as the dominant technological, economic, military, and cultural force of the century, perhaps the most powerful nation in history.

The story that tells every human being to be like America itself and every problem will be solved.

And so it came to pass that the English language adopted me at that crucial crossroads in twentieth-century history when its main carrier was embarking on its God-given mission to deliver the whole of humanity.

Just as I had been delivered in that Manhattan hospital. Because America whispered to me the same message, reinforced the same message I had whispered to myself so only I could hear it in that hospital: You can become someone else, you can give birth to your self all over again. You can reinvent yourself in an entirely new lan-guage in an entirely new land. I had taken a dangerous step, a step that must have filled me with guilt and apprehension, a leap into the unknown: and then America appeared on its shining horse and turned on me the full force of its power, the very power it was unleashing on the globe, and with the same energy and the same cheap and accessible and cheerful culture convinced me, as it was right then trying to convince the world, that tomorrow is another day, tomorrow will always be better. America reassured me that my act of betrayal of a useless past and useful parents was an act of rebellion, of self-reliance, of dignity, inevitable in any march to the future. America, made of immigrants and pioneers and entrepreneurs, told me that I was free, that I should not let others determine my life.

America told me I could be innocent again.

America, which had just won the Second World War and was out to save and possess the whole planet, promised me that, in return for my total loyalty, it would never abandon me.

I had nowhere else to go and no one else to turn to.

Bereft of a past and a language that told me who I was, what else was I to do?

I became an American.

FIVE

A Chapter Dealing with the Discovery of Death in the Late Morning of September 11, 1973, in Santiago de Chile

For many years, I refused to believe that Salvador Allende had committed suicide.

As soon as the Junta headed by General Pinochet had announced, the night of the coup, that the President had taken his own life, I knew they were lying. My only evidence was that, at that very moment, they were lying about killing hundreds of innocent patriots and lying about the death of Chile's democracy, the fact that they had betrayed Allende and the Constitution they had sworn to defend. Later, during my exile, the certainty that they were trying to cover up his murder congealed into a story about good and evil that we repeated over and over again as we campaigned across the world. Because Allende's death was the first death of the dictatorship, the preeminent death with which the terror had been inaugurated, we needed it to be an archetypal death, one from which all the other deaths would flow, we needed this to be an epic tale, tragic only in its simplicity, the good king assassinated by the generals who had sworn allegiance to him. And in this story we cast ourselves as the metaphorical sons and daughters of Allende, who would come out of the shadows, bent on revenge, determined to bring him back from the dead. It is a story that still greets me today everywhere I go, like an echo from people who are not—as I was not, during my years of exile—ready to face the tangled ambiguity of a hero who takes his own life, and prefer to return to my ears the stirring version that my mouth repeated for so long even as I suspected that it was false. Myths do not die as easily as human beings.

But it was not only political expediency that nourished for so long the legend of Allende fighting to the death, at least in my case. My automatic assumption that he had been murdered put his death in perspective, helped me to deal with its pain, make sense of my survival.

He was dying so we might live.

I knew it when I heard Allende's last words over the radio the morning of the coup, when I heard him admit defeat and tell us not to allow ourselves to be humiliated, when I heard him predict a time when, sooner rather than later, we would again be free. I looked at Angélica: these were the words of a man who was doomed and was saying goodbye.

Feverishly, I started to dress.

"Where are you going?"

Angélica asked me that question even if she must have seen in the wild grief of my eyes what the answer had to be. I was going to try to make it to La Moneda. She shook her head, I was out of my mind—and then, amazingly, Angélica, who was, and still is, the most pragmatic, down-to-earth being on this planet, decided to cooperate in my mad expedition: "I'll drive you down to the center."

She took me as far as she could, and then we hit a police barrier at the Plaza Italia, on the perimeter of downtown Santiago. Fourteen short blocks away, La Moneda was waiting for me.

I got out of the car, determined to find some way of talking the police into letting me pass. And standing there, I hesitated. I had been saved, up till then, by a series of fortuitous circumstances totally outside my control. But now my life is no longer in the hands of somebody else, in the hands of chance, in the hands of some unknown divinity who decides to cross my name off a list, a friend who decides to change places with me. This time, for now, for this one everlasting moment, I am the only one who can decide whether I live or die.

And then I turn, I turn after that moment's hesitation, I turn suddenly and decisively from the stolid faces of the policemen, I walk three paces back to the car, I get into it, I let Angélica drive me away.

It is a defining moment, that split second. I will not realize it till later, till much later, perhaps not till now that I have decided to probe that instant for its significance, only now have I realized that there, at the police barrier, I confronted the two basic dilemmas of resistance, two questions that have no easy answers, that I resolved then quickly and in haste, the same questions that at that very moment were challenging every Chilean man and every Chilean woman who had believed in the revolution. They are enmeshed in each other, these two questions, but they are not identical. They are as old as injustice, as old as the struggle against injustice, these two essential questions that cannot be avoided by anybody who, enduring violence or witnessing its dominion over others, decides to resist.

The first is by far the least interesting: Do I have the courage to do what my conscience asks? The least interesting because at times fear wins and at other times it doesn't and there is not much more to the matter than that. Or perhaps I find it the least interesting because I cannot help but wonder if, there at the police barrier the day of the coup, my resolve was not being fundamentally tested and somehow I was found wanting, I wonder if I could not have done more to press on to La Moneda, I wonder if I was not a coward, I wonder if I did not die at Allende's side because, quite simply, I was afraid. But with the years it is the second question, and not the enigma of courage, that has loomed larger, the second question that seems to embody the basic mystery of resistance, that plumbs what really went on in my mind the day of the coup, the start of a complex learning process that any survivor, in Chile or elsewhere, will always have to grapple with, that question: Do I have the wisdom to distinguish a death that I cannot avoid from a death that I must embrace? Or to put it differently: Given that some periods in history make it sadly inevitable that each small conquest of human dignity and freedom be paid for with enormous suffering and even death, and given the parallel sacredness of life, how to make sure that I die the right death? A question I will have to answer there, that day, and answer over and over again until the day the dictatorship ends.

If I decide for life at that moment when I confront the question for the first time, it is not only that it is patently insane to try to sneak past the police, cross the center of the city where snipers and soldiers are shooting at each other, in the vain hope that the troops besieging La Moneda will allow me to enter the building instead of executing me on the spot, it is not only reckless lunacy that I am defeating inside me, but despair, that handmaiden of death.

That is the real danger that confronts me at that police barrier, then and in the years to come.

When you have been defeated, when everything you believe in has been defeated, when the hope for change that a true revolution celebrates has been defeated, that is the moment when you can easily be drawn into the well of death. I could feel it calling inside me, that desire to destroy myself, as I contemplated where our dreams had led us. We had dared to make a prophecy, we had dared to believe that we could build a just society without shedding blood. And now the blood was ours, our peaceful revolution was ending in a massacre, yet another massacre in a Latin America strewn with corpses. And it was hard to reject the temptation to turn my death into the last way, the only way, to speak in the midst of failure, the only island of reality I could still control, my own dead body as the only proof I could now offer of my sincerity, my belief in a future of liberation that seemed forever postponed. That was the real trap of death: as the doors seem to close on every other possibility of expression, to hail martyrdom as a perverse way of subverting death itself, maybe even reversing its reign, force the future to listen to the dreams of the present, persist as a legend rather than a life.

If at that police barrier I finally did not take that road, it may have been because I was aware that someone else was taking it for me, taking it for all of us. Salvador Allende was taking responsibility for defeat, atoning with his life for all our mistakes and his, a ritual sacrifice which stopped me and so many others from throwing our lives away.

But it is not only protection that Salvador Allende is offering me, there, that day when I do not continue on to La Moneda. His death will also, in the years to come, make terrible demands on those who survive him, cast a shadow on our lives, burden us impossibly. There are some among us who will not be able to carry the sacred weight of Allende's death, some of us who will follow him into death.

One of those is his own daughter, Beatriz Allende. Taty—as Beatriz is known to her close friends—is Allende's constant companion and confidante. At the very moment that I am instinctively turning toward life at the police barrier, she is being ordered out of La Moneda along with all the women who are there that day. The President decides that Taty and the other women must leave when he realizes that he is going to die. When he receives the ultimatum from the Armed Forces to surrender or the Air Force will use bombs and Hawker Hunters to dislodge him, when he announces that he will never board the plane waiting to fly him into exile.

At first, Taty refuses. How her father convinced her is something I never found out, Taty never told me when we met many months later, in early March of 1974, in the little breakfast room on the second floor of the Hotel Havana Libre in Cuba.

I was on my way to my European exile. The Cubans had managed to get me out of Argentina, had paid my plane ticket, mine and Angélica's and Rodrigo's, and they had done it just in time. Two days after we left Buenos Aires, three men from the Argentine police had come to my grandmother's apartment asking for me. They did not believe her when she told them that her grandson had left the country. They interrogated her, my ninety-year-old grandmother, for an hour. Then they left. "We'll find him," they told my Baba Pizzi, who must have felt that time had stood still, that time repeated itself, who must have remembered how, seventy or so years before, she had heard similar words, in Russian, from the czarist police when they had come to her home to look for her revolutionary brother, "We'll find him, wherever he's hiding." The Argentinians never found me—but they would find lots of other people, in the years to come they would disappear thousands and thousands of others who did not escape.

How strange the paths to survival are, the bonding that occurs between survivors. I had last spoken to Taty the afternoon of September 10 at La Moneda, had briefly mentioned my ideas about Susana la Semilla, had prognosticated that if we could make it to the day spring would begin, eleven days away, we were going to win, mother nature herself would see to that. She had answered with a laugh, saying that I was an incorrigible poet, totally *loco*, but I should always stay that way. I remembered that laugh when I heard that La Moneda had been bombed, sure that she had died there. Nevertheless, here we were, six months later, together again.

I asked about her mother and her sister, she asked about Angélica and Rodrigo and my parents. I was curious, of course, about her last hours with Allende, but this was a delicate area for both of us, and I skirted it.

Taty had no such inhibitions. All of a sudden, she said: "Tell me about La Moneda."

I was silent. There was nothing to tell.

"About La Moneda," she insisted. "How did you manage to escape that day?"

She must have read the perplexity on my face.

"After the bombardment," she said. "Where did you hide? How come they never found you?"

I stuttered that I didn't know what she was talking about, that I'd never made it to La Moneda that morning.

"There's no need to be modest with me," she said. "Everybody knows you're a hero. *Vamos*, I've been waiting all these months to talk with you. You must have been one of the last people to see my father alive."

She had sighted me there, she fervently assured me that the last time she looked back I was standing at Allende's side, waiting for the end exactly the defiant way I had imagined it, exactly the way it never happened. And then she asked me again about Allende's last moments, she wanted to see her father's martyrdom through my absent eyes.

Her hallucination will taunt me then and still taunts me now, so many years later, because her vision of my body there next to Allende came as much from my imagination as from hers; it was the ghost of myself calling to me out of her mouth. She presented me, all over again, with the ending I had planned for myself, the way I would like to have been remembered, the way I had deliberately constructed my definitive revolutionary committed persona during the months that preceded the coup, she placed me boldly face-to-face with the radical Ariel I had sworn loyalty to, all the words I had chanted about my willingness to die for humanity, the easy words of liberation with which I had invented myself as an unequivocally political animal, the scenario that was filmed only in my head. She is a messenger of death, a messenger from her father: reminding me that in an alternative parallel version of my existence it would be my face on a poster while somebody else in exile accompanies the widow up the steps to meet some Minister of Foreign Affairs, somebody like me helps my Angélica to testify in front of the Human Rights Commission; in the life and death that I finally did not choose, my son would be demanding my body, next to other relatives in a teargassed Santiago street, my son pins my photo to his jacket and demands that I be redeemed from disappearance, demands the right to bury me, Taty reminds me that I am not one of the many Claudio Gimenos of this world.

I am eventually able to convince Taty that she has made a mistake, explaining how I was spared. But there is one thing I do not tell her: how I hesitated at the police barrier and did not join her at La Moneda, how her father's death saved me. I do not tell her that it took only a second for me to decide not to throw my life away.

I will remember what I told her and what I did not when, several years after she offered me that delusionary vision of my ending at La Moneda, I hear the news that Taty Allende has killed herself. Until her death, like so many of us in those first years of exile, she drives herself mercilessly, working for Chile's freedom, less perhaps as a tribute to the living who need support from abroad than as a way to placate the dead. But the dead will not be placated. When her father decreed, at La Moneda, that only men should die there that day, when he ordered his daughter out because she was a woman, he could not guess that he was condemning her to self-destruction. Taty would not let herself forget that, if she had been Allende's son, she would have been allowed, indeed been expected, to die at her father's side. She can never forgive herself for being alive only because of her sex. She belonged there. She could truly imagine herself nowhere else. The bullet she was certain was meant for her so many years earlier at that place where Allende died is the bullet that she belatedly fires at herself.

Did she know, at that moment when she took the gun in her hand, when she took her life with that gun, did she know that Salvador Allende had himself committed suicide? Was that the deeper ritual of death she was enacting, not to stand by her father's side at the moment of reckoning, but to *be* her father, follow his example by killing herself?

I have no way of knowing what went on in my friend's head. To be dead is, by definition, to be unable to tell the story of how we died. What is clear is that we ended up interpreting Allende's death in different ways—that she was finally engulfed by it and that I managed to break loose, the real daughter and the metaphorical son of the President taking divergent paths in a world where our father had ceased to exist, could only speak to us ambiguously from death.

That, at any rate, is what I think. And the fact that I survived and that she died gives me, irreparably, the last word. Even though she is there, looking at me still, staring at me from death next to her father, calling to me even now with the pale reminder that I could have chosen her path.

Reminding me that I will have to carry her and her father and all the other dead of Chile like an orphan till the day I die.

Telling me that perhaps I took the greater risk when I decided not to be devoured by the coup.

SIX

A Chapter Dealing with the Discovery of Life and Language During the Years 1945 to 1954 in the United States of America

It was not true, of course, that my Spanish had died in New York. My Spanish had resisted. When I had tried to smother it, my Spanish had hidden and then endured inside me, waiting for its chance to come out and find a way back into my life. I knew it was there, I knew it, but told nobody that I understood the language that my parents continued to speak at home.

How did I manage to stop Spanish from surfacing, how did I keep it at bay during ten years?

By shutting myself off, by closing the door, by throwing away the key. That is, if my first memory, the first one in my life, means anything at all.

I never wanted it to be the original memory, the moment when my consciousness begins. All I ever desired was to recall that day in the hospital, understand who I was before that day in the hospital, but what whirls up from the remote past is this: I am a child of three, probably going on four, I am sitting on the toilet, and outside the locked door my father is calling for me to hurry up or let him in. I am not sure what he wants but I am sure that he is angry and that I would rather stay here in this place where I can be intimate with myself by myself. That's it. Irrelevant, unheroic, only mysterious inasmuch as it happens to have clawed itself upward to the surface of my mind, there to remain scrawled indelibly to this day, as clear to me now in retrospect as it must have been when I lived it: the darkened bathroom, the mirror, my shorts and underpants wrapped around my ankles, the voice of my father, the certainty that I like to be here alone, the mild fear, the vague guilt. Nothing more. Nothing until now that revealed why I remembered this insignificant incident, why it should be there at the beginning of my remembered life, why I have forgotten everything that came before. Until now that, writing this, I realize that my father is calling to me in Spanish and that I am not answering him, that he is angry because I did not answer, that now he is switching to English and to this I reply, I call out something, anything, I flush the toilet, I wash my hands, I open the door. So that's what this is about: my refusal to let on that I understand his words unless he adapts to my language. My first memory: how I built a space of my own where Spanish cannot enter, where I can keep myself separate from its threat, forever apart, unyielding. The central act of my early life: I hide in the toilet with my nakedness and my privacy and my shit and my English, I reject that voice in Spanish, the voice of tradition that is echoed by words inside me that I refuse publicly to acknowledge. This is how I create, day by day, my identity. This is how I deny, day by day, the brother who is in my mind and understands Spanish, how I deny him the chance to resurrect.

It is a scene that, in gentler versions, will repeat itself over and over again. There I am at the dinner table a year later, maybe I am five by now. My mother and my father from time to time interrupt their conversation to try to catch me unawares, slyly direct a question to me in Spanish to see if I will acquiesce to whatever wonder is being offered, a toy, candy, an outing, a hug, a second helping, a movie matinee, but I do not bite, I repeat the same phrase from that first day at the hospital, "I don't understand," even if I do, because a few minutes later I pertinently erupt in English into the middle of their Spanish-language conversation. But when they turn to me and follow up, again in Spanish, again I clamp down: I am not ready to admit that my native language has any hold on me whatsoever, that there is an ember under the ashes.

I have been able to persist in this dismissal of Spanish because my parents do not use violence to make me desist. All it would have taken, as soon as we emerged from the hospital, was a quick slap the second time I stubbornly insisted on being monolingual in English, for my defenses to collapse. But my mother and father were very affectionate, not the sort to force-feed a meal to a child, let alone a language. And their own migratory experience probably made them tolerant of linguistic shifting, aware that languages are best learned through love. It was a *capricho*, they thought: a silly whim which would soon pass, would in fact pass, they proclaimed, as soon as the family returned to Argentina. Because my mother and father predicted, as exiles always do, that they would be back home by next year.

This was no idle dream.

I can remember a night when my parents waited anxiously by the radio with a group of expatriate friends—it must have been June 1946, so I was already a four-year-old Yankee enthralled by the Jack Benny Show and by Amos 'n' Andy perpetually trying to head North—waiting for news of the election back in Argentina. They were all certain that the nefarious General Juan Domingo Perón ("and his slut Evita," they added) would be defeated by a coalition of Conservatives, Liberals, Centrists, Socialists, and Communists, all of them supported by the United States: the anti-fascist coalition falling apart all over the world was still holding in laggard Argentina. I was waiting just as anxiously to hear that Perón—whoever he might be—had won. I had no idea what that far-off general represented: only that if he was defeated, my parents and their Spanish-gabbing pals would commandeer the first plane back to Buenos Aires to participate in the new government, and Vlady, of course, would have to tag along.

That was, I believe, the reason why I so ferociously repressed my Spanish self, because his threats to awaken, like a monster in the farthest recesses of the castle in the fairy tales, his threats to return from the dead like the youngest brother sold into slavery, were connected to a real place in the world, a recalcitrantly physical space that I could not erase from the real map of the world the way I had erased the Spanish perversely localized there.

But my bizarre ally, General Perón, saved me for English and America, he saved me for the Teddy Bears' picnic and for Burt Lancaster as *The Crimson Pirate* and for Joe DiMaggio hitting one more home, he saved me for the smell of hot dogs sizzling at Nedick's and for the Easter Parade on Fifth Avenue and for the Three Musketeers candy bar and for the infinite aisles of toys at Macy's and the buzz of the yellow cabs of New York and the icy excitement of skaters at Rockefeller Center and the little train that could and the Great Gildersleeve.

Perón! Who had never heard of the Great Gildersleeve. Like most of my readers, for that matter.

Perón saved me by doing something entirely unforgivable to the left-wing intellectuals of Argentina, including my own father: he stole the working class from them, the working class they had appealed to and supposedly understood and yet had never been able truly to represent. The *cabecitas negras*, so called because of their shock of black hair, pouring in from the hinterlands like an untamed horde, the masses of the Argentine poor who were fed up with conservative governments and didn't feel interpreted by immigrant European Marxist know-it-alls, were making sure that a little blond Jewish boy who spoke English in New York, for one, wouldn't cry for Argentina, that I could continue my accelerated process of Americanization, that I could lie on my tummy every Sunday with the *Herald Tribune* spread out larger than my body and follow the funnies while a mirage of voices on the radio acted out the roles. Not a bad example of how America enthralled me with its cutting edge of technology and marketing, striving already, with the harmonizing of sound and images right there in the living room, toward that most pervasive and invasive of media wonders that would soon conquer the world, including Argentina: television.

And while I watched the comic strips unfold like a screen before my ecstatic eyes, I knew somewhere in my head that a remote and apparently evil Argentine general's hold on power was all that kept me in the Land of Oz, and that the day he was forced to leave his Argentine sanctuary was the day I would be forced instantly to leave mine, the United States, never again to greet New Year's with clowning and revelry in Times Square, never again to exchange insults in Americanese—Ya Fatso, ya big slob, ya jughead—in the playground, in the schoolyard, and, ultimately, in the streets. Many years later, my own son Joaquín would be caught in a similar warped situation when Angélica and I were in exile in the States, longing, like my parents before us, for our own Promised Land. We longed for Chile. And all that Joaquín wanted was to stay in America. So it would be his turn to pray that his mother and father would not compel him to leave his friends and the English language behind and regress forever to the obscure Chile that they so desired and that our son born in Amsterdam hardly knew, perhaps repeating what his own grandfather Adolfo had felt when at the turn of the century he was forced to leave the Russia he loved, perhaps repeating my prayers about Argentina when I was a child.

I slowly came to realize, however, that the real menace was advancing, not from the Argentina where Perón was tightening his grip, but from my beloved America itself, where another sort of grip was tightening. History had arranged for me to adopt a homeland at the very crossroads of the twentieth century when this homeland was itself adopting a new post-war definition of its worldwide mission, an identity that would aggressively exclude from America my father and just about every friend and acquaintance he had made there, designating them, literally and specifically, as anti-American. Extraneous to the essence of the United States and therefore unworthy of living there—and, perhaps by implication, unworthy of living at all. If the war against Fascism had sent me North, the alliance between the Soviet Union and the United States paving the way for my Russian-infatuated father to be welcomed with open arms in the metropolis of capitalism, the falling-out of the two former allies was eventually to be responsible for sending me South.

This took time. Only in September of 1949, when I was seven, did I begin to understand that there was such a thing as the Cold War and that its existence had serious implications for my life and, yes, for my language.

Until then, I was largely oblivious to its effects. I was not yet four years old when Winston Churchill, in March 1946, proclaimed in Fulton, Missouri, that an iron curtain had come down on Eastern Europe, calling for "a fraternal association of the English-speaking people" to confront Stalin's plans for world domination. I was undoubtedly on that very day striving with energy and enthusiasm in some kindergarten in Manhattan to become a full-fledged member of that fraternal association, and couldn't have cared less about iron curtains: what was falling down in my life were London Bridge and Humpty Dumpty who sat on a wall, Humpty Dumpty who had a great fall, and me, I was falling down and laughing and squealing as I ran a ring around a rosy, pocketful of posies, all fall down! I didn't know that the curtain was coming down in the very middle of my life, splitting it as if I were a country occupied by two warring armies, that my father would be classified as a man who belonged on the other side of that curtain. I didn't know that the man who stood next to Churchill that day,

President Harry ("Give 'em Hell") Truman, was planting the seeds of my future banishment from America the Beautiful. As the elected guardian of the spacious skies and purple-mountained majesty that I had learned to praise in my foster home, he was already, before the war even ended, sending the Russians "to hell" and that day in Missouri was getting ready to "scare the hell" out of his fellow countrymen with the Communist bogeyman. It was only a matter of time (yes, time, which I imagined then as a mouse running hickory dickory dock up and down a clock) before the policy of containment of the enemy abroad would turn into a relentless, vicious assault on the presumed enemies inside. A year later, Truman ordered the Federal Loyalty Program to root out any employees in the Executive branch who might have had any links to Communism, and Congress, not to be outdone, increased the investigations of its House Committee on Un-American (*sic!*) Activities. The witch-hunt was on!

As for me, if I was able to concentrate on witches and activities of another sort, my first Halloween, my first trick-or-treating, the horrible, deformed, wart-filled stepmother in Disney's *Snow White*, it was because my father had taken the one job that helped to safeguard him and his family from the political terror that was seeping into the American bloodstream.

He had accepted, in August 1946 (two months after Perón's sobering victory), a high post in the recently formed United Nations: the second man in the Council for Economic Development. The world organization's charter did not permit the host country to interfere in any way in the lives of its foreign staff, and for many years my dad thought himself beyond reach of the Thought Police or the Red Scare, even as more and more of his American friends lost their jobs or were jailed or ostracized.

His diplomatic immunity not only meant that he couldn't be expelled from the country; it also translated into Parkway Village, a housing development in Queens that had been set aside for the United Nations staff who worked at nearby Lake Success; we moved in late 1947, once again—when else?—on the Day of the Dead. The arrival of families from all the nations of the world to those comfortable red-brick houses turned that piece of American real estate into an international village: all the colors, all the countries, all the religions, right there, in those twenty square blocks of suburbia, converging peacefully, living side by side. And all the languages—at home, that is, once the Norwegian and Ghanaian and Chinese mothers called the children indoors; but outside, in the gardens, in the playgrounds, and, above all, at the International School, which I attended for two years, the language was English. Everybody's preferred second language.

I was there at the outset, at that time and place in history when English became the first truly international language of humanity, the beginning of that language's conquest of the transnational spaces of the planet. Forty or so years before anybody ever heard of the Internet and the World Wide Web, English became, experimentally in my Village on the Parkway, the meeting place of the world, where children from every nation played excitedly on a common ground, cajoled and imagined and flamed each other.

Parkway Village—and the International School it harbored—dreamed itself, and managed to embody, an island of tolerance and olive branches and peace poised on the edge of an increasingly xenophobic and warlike America. My first two years there passed as if I were living and learning inside a magic circle: the bitter feud between the two superpowers, the struggle for Greece, for Berlin, for Italy, the intense U.S. meddling and intervention in what would become known as the Third World, the brutal Soviet crushing of democracy in Hungary and Poland and Czechoslovakia, all that transpired far away, as if the streets surrounding Parkway Village were a shadowland and our extraterritorial enclave the only reality. Nothing unsettled my fun and games with America in my beloved English, round and round the mulberry bush, the monkey chased the weasel. But my refuge of innocence and immunity in a world intent on racing in the other direction could not last.

In September 1949 two events, only one relevant to my personal life and the other of worldwide significance, coincided to explode me out of my cocoon, to bring the Cold War home.

The first was my departure from the United Nations Children's School. I had outgrown it, and my parents had no alternative but to place me in an American public school, P.S. 117, a few blocks away, on the other side of bustling Grand Central Parkway. I was suddenly outside the multicultural oasis where forbearance reigned, thrust straight into the frantic traffic of an America that was growing more paranoid by the day.

It was there, in that school, that the second event overtook me: there that I heard, one day in that month of September, that the Soviets had detonated their first nuclear bomb. The United States had been, in effect, chasing the Russians round and round the mulberry bush and now, all of a sudden, the enemy had stood its ground and threatened to do to the Americans what the Americans had been threatening to do to them since Nagasaki. "Pop goes the weasel" suddenly applied to the monkey chasing the weasel and the whole world: Pop goes the planet.

In the months to come, as hysteria swept the United States, I was unable to insulate myself from the mounting frenzy. How could I, when we kids were being terrorized by the siren sounding its dire shriek, made to scrunch under our desks during endless air-raid drills, waiting for the Russians to come and bomb, fry, vaporize us in one blind howling second, how could I ignore the Cold War when the enemy was portrayed everywhere as akin to polio—a sickness that could strike without provocation, creeping from some filth and sin inside and outside, prostrating children and leaving them in braces, on crutches, in wheelchairs? How could I ignore the red menace if my teacher had used the innocent word, apple, A is for apple, to lecture us on the danger and decay hidden everywhere. "There are people," she said, "bad Americans," she said, "who are like rotten apples."

Later, out in the playground, some kid had come up to me and asked the riddle/joke of the day, of the times: What is worse, he asked, than finding a worm in your apple? I blurted out the answer: Half a worm. What I did not tell him or anybody else was that I had a rotten apple at home, that I was the son of that rotten apple, that inside me was a worm I had swallowed, half a worm inside me as if I were the apple. For me the Red Menace was not something out there, foggy and vague.

The two worlds I had successfully kept apart, that of my family and that of my foster country, had finally collided. In that public school I was forced to come to terms with the confusion in my soul: my father was the enemy of the flag I pledged allegiance to every morning, the flag and words that had pledged to protect me in return.

At about that time, across the ocean, E. M. Forster was writing words that sadly applied to my dilemma (and oddly mirrored the predicament of so many Soviet children who, in their twisted totalitarian police state, were being asked, at that very moment, to turn in their own families): "If I had to choose between betraying my country and betraying my friend, I hope I should have the guts to betray my country."

I was about to find out if I had the guts.

The Cold War was going to submit me, before I was eight years old, to a loyalty test.

One incident has stayed with me, scuttling into my memory, there to remain like a crab. It must have been in early 1950. A day at breakfast when I was angry with my father or he was angry with me—the stupid details of our stupid quarrel have long ago slipped my mind, but not what happened next: I went to the door as I did every morning, to walk to school with a couple of friends who were waiting outside on the sidewalk. Suddenly I turned and pouted at my dad: "I'm going to tell my teacher you're a Communist." He went pale. But he said nothing. Just looked at me. My mother waited for a few seconds. And now, as I focus on that threshold moment, I realize that by then I must have known full well the perilous implications of what that word meant, because my mother and father had made sure that, when asked by anybody, I would get my father's profession right, that I would answer he was an economist. I had been made to enunciate each syllable separately, precisely, several times over, so my tongue could not blunder, however inadvertently, into the dangerous word Communist. My father—even though he had remained sympathetic to the Soviet Union—had not been a Communist for over a decade. He had kept that past affiliation a secret, even from me—one of the few acts of caution in his courageous life—but the guilt by association that was corroding America right then, the deduction of guilt from opinions, the guilt by silence, had penetrated my own mind. Children have a way of guessing when something is wrong, and I knew in my bones that my family was different. I knew that we led a sort of double life: that what was said in the intimacy of the home was never repeated anywhere else. I knew that the English language that was being corrupted by fear could not penetrate our safe haven where Spanish reigned, the language of secrecy, the language of clandestine emotions. I knew that the foreign language my parents spoke somehow protected them— but also set them apart, targeted them. And I knew other things: that a very important man named Alger Hiss (I had met him, he was an acquaintance of my father's) had been arrested for espionage and jailed for something called perjury. I had overheard that Aaron Copland, whose *Appalachian Spring* I had listened to, enthralled, at a concert at Tanglewood, that very same nice man who had talked to me after the concert and shaken my hand and rumpled my hair, that composer, in person, had been interrogated about his Communist connections by stone-faced men in Congress; and rumors abounded that the adored Charlie Chaplin was going to be deported; and . . . Now that I think of it, the signs were all around me, and had gradually dripped into my consciousness like a slow poison, the discussions at home, the worried friends of my father: Do you know who was called today before the House Committee? Do you know who's getting the boot? Do you know who refused to testify? Do you know who named names? It all comes back to me in bits and pieces, fragments swirling venomously in my mind which must have been smoldering inside me that morning, at the door, when I repeated the word, the dangerous one, loud and clear.

"Communist," I reasserted, so they would understand that this was no joke. My father continued to look at me quietly. No apology. No plea. And then my mother crossed the room, crouched down next to me, and looked me straight in the eyes. She must have told me she was sure I wouldn't do it, something like that, I can't remember her exact words, just the touch of her fingers softly on my arms, her kiss goodbye, her eyes sorrowful, trusting.

I didn't reply.

I shut the door, walked to school quietly, not clowning with my friends as usual, spent the whole day wondering if I should carry out my threat. I can still recall today how empowering it was to have the fate of my parents at my fingertips, rolling on my tongue, like a coin that could be flipped. Twice that day, my teacher expostulated about George Washington and Abraham Lincoln and freedom and both times I said to myself: Now's the time, just raise your hand and denounce your traitor father. When I returned home, my mother was waiting for me. She had been waiting the whole day. I told her that I hadn't whispered a word to anybody about my father or who he was. She hugged me and said I was a good boy. And never mentioned the affair again. Not once.

Faced with the choice that E. M. Forster had posed in that work I was not to read until several decades later in which he spoke about having to choose between country and friend, I had found the guts he wished for, I had preferred and would continue to prefer the two best friends in my life, my parents, to the country I had adopted, which had adopted me.

And so it came to pass that the Cold War managed what my parents, with all their nostalgia for Latin America and all their Spanish temptations, had never been able accomplish: to drive a wedge, the first in my life, between America and me.

I began to fear America.

The country I had proclaimed my champion in my search for an independent identity, the country that had nursed and guarded me, was out to get my family, would hurt them, send them running, perhaps even kill them.

And as if to prove that my fear was not abstract, almost like a sick echo, a name, two names in fact, attached themselves in that year of 1950 to that fear, the names of Julius and Ethel Rosenberg.

There were not just four Dorfmans at the table every evening: all through the early fifties, the ghosts of that other family sat with us, the four Rosenbergs, the mother and the father and their two boys, eight of us having dinner in the evening for three years, since the moment Ethel and Julius Rosenberg were arrested in 1950 until the night of their execution three years later, they were always there as a reminder of what could happen to us.

I remember it like a dagger: we all followed the ups and downs of the trial on the radio and in the papers, listening to the news that the father and the mother of those two boys had been condemned to death, for treachery, for spying, for being Communists, for passing secrets to the Soviets, for giving them the bomb, and then the appeals and then the calls for mercy from everywhere, and I can remember saying to myself: If they kill Ethel and Julius, then they can kill my mom and dad as well.

It was an early lesson on how terror works.

Across the world, Stalin had mercilessly sent millions of innocents to their deaths, slaughtering along the way the dream of socialism; in the United States, the government did not need to use genocide to tame its own dissidents. It was enough to make an example of two human beings, one of whom, Ethel, was obviously innocent; it was enough to liquidate them ruthlessly, trampling on due process and distorting the law, to demonstrate what awaited anyone who dared to oppose American policies. The rest is left to the imagination: those who survive are condemned to walk with those bodies to the electric chair, to place ourselves inside the minds of the victims when the switch is snapped. And once the truly rotten apple of *fear* corrupts the heart, it will not take long to infect everything else, paralyze the hand that would object, muzzle the mouth.

I learned the effectiveness of that strategy many years before the coup in Chile hammered that knowledge home. I was, I became, those two little boys who were orphaned. I stood next to my father and my mother and my sister in the sweltering night, and he hoisted me up in his arms on June 19 of the year 1953. My eyes covered the crowd outside Sing Sing, a multitude of fellow-travelers, I can remember the silence growing, the coughs being swallowed, as the hour of death approached, traveling with the Rosenbergs as they shuffled down the corridors toward their end and ours, waiting for the signal that Ethel and Julius had been executed, that we could all be next, that I could be next.

Unless I left the United States, unless my family left.

It was the murder of the Rosenbergs that started to reconcile me to the idea of losing America.

Because inside the fear that my parents would be punished was another one, more insidious.

Fear for myself.

They weren't American, Mom and Dad with their funny accents. Their foreign language saved them from having to deal with an enemy inside their own heads; whereas I lived, day after day, the corruption of the language I loved, its demeaning ride into jargon and intolerance. I did not have the safe haven of Spanish to keep myself pure, to help me fall asleep at night. I had nowhere to hide from my own betrayal of the land, from the voice that, in English of course, was salivating that the other Cub Scouts were going to find out who I really was and then they'd give it to me good, no way of stopping a gruff drawl in my head from suddenly erupting in the middle of a game with the accusation—it was John Wayne himself inside me—that I was a phony, that I could run but I couldn't hide. Watch your tongue, I said to myself: Watch each word. There they were, inside my language, the agents of my omnipotent country, its government and spies and armies and movie stars and radio personalities and neighbors and teachers and playmates, all of them ready to discover that I had double-crossed them, that I was not, and never could be, an all-American kid.

And the punishment, if not death, was something just as bad. The psychological, emotional, moral distance from America which the Cold War had instilled inside me threatened to be transmuted into physical space, to send me thousands of real miles away. There was a man who would do it. The name had surfaced back then, in that year of 1950, made its way into my haunted vocabulary next to the Rosenbergs: the name of Joe McCarthy. The Republican senator from Wisconsin who, around the time when I decided not to denounce my father, had summoned America on a crusade to sweep "the whole sorry mess of twisted, warped thinkers from the national scene so that we may have a new birth." It would take him until 1953 to set his sights directly on that twisted, warped thinker called Adolfo Dorfman, but in the intervening years there was not a day I did not evoke him, the nemesis who would hound my family out of the United States. What would he have said if he had known that his cleansing of America would have the unintended effect of sending an Argentine kid who adored Disney back to Latin America, where he would be corrupted by all the rotten apples down there and end up writing the first left-wing critique of that most imperialist of creatures, Donald Duck? Think of it: Joe McCarthy parting me from Charlie McCarthy.

The net around my father was tightening.

As 1953 rolled on, the persecution finally reached the United Nations, where the administration buckled under U.S. pressure: nine of the ten Americans working in my father's division were dismissed. But he, stubborn as a mule, defiant as usual, did not cover his tracks, camouflage his movements. On the contrary, my dad would make it a point to go to the cafeteria and sit noticeably next to those who had been sacked, make a point of talking to them on their last day of work, posting goodbye notes on the bulletin board and protesting in letters as impulsive as the one which had got him into trouble with the Argentine Army.

If he had been less imprudent, if he had "played ball," as one of his superiors had suggested, perhaps things would have turned out differently. But he was about to commit—isn't it always so with exiles?—one more rash, unpardonable act.

An old friend of his, Maurice Halperin, was in trouble.

Maur, a prominent fellow-traveler, had during the war been given a high post by Wild Bill Donovan in the COI (Office of the Co-ordinator of Information), soon to become the OSS and later the CIA. As head of the Latin American division, Halperin had be-friended dozens of exiled left-wing Latin Americans, including my father, who shared his obsession with getting rid of the Nazi-loving Argentine military. Maur had landed my father his first job after the Guggenheim, helping him bring his family from Argentina. (It seems curious that the forerunner of the very CIA that would flush me out of Chile thirty years later was instrumental in helping me leave Ar-gentina as an infant.) After the war, Maur and Adolfo had grown even closer—and when my father read, one morning in late 1953, that Halperin, then a professor at Boston University, had been ac-cused of espionage by HUAC and would be called to testify, he grabbed the phone and offered Maur his solidarity, without caring if J. Edgar Hoover himself was listening to the conversation.

The only support Halperin needed was a place to stay in New York. When Maur and his wife, Edith, arrived—it must have been October, perhaps November, of 1953—they told us that their secret intentions were to drive on to Mexico, to leave the country before something worse happened to them. I was disturbed by that visit, that night they spent with us at our Riverside Drive apartment, impressed by the haste with which they had fled, the consequences for the family, their sixteen-year-old son, David, left behind to finish his studies, their voices cracking as they spoke over the phone with their married daughter, Judith, to tell her yes, they were okay, yes, they would call tomorrow from Washington, heading South, heading South. How strange that the first political refugees I remember in my life were American citizens, sleeping in our midst as I would sleep many years later with my family on the floors of foreign friends' homes, my parents giving them the same sanctuary Angélica and I would give other exiles in the future. The two Halperins sitting down without their two children at the table where the four Dorfmans had hosted the four phantom Rosenbergs.

Next day, they were gone, Maurice never to return to his native land. He would spend five years in Mexico and then continue on to the Soviet Union for another four and then Cuba until 1968, finally ending up in Vancouver for the rest of his life, sadly disillusioned with Communism, the cause for which he had lost his country. I watched him and Edith load their packed suitcases into their Studebaker, watched them embark on that long trip they were not coming back from, watched them turn the corner and disappear from my eyes as if I were previewing my own future.

I was. The asylum my father offered to the accused spy, the man without a country, probably turned out to be the last straw. A few days after we had seen the Halperins off, Adolfo was summoned by a UN official, who informed him that Senator McCarthy himself had called up the Secretary General and warned him to "get that troublemaker Dorfman out of here. Or else." Or else—meaning? Probably deportation. If he was lucky. The functionary pointed out that, since mid-1950, coinciding ominously with the outbreak of the Korean War, my father's visa had been revoked and invariably he had been detained and interrogated every time he returned to the United States from abroad; on each ocasion he had been allowed back in only after the UN authorities had lodged strong protests. They were no longer in a position to continue defending him. Choose: resign or serve at UN regional offices in Bangkok or Santiago.

Two days later, my father was on a plane to Chile, and eight months after that, having finished school, I found myself awakening to the last day of my stay in America—everything boxed away—

ready to board a ship heading South with all our possessions. I can remember so clearly, almost as if I had a jagged mirror in my head or in my heart, I can remember like a reflection in the pool of the past my last hours before we took the taxi. Every afternoon of that summer I had been playing baseball in a park near our apartment overlooking the Hudson, every game I had been getting better, and that last day I went off banging my fist into my glove, headed for my last game. It sounds so corny that I almost hesitate to consign it here, I almost wonder if my memory has not made this up: but I stepped up to the plate the last time I was batting and with my eyes wide open I swung at the ball and I hit a home run and I jogged around the bases slowly and landed with both feet on home plate and the game was over and we had won. All too literary to be true, but what can I do if that is how it happened, if I was making things harder for myself by playing the end as melodramatically as I could? The coach came over and grinned at me, talked about tomorrow's game. I didn't have the heart to tell him I was leaving, couldn't even begin to explain. I answered sure, I'd see him tomorrow, knowing that they would wait for me awhile and then the coach would shrug his shoulders and point to somebody else to take my place, knowing they would forget me. It was over: the day I had been fearing for almost ten years had arrived.

And yet I had been rehearsing this moment for a long time, ever since I had sworn that I would not allow the crazy and futile polarization that the Cold War had transferred into my human heart to destroy my idyllic relationship with America.

I had trained myself for the loss that I saw looming over me, not, as might have seemed logical, by responsibly rebuilding my bridges to Latin America with whatever driftwood of my shipwrecked Spanish might still be washing around my life. On the contrary. What I did was even more ferociously burn those bridges. The fiercer the confrontation between East and West and the closer my departure, the more determined was I to plunge in the opposite direction, deeper into the vibrant maelstrom of the American dream, spinning more recklessly than ever into the neurosis of English. Or perhaps I gave myself even more fully to the country I was going to leave because I had already left it in my mind by betraying it, perhaps the passion was intensified by the distance that was already growing, trying to pretend that the rift had not cloven into me. Readying myself for a future when I would not have America nearby, as if I had to frantically accumulate it inside me. Like lovers before a separation exhaust themselves, try to put off the dawn when one of them must depart for war and the other remain behind, I was like him, like her, trying desperately to bring the other body into my own body, sweat and rub and touch and smell so that he, that she, would not be effaced by any mortal coil of time or geography.

I did so by proclaiming and parading my loyalty to the only permanent America I could accept as my guardian: not the transitory, superficial America whose government harassed my parents and their friends and intimidated me, but the more profound and loving culture of that America which I disassociated from politics and policies. On the verge of leaving for another continent, I melted, I tried to melt, I wanted to melt and dissolve, bewitched, dazzled, and bewildered, into the gigantic melting pot of America. I lived the early fifties as if America was a permanent shower I took as often as I could, trying to "wash that man right out of my hair," one of my favorite songs which I had heard the incomparable Mary Martin sing in person at the Broadway show of *South Pacific*, the man in question being, in my case, the residue of my Argentine self, my Spanish-speaking side, the Chiquita Banana kid. At a time when the United States was waging a war against everything foreign and alien, I waged my own internal war, determined to sweep away like a beggar whatever had been malevolently deposited in me by the language of my birth; so that, if I was forced to return to Latin America, I would at least not be tempted to stay there and forget my fatherland, the United States that was paradoxically sending my true father away.

I took this crusade against my past to its extreme. Because there had been, all these years, one vestige from my previous life that reminded me and everybody else how different I really was: my name. It stood between the United States and me, forced me to recollect every day, every moment of the day, how far I really was from being irreversibly American, how tainted I was by both Russia and Latin America.

I hated being called Vladimiro, but hated Vlady even more. The kids at school deformed my name without mercy: Bloody, Floody, Flatty—and especially the terminal insult, Laddie and Lady, names for dogs. Kids are cruel. But adults, who are not inevitably cruel—at least not to children—would also make me feel thoroughly self-conscious about who I was. Where did you get that name? What does it mean? My parents, absurdly, had told me to allege I was named after the pianist Vladimir Horowitz. And I obeyed. What was I supposed to proclaim in red-baiting America? That my dad worshipped Lenin and was glad that Uncle Joe Stalin had the bomb so he could defend socialism against the imperialists? What did my name mean? It means that I can't conform, that I can't make believe I'm from here, that's what it means.

Slowly, when I was alone, I had begun to call myself by another name. A fantasy that many children indulge in—we are not really the offspring of our parents, we were exchanged as babies, we are princes and princesses, our lineage secretly royal. The name I chose for myself, accordingly, was Edward, a name I had first come across in the Classic Comics edition of Mark Twain's *The Prince and the Pauper*—though later, as obsessively it became my favorite story, I managed to ingest the Errol Flynn film version and also read over and over again an abridged edition of the text. I was fascinated by the tale of the two physically identical boys born the same day in Renaissance England, one to poverty and hardship and the other to opulence and power, and how they switched places, the beggar and the Prince of Wales. It may have been the first time I came across the idea of the doppelgänger that was to haunt my literary work, the certainty that out there (in here?) somebody just like us suffers and watches and is waiting for his chance to take over our lives. Or the opposite idea: we may seem marginal and powerless to ignorant eyes, but someday our majesty will be recognized and the world will bow down before us. Twins, doubles, duality, duplicity, there at the start of my life. So I told myself that in reality I was Edward the Prince, but not content, like most children, to secrete my fantasy within my own closeted world, I decided to force the world to acknowledge, if not my princehood, at least my Edwardliness. With the same deranged determination with which I had succeeded in coercing my parents into speaking English back to me, I now carefully planned the demise of Vlady and the crowning of Edward.

I was not so far gone that I deluded myself into believing that I could manage this metamorphosis ensconced in my regular surroundings: the only way to force my mom and dad to accept a change in designation was to spring it on them in a location where I controlled how I was called. So when my father announced one day that he would have to spend many months in Europe on United Nations business and wanted the whole family to come along, London, Paris, Geneva, Italy, and then a visit to Argentina on home leave before returning to the States, I was delighted: no school for half a year, the legendary Old Continent of castles and adventures, the home of the Grand Masters of Painting. But more important: here was my chance to throw Vlady into the sea, drown the sonofabitch, and baptize myself with my true and princely title. I did not inform my parents of my intentions when we boarded the French ship *De Grasse* in June 1951. First I carefully spread my new English name among the other children on that ship, then engaged their parents, the crew members, the waiters, the stewards, until everybody was calling me Eddie. I would have preferred the lofty and lordly Edward, but what the hell, a small price to pay, that tacky diminutive, for getting rid of the detested Vladimiro. By the time my parents began to realize what I had wrought, it was too late. I informed them that I would not answer if called Vlady ever again. Not quite true, because when we returned to the States many months later, Vlady was waiting for me there in the memories of the neighbors and the school, and during the next few years my two names fluctuated back and forth, until our expatriation to Chile in 1954 gave me the opportunity to start afresh and definitely cut Lenin's embalmed name out of my life, to the point that my high school graduation certificates are all made out in the name of Edward Dorfman (a crazy thing to do, because my legal name was and in fact still is Vladimiro). Many of my friends from Chile still call me Ed or Eddie, and not the Ariel which I was eventually to adopt.

But it was on that French ship that I made the real transition and I could not have conceived of a more appropriate locale: a floating hotel in the middle of nowhere, a site of exile where you can craft your identity any way you want, where you can con everybody into believing anything because there is no way of confirming or denying your past.

And it was also on that ship that I was to begin a different sort of transition, one which was to prove far more crucial in the decades to come in defending the self I had come to identify with English. A transition to what might well be called the biggest con game ever invented by humanity: literature. The game I am still engaged in right now, the reader believing in the truth of my perishable, sliding words, lending faith to them without a shred of proof that I am not making everything up, inventing a self in this book as I invented (or so I say) a name for my future on that vessel.

But that was not the reason, at least not initially, not then, why literature entered my life so forcefully so early. During those six months in Europe, a rehearsal for the more permanent departure I was envisioning, literature was revealed to me as the best way to surmount the question of how to hold on to the language that defined my identity if I did not inhabit the country where it was spoken.

Until then, writing had played a negligible, indeed minimal, part in my existence. English had been for me, as it is for all native speakers, an oral experience. From the start, in that hospital, it had been a way of charming adults and forging alliances with the other children, dancing my words into their foreign hearts. As soon as I encountered the world of America, my repetition and learning of English quickly turned into a ritual of belonging, another way of combating loneliness, perfecting accent and grammar and vocabulary as evidence that I was not an immigrant recently stranded on these shores. As a child, I was always performing, partly because of my exuberant personality (today I would be diagnosed as having a mild form of ADD, Attention Deficit Disorder), but also, I believe, as a way of incessantly staking my claim to the public space in an English that I knew I had not been born to, endlessly acting out for the benefit of my fellow Americans.

I didn't have the means—or the desire—to pin down those early performances of mine in any permanent form, to transform them into letters on paper, to make them "literary": it was enough to play with words and horse around endlessly for the delight (or to the groans) of others. These vociferous demonstrations got so out of control that my father and mother instituted a "silly hour," an hour a day when my imagination was officially given freedom publicly to invent alternative babbling worlds. But even this was not enough. I built a soap-box theater where I animated puppets and drawings, parading them for my family and for their guests and for the neighbors, for the other children, my teachers, and anybody else I could conceivably drag in. Given the range and variety attainable by the human voice, it is not surprising that when reading appeared timidly on the horizon, I showed no interest: Look at Spot. Look at Spot run. Run, Dick, run. I was running other sorts of linguistic circles, running so fast with my loud mouth that I ended up lagging behind in my reading skills. And when my mother tried to remedially teach me, I drove her dizzy, running (sic!) around her chair, from one side to the other, unable to sit quietly, unable to concentrate. Look at Vlady run.

If I couldn't slow down to start reading, the laborious, agonizing crucifixion of writing was even less appealing as a creative vehicle. My first texts were, in fact, limited, secondary, and parasitical, serving to support illustrations, like the bubbles in the mock comic books I began to create. Even my first "novel" (a twenty-page cowboys-and-Indians extravaganza scribbled as a present for my father when I was a bit over seven) was no more than a series of drawings with a few written words scattered here and there.

Until that trip to Europe, in fact, it was assumed that I would devote my life to the plastic arts when I grew up. Drawing, from the earliest age, was the only way of nailing me down for hours in one spot, my preferred way of marking the world with the immediacy of my feelings. If colors so quickly came to dominate my life, it was because, like language, they were a way of loving and exploring myself, but also, almost simultaneously, a way of being loved, being explored by others—initially my parents but later on the wider world beyond them—ready to respond to and recognize the shape, the beauty, they called it, of those revelations I was extracting from some miraculous source within me. There was no greater joy then, there is no greater joy now: finding a refuge inside others for what had been inside me, like seeds settling into them, the pleasure of transferring those visions born of my pleasure to other hearts and eyes. Perhaps because I had such a supportive environment, parents who were fawning in their devotion, my art quickly announced itself as *powerful,* by which I mean that it both radiated power and conferred it, integrated me to people out there and yet also made me distinct and special, made me belong while allowing me to be different.

When we journeyed to Europe in 1951, there was not the slightest indication that the plastic arts were about to be supplanted in my life. On the contrary, I had just spent a whole year at an after-school program for gifted young artists at Queens College, where another scholarship awaited my return.

When I came back from Europe many months later, however, I rejected that potential career. I thought of myself—at nine years of age—as a writer, having discovered on that sea voyage that it was literature, and not painting, that could shield my identity constructed in English.

This discovery of how the literary imagination could protect me had humble origins: a small notebook, bound in red leather, presented to me by my parents when we boarded the *De Grasse*. They suggested that I record there, and therefore keep forever (I remember that word, forever), my recollections of the trip. It was in that diary—unfortunately lost in the coup in Chile many years later—that I first tentatively anticipated the specific marvels of writing. After the day's harrowing conglomeration of activities, I would sit myself down and watch my hand painstakingly preserve what otherwise would have become ephemeral; I fixed time, stopped it, calmed it; I read over the next evening what I had written and found it wanting, crossed out one word, put in another one, tested it, forced myself to work. Nobody would ever read this, I said, but once in a while I would show my mother what I'd written (always looking for approval, obsessed with contacting others) and I realized that I could be absent in my body and still be there, with her, or anybody else for that matter, through my words. More important, perhaps, than replicating myself in others was the intuition that writing was first of all a private act whose audience was primarily one's own self, so that loneliness did not need to be mastered by escaping from it into the outer world of performance, demanding the frantic fraternity of others, but by journeying with written words into the loneliness itself. A dangerous discovery: because I think I began, from that moment, to live in order to record life, that the register of that life started to be more essential than life itself. It was then that I began formulating the expression of what was happening while it was happening, often before it happened. But I was unaware of that peril: by expressing my English entirely independent of the oral or, more crucially, of performance, I took a pivotal step toward answering the question of how to keep alive the language I had adopted as my own if I was to leave the United States. In that diary, for the first time, I created an imaginary space and self outside the body and, perhaps as fundamentally, beyond geography, a dialogue with language which could be deepened regardless of where that body happened to be, what contingent geography surrounded me.

These faint glimmerings of literature's power and how that power could answer my specific needs were reinforced and in fact received a boost from an unexpected quarter.

One morning, my father stopped me as, hurly-burly and zany as usual, I rushed by him on the deck of our steamer headed for Le Havre.

He pointed to a man, gaunt I remember him somehow, his back to us, holding the hand of a woman, standing at the bow.

"That's Thomas Mann," my father said in a hushed tone I had rarely heard from him. We were not religious in my family: at that point I don't think I had stepped inside a church or a synagogue. Though in a few weeks' time I was to discover the interior of the great cathedrals of France and England, and the quiet that greeted me there, the lowered voices of my parents as they crossed the threshold, would remind me of the sacred awe that had overcome my father as he spoke of Thomas Mann.

"He's a great novelist, perhaps the greatest in the world," my father whispered. "Do you want to say hello to him?"

I nodded.

We went up to him. Thomas Mann was looking forward, in the direction of the Europe where he had been born, to which he was returning for the first time since he had fled the Nazis in 1938. Mann turned from his vision of the homeland that awaited him, scrutinized me intensely, shook my hand. I was unabashed and looked right back. I don't remember what petty phrases we exchanged, probably about the trip, the weather, some such nonsense. I must have conned him, informing him that my name was Edward—an ironic act in retrospect, given that all too soon the German writer would be laboring away at *Felix Krull, Confidence Man*, may even have been gathering notes about that profession so akin to writing, there in his stateroom. But it is not primarily the accomplishment of presenting myself to a great man with my new personality that remains with me today.

I would be mythifying grossly if I stated that our brief and vapid exchange of pleasantries altered my life, disclosed to me in a flash my true calling. It is true that for one intense moment, confronted with the brooding, famous, implausibly eternal bulk of Thomas Mann, I suddenly knew what I wanted in life: to be him, be Thomas Mann. I wanted that power to reach all humanity. I wanted the world to admire me the way they admired him, the way my parents admired me when I came running with my minor artistic wares in search of adoration, the way my parents admired him even if he was not their son.

Far more essential to my transition to literature, and specific to Thomas Mann's providential and ultimately evanescent presence on that ship, far more interesting than that accidental flicker of envy at success, was a question, provoked by Mann's thick, strange accent in English, that I fired at my father as soon as we were out of earshot.

"In what language does he write?"

The answer, that Mann's language was German and that he had continued to produce extraordinary works in his native tongue when he had been forced to flee the Nazis was simple enough and would have meant nothing to me a year before, but I was to return to it often in the following months as I traveled through Europe, rehearsing for that other, longer voyage that I saw coming.

And when it did arrive, when another ship, three years later, approached the port of Valparaiso, a twelve-year-old boy found himself ready to confront the terrors of Spanish and Latin America, armed with literature as his ultimate defense. It would take me less than a decade to start thinking of myself as a Chilean. The distance that the politics of the Cold War had created inside me would grow into a divorce from North America. But English's alliance with writing, its merging with literature, that was to be another matter. By the time I disembarked in Chile, English had become the efficient instrument of my intimacy, the inner kingdom I could control, and also the foundation for what I already called my profession, convinced as I was that my place in the world and in history would be determined by the way in which I affected and shaped that language permanently.

Spanish and history had different plans for me.

SEVEN

A Chapter Dealing with the
Discovery of Death on
September 13 and 14, 1973,
in Santiago de Chile

Almost as soon as Allende dies, I begin to run.

But do I need to? Is this really the only way of saving my life?

My name is not on the most-wanted list. In the late afternoon of the 11th of September I listen to the names on the radio, the infamous Bando Número Cinco, the men and women who yesterday were Ministers and senators and trade-union presidents and chairmen of the governing parties and today are fugitives and outcasts, who are being asked to give themselves up to the proper authorities or face the consequences. I am at Manuel's house. We had agreed, with the other members of our Party cell, that this would be the place to gather in an emergency. I made my way here when I realized that I would not be able to make it to La Moneda. Six others turn up. All of us awaiting instructions.

When our Party contact arrives, he has one word for us from above: Retreat.

"What does that mean?" we ask him.

"That means what it means," he says. We wait for something more. "It means we're fucked," he says. "It means we lost. It means we don't get ourselves killed unless we have to."

He reviews the channels through which we will communicate with him, which we have been setting up for the last two months, and promises more information and analysis when it comes. Anything else? "Yes," he says, "one more thing. The Party says to make sure Ariel is all right, that you can all go home now, except Ariel."

There is something perversely satisfying about being singled out. A bit later, however, when the names of the new public enemies of Chile are read out on the radio, it becomes clear that I am not as notorious as I presumed. And along with relief at the fact that nobody is hunting me down at this very moment, I acutely feel the humiliation of being denied the sick mark of distinction that comes from being included among those most wanted by the military Junta, my enemies' refusal to validate me as a supreme pain in the ass. Years later, when the first prisoners from the Chilean concentration camps were freed and began straggling to Europe, I heard of a similar sort of bizarre masochism: "When we read the list of those who were about to be released," they told me, "those of us who were favored felt—well, it was shame, a grotesque shame at the fact that we weren't being kept there for a longer time, that this somehow reflected on our manhood, that the ones who remained behind had suddenly become more legendary and intrepid. We wanted to be the most dangerous. Even if it meant not being free."

These men had been imprisoned for three years without a trial, they had been put in front of mock firing squads, they had been tortured, but they still needed additional proof of how much the fascists hated them—little wonder, then, that I should have desired my selection by the new rulers of Chile as public enemy number one. Though in my case, it was not only a matter of having my revolutionary persona recognized. What Pinochet was in effect refusing me, and thousands and thousands of Allende supporters who were not on the list read over the radio, was the most precious piece of knowledge under a dictatorship: clarity about how much danger you are really in, an answer to that most vital of questions, what to do?

Should I go home? Proclaim to my neighbors and colleagues that Allende had betrayed us and led us to disaster and that I had learned my lesson and would now work for the greater good of the *patria?* Maybe the Junta would heed the call of the Church, of the Christian Democrats, to be merciful to the fallen adversaries. Or perhaps it would be better to leave? But why panic? Why remove ourselves from the country out of unfounded dread, do Pinochet's dirty work for him? Wasn't this, the gray zone of uncertainty we had been thrust into, already a sign of our enemies' victory, their ability to force us to internalize their power, bringing them into our minds and houses and beds, wondering who's next?

Unless you are on that list, there is no certain answer.

And so I go on the run. More than from real danger, I run because I need time to figure out if I really am in danger, I run until I can be certain that I don't need to run anymore.

The first signals I get will not be promising.

On the afternoon of September 13, as the curfew is lifted for a few hours, I leave Manuel's house. It's not safe for me to stay there anymore, so one of our group, a lab technician whom I will call Alberto, has suggested that I spend the next week at his small apartment with his wife, three kids, and mother-in-law, in the sort of unassuming neighborhood where people mind their own business. Before I leave, Manuel takes me to a nearby house, where there is a phone. I am able, for the first time in two days, to speak to Angélica. She has spent yesterday, her birthday, under curfew, alone with Rodrigo and my parents, unable to leave the house, mourning Allende, fearful for me and all our friends. The city, she tells me, is wild with rumors: factories have been bombed, prisoners are being executed, the embassies are besieged by people seeking asylum. One piece of good news: our own house hasn't been raided—maybe a sign that they won't come for me or track us down to my parents' home. But she really doesn't know, for once my sorceress wife who seems to fathom the future and see through people and situations as if they were transparent is at a loss. Her best guess is that I'm probably in danger, but we should wait and see.

There are no buses, so Alberto and I have to walk miles across the city, and everywhere there are people like us, their heads to the ground, avoiding each other's eyes, hurrying by, atomized. Already what was just two days ago a collective is beginning to disperse under the pressure of fear. Close by we can hear machine-gun fire, an indication that the fighting is not over. We try to hitch a ride, but nobody stops. Then, on the sidewalk, striding toward me, I catch a glimpse of an old friend, a socialist militant from way back. During the last year we've been too busy to see each other but I'd heard he was splitting up with his wife. Now he is there, a few feet away, a tiny baby cradled in his arms, a woman I've never met clutching him. As he passes by, dazed, I look straight into his face, but he doesn't see me: there is in him such an abyss of sorrow that I am forced to look away, as if I had been caught watching a man's soul melting, disintegrating in front of me. But there is no time for this man with whom I have studied and played soccer and drunk wine, no time for anything but Alberto pulling my sleeve, Alberto who has finally managed to flag down a car that is willing to take us the rest of the way.

When we get in, the driver shifts the run-down engine into first gear, throws us a glance through his glasses, then looks at the street, then back at me. "Hey," he says, fixing me in his bohemian gaze, "you're Ariel Dorfman, aren't you?" I don't answer. He insists, he's sure it's me: I'm so ethnically different from most Chileans that I'm easy to identify. "They must be looking for you, *hombre*," he adds, cheerfully. "They sure must be looking for you."

I glance sideways at Alberto. We had both expected more anonymity. "Oh, I don't think they're that interested in me," I answer. "I'm just a writer. I'm not mixed up in politics."

"Yeah, nobody's mixed up in politics anymore," the driver says. "But try to make the *hijos de puta* who're in control believe it."

My disappointment at not making the Junta's priority list has come back to haunt me. It is far from exhilarating to get what I so fancied: to be distinguished as dangerous, to be held in awe by people I've never even met. I can feel Alberto next to me stiffen, as he thinks of his family. We stop at a traffic light and it is as if every stranger passing us is a threat. A jeep full of soldiers pulls up next to us, its motor idling. One of the recruits stares into my eyes, as if he could read my thoughts. I half expect him to pull my photo out and start firing. I feel naked: if this man who's given us a ride thinks I'm in trouble, if this man who represents in some way the voice of everyman . . .

My worst fears are confirmed that very night. A tense dinner at Alberto's house. Hardly anybody at the table says a word. Later, I am shown to my room; the two oldest girls have gone camping for the night in the skimpy living-dining-room area. Alberto and his wife are arguing in their bedroom right next to mine. The walls are paper-thin. Alberto's wife is worried sick. For the last two days she had not known whether her husband was alive or dead. Now that he's back, she's bright enough to anticipate that he's going to be investigated at the university, that at best he'll lose his job. And now he's brought home a man who can get them all murdered. Just yesterday, she says, her voice rising shrilly, a whole family was taken away a few streets from here. They were harboring somebody. Did Alberto want—? Alberto tells her to hush, to keep her voice down. Now I can no longer hear what they're saying, just the urgent whispers, her fear, his anger.

An hour later, he comes in to see me.

"Listen," I say to him, before he can get in a word. "I'm leaving tomorrow."

"You're staying. I told her you're staying. And she'd better believe it."

"If I were her," I say, "I'd be scared, too."

"Everybody's scared," Alberto says. "If we end up so scared we don't do what's right, then they've really screwed us, *perdimos de verdad,* we've really lost."

The next day, I leave.

Alberto's wife stays in her room, does not say goodbye. His girls hug me and beg me to stay, when is the *tío* coming back, they love to have visitors, please say I'll be back soon, please? I lie to them, tell them soon, very soon, and Alberto nods unhappily.

Then I'm on the street again, headed for a meeting with a contact from the Party that Alberto has set up to see if someone else can help me. I feel like a piece of baggage. Alberto himself insists on accompanying me.

There is still hardly any transportation, so we have to walk. We go through the center of the city and both of us head, almost automatically, without sharing a word about why we are taking this detour, for La Moneda.

There, as I face the ruins of the Presidential Palace where Allende has died, a rage surges through me with such sudden ferocity that I fear it will kill me, I fear that it will destroy me unless I can exorcise it by letting it out, unless I kill the men who have done this to us, to me, to our land.

It is a lust for murder and revenge that will all too soon have a chance to be fulfilled.

As we continue on our way through the shattered Santiago streets to meet our contact, we see, perhaps four blocks away from La Moneda, a young recruit slumped against a peeling wall. At first he seems to be dead, a sniper must have got him, but no, he's asleep, his face half in the shade, half in the sun. He's probably spent the night on duty, put his head against the wall to rest his eyes, slid into sleep, and here he is, barely out of adolescence, his legs innocently sprawled open on the narrow sidewalk, his submachine gun at his feet.

Alberto and I stop. We look at the soldier, we look at his weapon, we look at each other.

There is nobody else present. Not even a witness. A thought crosses my mind and, as if in a mirror, I can see it reflected in Alberto's eyes. It would be easy to steal the gun. And if the bastard wakes up, we just pull the trigger, one less murderer. They wanted war? They'll get it.

We both hesitate there, our eyes fixed in fascination on the sleeping soldier not one yard away, we hesitate for two more seconds as if we were on the edge of eternity.

That's how long it takes me to dismiss the idea as mad, that's how long it takes me to watch it disappear simultaneously from Alberto's face, as if we were synchronized to some internal common clock. One more instant passes and then we are gone, we leave him and his weapon behind, there on that corner.

Those few seconds are to be as important and prophetic in my life and the life of the country as the brief moment just three days before when I turned from the police barrier that blocked passage to my death at La Moneda, the death that Taty imagined for me. What both Alberto and I have instinctively rejected is armed struggle as the way to bring back democracy. In retrospect, it will look to me as if we were symbolically deciding with the whole nation, because many other Chileans must have been mulling over at that same time whether to answer military violence with their own violence, we are collectively establishing the strategy of peaceful resistance to the dictatorship that will culminate, seventeen years later, in a return to democracy.

In my case, though it takes only a couple of seconds to be resolved, it is a strategy rooted in deeply held convictions that go back to a discovery about who I am and who I want to be, made more than thirteen years before, in March of 1960, when I started my studies at the University of Chile, when I found myself on the second day of classes doing battle with the police for the first time in my life. That morning's session of Comparative Literature had focused on more abstruse battles with authority and repression, as we brainily dissected a story by Kafka about a crow pecking at somebody's feet. But the next class was suspended to give way to a rousing student assembly where the miserable state of public education and the low salaries of the secondary-school teachers were denounced. The fiscally conservative government had refused to negotiate and a strike was being called for the following week. A motion was made and passed that we immediately cease all Faculty activities in solidarity with the teachers; and then another was approved by acclaim that we stage a protest right away, a lightning sortie into the streets to let President Alessandri and his right-wing coalition know that we aren't going to take this sort of treatment sitting down. I joined the fervent multitude as we marched and chanted down the wide tree-lined avenue of Macul, handing out pamphlets to unconcerned passersby, disrupting traffic and, in truth, not appreciably advancing the cause of higher education. I was a bit wary of showing solidarity with teachers who in high school, just a few months ago, I had considered the mortal (and boring!) enemies of the young. My skepticism vanished as soon as I joyfully merged with the other peaceful marchers. Peaceful, that is, until the police arrived and ordered us to disperse and then grabbed a couple of our ringleaders and began to beat them, although, I must admit, not with excessive savagery. That was the first day I saw Freddy Taberna in action, a tall, lithe, hawk-nosed geography student who was to become one of my dearest buddies, Freddy who would be executed by a firing squad in the north of Chile four days after the coup, Freddy, whose dead body was never returned to his family, that body of Freddy's alive back then, shouting at the police, prancing in front of them, taunting them, I saw Freddy go down under a blow from a nightstick and saw him get up again as if it had hardly happened and then an officer gave the order to throw tear gas, and we all fled back down Macul, coughing and gagging, toward the university, which, according to Latin American custom, was out of bounds for the police, as extraterritorial, in fact, as an embassy. We stopped at its gates and, made valiant again by the proximity of the hallowed halls of higher learning, turned to confront the police one more time, and I saw them dragging a young woman by the hair and I felt inside me a mild version of the rage I would be filled with many years later at the bombed walls of La Moneda. All around me students were picking up rocks and soon the air was thick with missiles, most of them falling far short of their objective. So I stooped down and picked up a rock as hard and round and manageable as a baseball and, taking aim, threw it into the air and watched it go much farther than the other projectiles, landing with a thunk against the shield of a beefy policeman. Everybody around me cheered. I had one hell of an arm. The fact that I was using my prowess at the Yankee sport of baseball to outthrow my soccer-playing classmates and attack a Chilean police force trained and armed by the United States was a cultural contradiction I did not stop to analyze. It was not a time to wonder how Yogi Berra would have judged one of his erstwhile fans applying his technique to street-fighting tactics in faraway Chile.

Encouraged by my unexpected popularity, I let fly another rock, and this one whistled by another cop, barely missing his head. Another cheer went up and I picked up another rock and got ready to let loose with it and then . . . And then I dropped it. Those were the first and the last two rocks I ever hurled in what was to be a long revolutionary career.

What happened between the second rock that flew through the air and the third rock that would not leave my hand was the fear that I might end up hurting somebody irreparably. In that lull between two actions, I identified with the unknown cop I had almost felled with my gringoland arm, identified not only with him but with his wife and his children and his family. I was certain that hurting him or anyone else if there was a way of avoiding it would transform me into somebody I couldn't live with. I think that in the hand that dropped the rock something that was most viscerally mine rejected violence as a method, as a solution, as a way of life.

Does that mean that during my baptismal moment in the line of fire I suddenly converted to pacifism, ready to preach tolerance to my enraged university classmates? Not at all. As for most of my generation, Fidel Castro's homegrown revolution, the first in Latin America successfully to stand up to the gringos, was for many years our touchstone, our Mecca, our guiding macho light. I praised its accomplishments as well as its excesses. I justified its disastrous export of armed struggle. I even admit with a shudder now that I thought Fidel's execution and exile of his opponents was absolutely necessary. Them or us, I would say: take your pick, I would say, ten million starving children or a couple of bourgeois counterrevolutionaries. It was not a time for subtleties.

So I am not trying, more than thirty years later, to recast myself as a saint, suggesting that during my first street protest in early 1960 I was visited by a Gandhian epiphany. But that incident does signal my deepest, most intimate preference for a revolution that could take power without killing its adversaries—or its followers, for that matter.

My defense of armed violence during the sixties was to be enthusiastic and outspoken, but it was, primarily, that: spoken, defended with my mouth, but not carried out with my body. And what if, in order to save the people, save the revolution, stop children from starving, I was asked to kill that cop? Then what? A question which was to return in café discussions and smoke-filled cabals at dinner tables all through the sixties, a question that I never had to answer, basically because my father had, by absolute accident, ended up in Chile when he had to flee the United States in the fifties. If the Chilean workers had not, for forty years, been working toward a peaceful revolution that Allende was to embody, perhaps my commitment to the liberation of the Latin American poor would eventually have led me, like so many of my generation in other countries of the continent, to hills and slums where, gun in hand, I would have been hunted down and slaughtered. As it was, I was fortunate enough to find one of the only mass movements in the planet that reconciled my drastic need for structural, earth-shattering change and my desire that this change be accomplished without harm to others.

All revolutions, up until the victory of the Unidad Popular government in 1970, had invariably been violent, based on the premise that radical changes in society and the economy could not be accomplished without first smashing the military machine through which ruling classes ensure their ownership of wealth and power, and then going on from there to a complete—some would say total—takeover of all the organs of the state (executive, legislative, judicial), all the means of communication, and, eventually, all forms of property. This had been the orthodox doctrine of the left since the Bolshevik Revolution; in fact, since the Paris Commune in 1870—exactly a century before our triumph in Chile—had first been held up by Marx as a model for the coercion that any successful revolution would have to resort to if it wished to remain in power; only ten years earlier, it had been launched in Latin America itself with the Cuban Revolution. Allende believed, and with him the majority of the Chilean people, that it was possible, and indeed desirable, to effect those changes through democratic means, that one did not have to persecute and kill one's enemies in order to neutralize them, that one did not have to limit anyone's basic freedoms in order to be rid of the plagues of hunger, unemployment, homelessness, exploitation, that one did not have to install a dictatorship in order to defend the gains of the revolution.

Critics of this Chilean road to socialism predicted that this strategy would fail, that the ruling classes would never give up their power willingly, that it would end in a bloodbath, pointing to the same Paris Commune, where the counterrevolution, when it restored order, had massacred the communards. Allende's answer was that he had no illusions about the peacefulness of his adversaries. Once democracy could not be counted on to protect their interests, the former rulers of Chile would conspire to destroy and vandalize that democracy, would undoubtedly try to subvert the military. But they would be isolated, our theory went; we had disarmed them, stripped

them of any justification for their terror by renouncing terror ourselves as the inevitable midwife of change. This was our strategy of
persuasion as a moral force in history, this was Allende's way of
escaping the spiral of violence and counterviolence that had fed on
each other voraciously throughout the twentieth century. We were
trying to keep not only our own hands clean of blood but those of
our foes as well.

I say we, but the truth is that at the beginning of the Allende
period I was myself brimming with doubts about the feasibility of a
gentle revolution. By the end of those three years, however, I had
become a true believer, in great measure because I witnessed a small
but vocal minority on the Chilean left, brimming with bookish
theories to which reality was supposed to conform, sabotage our
revolution. Knowing that Allende would not repress them, they irresponsibly accelerated social change to try to force an armed outcome to the conflict. Their incessant mobilization of the poorer
sectors of society, their indiscriminate takeover of industries, housing
projects, and fields, their push to radicalize the revolution, ended up
alienating the middle classes, which were essential for our triumph
if we were to keep the military on our side.

But hadn't the ultra-left been correct?

Now that someone like the cop who had been giving Freddy
Taberna a couple of whacks with his nightclub in 1960 was going
down the steps of a cellar in 1973, to torture someone just like
Freddy, now that the armed men whom I had delicately not wanted
to hurt back in 1960 were shooting at us, now that they were in-
flicting on us the violence we had refused to inflict on them, did I
still think we should turn the other cheek? Did I still think there
was no justification for throwing even a rock at them? Was I going
to leave that weapon in the hands of the sleeping recruit, who, when
we awoke, would be more than ready to pull the trigger? Did I still
believe that violence was not a solution?

My belief was put to the test by that young soldier whom we
refused to kill that day.

So the coup was not only bringing me my own death as a possibility but was visiting me now with another variety of death altogether, in a different and vicious disguise. For one moment, however brief, there on September 14 of 1973, fortune had made me into the hunter rather than the hunted; I had become the god who decides if somebody lives or if somebody dies.

Someone with power had spared me during the coup, death had brushed near me in the dark and passed me by, as if I also had been asleep, watched over by someone more powerful.

Now it was this young soldier's turn.

While he slept, I had decided that he should live.

We left him there, Alberto and I, half in the sun, half in the shade, we left him breathing there, and went on our way.

I never even knew his name.

EIGHT

A Chapter Dealing with the Discovery of Life and Language During the Years 1954 to 1959 in Santiago de Chile

It would be fourteen years before I returned to the States and by then it was too late.

Sitting in a small room one day in Berkeley, California, in front of my typewriter—it must have been late in that turbulent year of 1968—abruptly, just like that, in the middle of a sentence I was writing, I stopped. I looked at those words in English perched on that piece of paper and I told myself, it popped up into my thoughts without warning, a simple revelation whose obviousness had never-theless been brewing in my mind for some time and that only now, far from Chile, back in America, had finally surfaced: What was I doing here, making believe I was a gringo, writing in this language that suddenly seemed an alien script? I was not from here. I was Latin American.

And then came a decision perversely opposite to the one I had made so many years ago, on the New York coast of the United States, but symmetrical to it and just as fierce: I proceeded, in that room not far from the Pacific Ocean, to renounce English along with the America of the North and its empire and its culture, renounce and denounce and try to suppress henceforth the man inside me who had spent his life identifying through that language, speaking and writing himself into personhood in that language. As nobody can, at the age of twenty-six, forgo and forget a language, as languages cannot be unlearned by decree that late in life, I did what was second best in order to establish the intensity and credentials of my convictions. Needing, like all converts, to burn what they have adored, I swore never to write another word in the English language. Spanish was to be the love of my life.

I willed myself to become monolingual again.

Not the outcome I would have foretold in 1954 when I arrived in Chile with a siege mentality. Spanish was everywhere, surrounding me with its babbling, sticky, suffocating sea of sound. But now the tactic that had served me so well during the last ten years—to pretend that the language I had been born into did not exist—was useless. All I could do was promise that I wouldn't admit it to my heart, that I'd leave this foreign dump as soon as I was old enough to return to my own beloved United States.

I am not sure now, as I write this, how strong the wall of my isolationist position really was, if it might not have crumbled into dust if I had been made instantly, gloriously welcome in Chile. But that was not to be the case: as soon as my mother, the day after we disembarked in Valparaiso, set to solve the pressing issue of how I would be educated, my prejudices against the country and against Spanish in particular were trenchantly reinforced.

Entering the Chilean educational system proved a nightmare.

A transition that would have been difficult for any child was complicated by the fact that in my last two years in the States I had found a school that was perfect for me: Dalton, a progressive private establishment on the East Side of Manhattan where my mother taught Spanish—a circumstance that, combined with a scholarship my artistic talents had won me, helped to reduce the tuition.

My parents sought to ease the pain of the loss of that school built on the premise that children flourish if they are given freedom, by applying to the Liceo Manuel de Salas, an experimental public high school in Santiago presumably dedicated to the same philosophy. My mother, with her incurable cheerfulness and her assumption that everyone had to admire her son as unconditionally as she did, expected that I would have no problem being admitted.

We got as far as the principal's office.

She was a stern, prim woman. On her desk were a series of glowing letters of introduction and recommendation from Dalton, which my mother had meticulously translated into Spanish and sent ahead. The principal feigned enthusiasm. I was twelve years old but I could tell she was faking it. How wonderful to have someone from Dalton, she cooed, a school that is like a sister to us.

Good. My mother asked when I could start.

The principal pursed her lips and said, *"Bueno . . . weeeelll . . ."* There are, she said, some problems, she said. She ticked them off with a long index finger, adressing my mother, hardly looking at me. First: Chile operated, perhaps we were not aware of it, on the French model. In the United States, he, Vladimiro (meaning me, Eddie, sitting in front of her), was considered a child—*un niño*—with two more years of elementary education to go, but here, and now my mother tried to interrupt, but the principal waved her aside, here, she insisted, he is a *joven,* a young man, a pre-teen. At the age of twelve, he is supposed to be in high school here, because here, she accentuated the word, *aquí,* there were six years of higher education and not four as in the United States. And not every student is automatically allowed to enter high school here, she said, this is paid for by the state and by the Chilean people, and therefore it is the state that decides if the child is ready to commence higher forms of instruction, and there is a battery of tests to which every pupil must submit before being allowed entry. Tests which *este joven* had not undergone, she said. Again my mother tried to put a word in, but the principal was unrestrainable. That is not all, the principal said. There is a second matter, she said, waving that long index finger; second was the fact that we happened to be in the Southern Hemisphere, perhaps we had not realized that here, *aquí en Chile*, the seasons were reversed, she pointed in the general direction of the schoolyard, where kids in overcoats milled around, some of them peering into the principal's office to see what the hell was going on, all of them shouting at each other in Spanish, not a friendly English insult sullying the clean Chilean air, which meant, the principal proceeded, that school had started in March, and it was now late August, so I had already lost five months. However, she said, given the recommendations, she said, basking in the smugness of her own fiefdom, yes, she felt *el joven Vladimiro* would be well served to pursue his studies at her model institution.

My mother breathed a sigh of relief.

So it was settled.

Not really. The principal now turned her attention to me. She asked me a question. I began to stammer a few words in Spanish, gringo, pidgin, ungrammatical, mispronounced, mixed-up Spanish, the first words I had uttered in that native language of mine in ten years. I extracted them tentatively and against their will and against mine, and the first thing I told her, foolish and arrogant and defiant, was that my name was Edward, tried to convey, tongue-tied, that I answered to a different name than the one on my birth certificate. My first conversation with a Chilean citizen. And she heard me out, she let me have my say, if you could call it that, watched me splutter every hunchbacked word into the air, make every mistake in the book, she let me grind to a halt and stumble and cease my massacre of the language of Cervantes. And with every blunder I could feel the principal's mistrust turning into a more drastic hostility.

She didn't like me. No. It wasn't me she didn't like. It was my

language. It was that I was a Yankee. It was that I called myself
Edward. That I felt that I could just barge in here, into this sanctuary
of hers where the best and the brightest young Chileans were being
trained in freedom and independence with taxes paid by her fellow
countrymen, that I could presume to gain admittance, leaping over
the thousands of deserving native applicants, merely because I was
from the North, this child who had denied his name and his heritage.
This child who had betrayed the cause of Latin America, had forgotten the language and the culture in those ten years in the North.
Payback time.

Am I exaggerating? Am I injecting what I know now into what I
did not know then? Probably. But the animosity was there. I felt it
then, I can feel it now so many years later, emanating from some
cold center under her skin even if I had no way at that time of
grasping its dimensions, not enough knowledge of Chile to realize
that many people here—particularly among the intellectual elite—
begrudged and even hated the United States, blaming it for their
country's poverty and backwardness. The Cold War that had chased
me from the United States was not going to leave me alone now that
I had journeyed to the farthest reaches of the American sphere of
influence, about as far South as you could go: how was I to guess,
sitting there as the icy strutting resentment of the principal glazed
over me, how was I to know that I was being categorized as a rep-
resentative of the North, of the gringos who had come down to Chile
and taken over the economy, who owned the copper mines and the
banks and the major industries and the foreign policy and the steam-
ships. It was her duty to educate a generation of young men and
women to stand on their own feet and defy these foreigners who
believed that their dollars and their technology and their language
gave them the right to dictate terms to a sovereign land.

I would come to understand how she felt because many years later
I turned into somebody very much like her, fiercely proud of Chile,
resolutely nationalistic, fanatically defensive of our right to decide
our fate without foreign influence or intervention. I would become

that principal whose name I never knew, I would join her camp, her battle for the liberation of Chile would become my battle. Yes, that same woman would gladly have given me refuge in the days after the coup against Allende, taken me in and risked her life and her family's life to save me, if she herself, as seems probable in retrospect, had not been one of those hunted down. But at that moment when I first set foot in my future country, she was not willing to give me refuge then and there, to ease me into Chilean society, to welcome me charitably into the Spanish I had forsaken.

She turned to my mother and pointed out that my Spanish was— what words did she use? let me invent here because what I remember now is the tone rather than the vocabulary, her piercing desire to draw lines, to exclude, to exercise her petty sectarian quota of power—yes, she said something to the effect that *Este niño no sabe hablar castellano.* This child can't speak Spanish. No longer a *joven:* demoted in age, demoted to helplessness. However she said it, her conclusions could not have been more dramatic. Vladimiro, she said, accentuating each syllable of the Russian revolutionary name, will have to wait seven months, until March of 1955, to be admitted, and he will unfortunately have to lose a whole year, start high school from scratch in the first year, and we should be grateful that she was waiving, in homage to the sister school of Dalton, all entrance examinations, grateful that I was not losing two years.

Five minutes later, we were out in the corridor, my mother and her twelve-year-old son. Five minutes later, as soon as the door to the principal's office was closed, I blurted out, in English of course, my decision: "I'm not coming to this stupid school!" I can remember the startled look on the faces of two young girls who were skipping down the hall, their surprise, whether at the foreign sounds coming from my mouth or at the passion with which I was spewing them I could not tell, but I can remember their look and how it made me feel even more alien to them and to their establishment and to their country, how it verified my decision to shun that sort of look if I possibly could.

My mother shook her head in despair. "But then where in heaven will you go to school?"

Within two days I was sitting in the office of Mr. Jackson, the British-born headmaster of the Grange, a prestigious English prep school that had been established as a way of insuring that the descendants of British merchants and entrepreneurs who had migrated to Chile in the nineteenth century would be brought up in the best Victorian traditions—and keep the language of their forefathers. My dad had looked into that school as a possibility and decided against it and now warned me: the Grange was the opposite of Dalton in every possible way. It was a boys-only school, resolutely hierarchical, run on the theory that young males are savages that need to be disciplined and threatened and toughened up for a life where they will have to exercise cold control over other, lesser beings in order to succeed. Uniforms and ties were compulsory, students were beaten with a cane if they stepped out of line, showers were freezing, in the chill of early mornings the kids were marched out onto the gravel of the driveway and forced to endure half an hour of excruciating physical exercises. And if they cut their hands on the stones, better still. Nor was I going to be able to avoid the detested Spanish language: the Grange, like every other educational institution in Chile, also taught the full official curriculum in Spanish.

"Why's it called an English school, then?" I asked.

Because the system was modeled on British public schools, came the answer. Because boys at the Grange played rugby and cricket (and not, my parents pointed out, baseball or American football or basketball). Because a series of subjects were additionally taught in English—language, literature, history, current events, geography, even mathematics—which meant, my parents hastened to explain, hoping that maybe this would dissuade their recalcitrant son from going to an authoritarian school, that in order to accommodate these extra classes, days at the Grange were several hours longer than at other Chilean schools. There was even instruction on Saturday mornings.

"And what do kids speak in their free time, when they're on break?"

"English is enforced," my dad said. "Drastically, it seems."

That was all I needed to hear. Even before I crossed its august gate, saw its spacious green fields, walked into the ivy-covered buildings, I had decided that the Grange was the place for me.

My preconceptions were confirmed by a small incident I witnessed as my parents chatted for a few minutes with the school's Secretary of Studies at the entrance to the main building. Nearby, three young boys in gray jackets were playing marbles in the dust, heatedly arguing in Spanish about whether one of them had cheated. Their excited jabber was interrupted by an older boy in a blue jacket. He came upon them gliding out of nowhere, like a blue shadow out of nowhere, and barked: "English!" That word. No more. The boys looked up guiltily, fell silent, rose to their feet. The older boy (I would later learn he was called a prefect) stood there for a few seconds, rocking back and forth, policeman-like, his hands behind his back, the youthful caricature of a Dickensian stepfather. The prefect let the marble players wait a bit more, then demanded their names and delivered their punishment in crisp, Laurence Olivier English: "You should be caned. But this morning I'm feeling merciful. Two hours' detention. Saturday afternoon! Copy a thousand times: I am not to speak Spanish during break. Say it."

Each of the boys repeated the phrase over in an English heavily accented by Spanish, floundering over the words as if they were extras in some Western where the Mexicans can barely make themselves understood.

"Next time . . ." the prefect said, and he lifted his arm up in the air and brought it down, making a whistling sound with his mouth and smacking one palm against the other with a great white whack.

Then he was gone.

It would be nice to report that I felt a wave of sympathy for the victims, who, like me, had been stripped of the language that gave meaning to their lives, their games rendered joyless, as they were obligated by older people in power to stutter halfhearted words in a foreign tongue they hated. But there was no room for compassion in my barren exile's heart. That trio of marble players was persecuted here at the Grange. Well, too bad for them. I would have been persecuted for my language at the Liceo Manuel de Salas, that would have been my daily bread, doled out by kids like them, in the jungle of the Chilean schoolyards. That blond prefect in his blue jacket, coercive, driven, bleak, was defending my interests, my language, my colonial enclave at the Grange, an outpost of civilization in the midst of semi-savage territory where I could practice my English un-opposed. He was like a barbed-wire fence, keeping Chile out, ban-ishing Spanish to the streets outside the Grange, where it belonged: an inferior, barbarous tongue mumbled by the natives.

Even so, I would have to learn that language. The headmaster, Mr. Jackson himself, notified me of this requirement when I finally met him a few minutes later. He was ready to admit me to the Grange and didn't mind at all that I preferred not to call myself Vladimiro. Here the boys answered to their last name, and besides, Edward seemed a reasonable choice. He couldn't, however, let me into school this late in the year. He did have a suggestion, however, that the principal of the Liceo Manuel de Salas had not even broached. Why not use the few months left in 1954 to study all the subjects taught in the first year of high school and take the exami-nations on my own? Then next March he could place me in the second year. My parents explained that my Spanish was not quite up to that sort of testing.

Mr. Jackson looked me squarely in the eyes. Nonsense, he said. You can do it, Dorfman, he said to me, placing both his hands on my shoulders, you can show them the sort of stuff we're made of, you can learn Spanish in a snap, he said, even though I was later to discover that his own Spanish was atrocious, that he had never mas-tered the language. We'll pull through, won't we? he said.

And I nodded.

I would stop feeling sorry for myself and pull through.

And that is how, in the first days of September of 1954, I forced this throat of mine to make up for ten years of neglect of Spanish, I studied my way back into the language. I did it out of love of English. I did it because I had been encouraged by a defender of the British Empire to believe in myself, to be self-reliant, to keep my head, as Rudyard Kipling had put it in "If," Mr. Jackson's favorite poem, when all about me were losing theirs. I did it to spite the Chilean woman principal who didn't think a gringo kid could be worthy of her school. But above all I did it because my parents had cautioned me that enough was enough: if I did not pass these exams, I was going to enter the first year at Manuel de Salas and that was that.

I had one chance, therefore, to defend my English-language identity and I tried hard not to blow it. If it had only been Spanish . . . But there was also arithmetic and geometry and botany and the rudiments of Chilean history and Chilean geography and Chilean flowers and fruits and battles, a crash course on the heritage of that country I disdained. Above all, my challenge was the language that Pablo Neruda was at that very moment furiously hurling to the winds not ten blocks from where I was studying, hating every moment of class, at a private Academia. A highfalutin name for a dingy couple of catch-up classrooms in the dirtiest corner of the center of Santiago, where children in trouble were being drilled for their exams, kids mostly older than I who were either dyslexic or had other learning disabilities or had been expelled from their schools. It was there, among a group of outcasts and misfits, that I reluctantly reestablished a relationship with the language I had repudiated in that hospital in Manhattan.

Given that I detested Spanish, it seems a miracle that I finally was able to pass the exams in December, do tolerably in math, and scrape by in Chilean history. Spanish, however, was a different story. My written test was such a shambles that the examining committee of government-named teachers decided to grill me orally. They indignantly showed me the results of the test. One of my errors was so egregious that I can still remember it. Among the words dictated to me by a foul-breathed examining teacher was *azucena*, water lily, undoubtedly chosen, not out of admiration for the flower, but in the hope that the student would confuse the *z* and the *c*, both pronounced like *s* in Latin America. I didn't fall into that trap, however, because I had never heard the word before. I timidly asked the teacher if she could repeat it. She looked at me furiously, as if I were deaf, and sidled up to me, hissing the four syllables even more incomprehensibly into my ear. What I heard this time, perhaps under the influence of the smell of poorly digested pork and fried garlic that wafted down from her mouth, was *a su cena*, "to her [or his] dinner." I gagged, I shrugged, I scribbled down those three words. When the examiners got my test, they must have thought I was a cretin. But as soon as they started to question me, they realized that I was merely a silly gringo who had just arrived in the country, and that my resolute effort to learn the language in three months should be commended rather than penalized. They gave me a passing grade. Something like a C minus. Maybe they wouldn't have been so generous if they had been informed that I was born Latin American, that my parents were Argentinian, that I should have breezed through that test. Or maybe they would have passed me anyway, in return for the portentous lunch offered them by the "Academia," the meal whose greasy residues the dictating lady had been burping into my ears. What did I care? I had outsmarted them. I was heading for the Grange, English-language heaven where Spanish was subordinate, tenuous, irrelevant.

Well, not quite, as my first teacher of Spanish at the Grange was quick to proclaim as soon as I had the misfortune to meet him, on a day in March of 1955, when I started classes at Mr. Jackson's British institution. My first two periods in the morning went like a dream: they were current events and literature, both in English, and I shot my hand up repeatedly and tried out a phony British accent and ingratiated myself with the instructors, and then, during break, had trotted out to the yard to excitedly show off my English-language prowess to anybody who cared to hear me—and to many who probably didn't. I then marched back into the classroom, flushed and self-satisfied, ready to continue the triumphant defense of my heritage. And found myself face-to-face with the professor of *castellano*. Castellano? The name given to the Spanish language in many Latin American countries, a reminder that what we call Spanish is in fact the dialect of Castile, which the same Catholic Kings, Isabella and Ferdinand, who expelled the Jews, established the Inquisition, and financed Columbus, imposed on the rest of the peninsula. And which that teacher was about to impose on me.

He called the roll and had only to hear me answer with my excruciating un-Castilian Yankee accent to curl his lip sarcastically and ask me to come to the head of the class. He handed me the second-year textbook and made me read a poem. My first poem in Spanish: *"Nadie dijo nada,"* by a nineteenth-century Chilean writer named Carlos Pezoa Véliz, about a homeless man who is being buried anonymously, and as the gravediggers throw earth on the body, *"nadie dijo nada, nadie dijo nada,"* nobody said a word, nobody said a word. In the poem, that is—because I was forced to pronounce each word, and as I waffled on, the teacher was more than happy to correct me and then asked for a couple of synonyms. I grubbed in my mind and found an empty blank space: like the people in the poem, I didn't have a word to say, I felt that I was the one being buried. The teacher provided some choices, however, and commanded me to write them on the blackboard and mocked both my script and my spelling. Then he made me pronounce over and over the phrase *"Hablo este idioma en forma execrable,"* I speak this language execrably. After a few minutes of this sort of merriment, he sent me back to my seat, where I stewed, publicly humiliated, for the rest of the class.

When it was over, I hurried after that teacher, approached him in the hall. I didn't know what I was going to say, and may have been as astonished as he was by what dropped out of my faltering mouth: that before I graduated from the Grange I would win the prize for excellence in the use of the Spanish language. He looked at me for a few seconds, perhaps wondering whether this gringo brat was making fun of him or just crazy. Unable to decide, he settled on one word: *Nunca*. Never. He turned smartly on his heel, as if executing a military maneuver, and left me there in the hall nursing plans for revenge.

He ignored me for the next few weeks, and then one day he didn't turn up for class and we heard he had resigned from the school to seek his fortune abroad, gone off to a small college in the United States no less (so much for his anti-Yankee sentiments!). He was replaced by another teacher, mouselike and dreary, who couldn't have cared less if I was gringo or Martian. So my tormentor was not around to eat crow when almost five years later, at the end of 1959, at the final graduation ceremonies, I received, just as I had vowed, the prize for Spanish. I did meet him once more, however: many years later, when I was in exile. It was late December of 1977 and I had flown from Amsterdam to an MLA convention in Chicago, where I had been invited to deliver the keynote speech to over a thousand U.S. university professors of Spanish and Latin American literature. By then I had made a name for myself, had penned several best-selling essays and won a major literary prize for a novel. When I finished my speech (which dealt with the Chilean cultural resistance against Pinochet and the mistakes that had been made during the Allende period), I was approached by none other than my former *castellano* teacher at the Grange. I had vaguely heard about him, that he was about to retire from the small college, but I hadn't expected to see him here. He was all gushy and sentimental: *Quiero que usted sepa, señor Dorfman*, I want you to know, Mr. Dorfman, how much I admire your writings, *cuánto admiro lo que escribe*. Would I care to autograph a copy of a book I had written on imagination and violence in the Latin American novel which he had been using for the last few years with students at his college?

I looked at him, speechless at this opportunity for vindication: it was clear that he didn't recognize in this Ariel Dorfman the Edward he had insulted in his classroom back in Chile. My youngest son, Joaquín, upon being told many years later about this encounter, has scolded me for not disclosing my identity with a Count of Monte Cristo flourish and humbling the bastard. Instead, I confess I murmured some inane nicety and let him toddle away with my autograph. I had been as tongue-tied as the first time our paths crossed, but this time it was not my lack of Spanish which paralyzed me but my excess of it. Nothing I could have said to him would really have explained what had befallen that tongue in the twenty or so years since our last exchange. Yes, he had been unjustifiably harsh to a boy without a country who could not defend himself. And yes, I hate tormentors of children. But I had come to the absurd conclusion that I owed him a favor; I bizarrely contemplated whether I shouldn't thank him for having been so cruel. There at that MLA convention in Chicago he was suddenly revealed to me—and the revelation is confirmed now, as I write this—as an avenging angel of the Spanish language, an envoy of history come to shake me out of my arrogance, an instrument secretly sent by the unknowing Chilean people to shock me into understanding once and for all that I could not continue acting as if the language I had been given at my birth had no right to exist.

That teacher was indeed abusive, but I had been abusive as well, to the language he had dedicated his life to nursing so it would grow among the young. I deserved his contempt and that realization jolted me into opening a space for Spanish in my life, a minor space, ridiculously dwarfish compared to the gigantic area in my brain seething with English, but that was enough: once it was accorded respect, once it was given a chance to establish itself in my life, there was no stopping it.

English had used America as its secret weapon. Now it was time for Spanish to use Chile, to draw me into its net. Out there, just beyond the oasis of that British school rememorating an old empire that no longer existed, just beyond the boundaries of my body straining to return to the newer empire of the United States (soon to be on a collision course with the Chile I had hardly taken the trouble to gaze at), out there, at the edge of my tongue, within reach of the Spanish words I hardly knew how to formulate, a real challenge was lying in wait for me: the people who spoke that language, the guardians of a plenitude of things and experiences that were to sensually surround my body and demand a name. That Spanish out there contained my future. It contained the words of García Lorca I would say to Angélica one day, *Verde que te quiero verde*, the lover-like green of desire, and the words of Quevedo I would say to my country, *Miré los muros de la patria mía*, watching the walls of my fatherland crumble, and the words of Neruda I would say to the revolution, *Sube a nacer conmigo, hermano*, rise and be born with me, my brother, and the words of Borges I would whisper to time, *los tigres de la memoria*, the tigers of memory with which I would try to fool death once again. I would realize one day that the word for hope in Spanish, the word *esperanza*, hides within its syllables the sound and meaning of *esperar*, to wait, that there was in the language itself a foretelling of frustration, a warning to be cautious, to hope but not to hope too much because the experience of those who forged those syllables tells them that we end up, more often than not, being violated by history.

Not only wonders, in Spanish: also learning with it how to avoid responsibility. A day comes back to me—I must have been sixteen—the first time I realized that Spanish was beginning to speak me, had infiltrated my habits. It was in carpentry class and I had given a final clumsy bang with a hammer to a monstrous misshapen contraption I had built and it broke, fell apart right there, so I turned to the carpentry teacher and "*Se rompió*," I said, shrugging my shoulders.

His mouth had twisted in anger. "*Se, se, se*," he hissed. "Everything in this country is *se*, it broke, it just happened, why in the hell don't you say I broke it, I screwed up. Say it, say, *Yo lo rompí, yo, yo, yo*, take responsibility, boy." And all of a sudden I was a Spanish speaker, I was being berated for having used that form of the language to hide behind, I had automatically used that ubiquitous, impersonal *se*, I had escaped into the language, *escapé lenguaje adentro,* merged with it.

I became conscious then of the other elusive ways in which the language allowed its devoutest followers to pass the buck onto others, the proliferation of passive forms and the overemployment of the *hay que, había que, habría que* (approximately, "it should be necessary to . . .") which, in years to come, would drive me crazy, people all around me endlessly discussing in smoke-filled rooms what should be done and very few of them effectively doing anything. But by then I had gone deeper into the language and learned that this multiplication of possibilities and parallel paths could also be a virtue, could also enrich the language. I had come to explore the verb system in Spanish, perhaps the richest in the Indo-European family of languages. I had come to adore the fluid use of time that Spanish plays with, I had internalized the subjunctive, to mentally live a plurality of forms of time that had not yet occurred, a time that was suspended and waiting to occur, a time that existed in the mind even if it had no chance of materializing in history, the construction of alternative imaginary universes always haunting the hard reality of our hearts trapped in the prison house of today and now and right here.

I was not aware of what was happening to my mind: it was a subtle, cunning, camouflaged process, the vocabulary and the grammatical code seeping into my consciousness slowly, turning me into a person who, without acknowledging it, began to function in either language. Although from the very beginning I did not allow my new language to enter into a dialogue with the older one. I stubbornly avoided comparing their relative merits, what one could offer me that the other could not. It was as if they inhabited two strictly different, segregated zones in my mind, or perhaps as if there were two Edwards, one for each language, each incommunicado like a split personality, each trying to ignore the other, afraid of contamination. I did not attempt—or even contemplate the possibility—of cross-fertilization: to weigh the caliber and performance of one against the other would have meant creating a territory from which to think the phenomenon, a common space they both shared within me. It would have meant admitting that I was irrevocably bilingual, opening the door to questions of identity that I was much too vulnerable and immature to face: Who is it that speaks Spanish? Is it the same youngster who speaks English? Is there a core that is unchanged no matter what dictionary you reach for? And which is better equipped to tell a particular story? And how is it that your body language changes when you switch from one to the other? Is it a different body? Questions that only many years later, only now that I have agreed to their coexistence, can I begin to register. Questions which, if I had asked them when I was first starting this journey toward duality, would have made me clamp down, suffocate Spanish again, deny its right to a voice. And my Spanish knew this, and cooperated, was glad to be once again inside my head, did not call attention to its gains, was not stupidly going to let itself crow victory when suddenly, in the middle of a sentence in English, a word in Spanish would make its upstart appearance as if nothing was more natural in the world, given that there was no English equivalent for that untranslatable turn of phrase. My Spanish did not demand that I examine why I needed that precise word when I had an infinitude of English at my tongue's end, why it was irreplaceable. Having smuggled itself in, my Spanish was wise enough not to corner me. Instead, quite simply, it grew. And grew. And grew.

If I had realized how radical that process of learning Spanish was to be, how it was to change my life and chain me to Chile, I would undoubtedly have rebelled, preferred to endure hundreds of abusive teachers and mocking schoolmates than jeopardize the predominance of my English-language identity, my determination to return to America.

I did not think at the time that there was the slightest danger of Chile, or Spanish, enchanting me forever. My head was firmly turned North, living the archetypal colonialist dream, looking to the mother country for everything of value, and because my father happened to be a diplomat, it was not only my head but my stomach as well that was able to make believe we still inhabited the United States.

A few weeks after my first Spanish lesson at the blackboard of the Grange had launched me in the direction of Chile, my Yankee past reclaimed me in the form of an enormous box my father brought home. Imported straight from America. He handed me a knife and told me to cut into it. I didn't hesitate and stabbed the heart of the box, and the loot came pouring forth and was parceled out. Corn-flakes and Hershey's syrup and Campbell's tomato soup and Aunt Jemima's pancake mix and Schrafft's almond crunch, along with magazines and books and records and shirts and bathing suits, to be shared by one and all. And one kind of booty that was only for me: an assortment of twelve candy bars. Every three months, my dad said, there'll be a new shipment. I went whooping up to my room and proceeded to hide and hoard those candies in the bottom drawer of my desk, under my most precious manuscripts. Food and litera-ture, the twin obsessions of my life, side by side. My stock was supposed to last me exactly twelve weeks, until the next shipment would bring relief. If I disciplined myself, I could, like Robinson Crusoe on his island, resist the siege of the savages and the brutal wheel of time; if I resisted temptation, the candy bars would allow me to remain the child I had been, flash back piecemeal each night to the States until the day when I could really journey home and gorge myself at the local drugstore.

I had not read Proust yet nor knew how to pronounce the word *madeleine,* but during those first years in Chile my candy bars helped me indulge in a Proustian struggle to recapture the past, though in my case the attempt to prove that time was an illusion was not left to chance but turned into what I thought would be a cold and calculating scientific campaign. Before going to sleep each night, I would gnaw at the edge of, say, a Baby Ruth and carefully, almost religiously, return the rest to the wrapper; and then I would go to bed and lie awake ruminating, not on death, as I did when I was a child, but on who in the hell Baby Ruth had been and whether she had been able to eat all the concoctions she wanted, and then my mind would inevitably turn to the candy bar there, in the drawer, so close at hand, so lonesome, so willing to take me, salivating, back to my lost and faraway land, and I would creep out from under the covers and open the drawer and take that delectable Baby Ruth out and peel its paper like a flower and smell it and bring it almost to my lips and then put it back to sleep sexually inside its wrappers without even licking it once and then back to bed and more thoughts and then a flood of distance and the abysm of desire and finally a rush to open the drawer and pull back the wrapping, and open the soft heart of the candy, and a tiny bite, the hope that the morsel of chocolate would melt me toward the States. But it was never enough and all too soon I was taking another bite and another one until the last crumb was gone and often, all too often, on I would go to the next Baby Ruth and then a Mars bar and just one more, only one more, I promise, I swear! and all of a sudden there I was, stranded in my room in Santiago with all those empty wrappers on the floor and the hint of a tummy ache and the realization that I had just swallowed in one sitting a whole month of secret passages to America, uselessly telling myself what all exiles tell themselves as they fantasize about returning home tomorrow: this distance is a mere parenthesis, a punishment that will end if I can only stay the same, if I can only foil time. Not knowing that many years later, in my next exile, I would devour *empanadas* with the same expectation that those Chilean meat pies could act as my adult ticket to the past, to the country of the past where my body was forbidden to go. The country I wanted to escape during my adolescence, the *empanadas* I hardly wasted time on then, obsessed as I was with my Milky Ways.

I had, of course, less precarious ways of returning to the place I insisted on calling home, subscribing to more magazines, from *Mad* to *The Saturday Evening Post*, than I ever had read in the States, trying particularly to keep abreast of sports. And comics and mystery books that, unlike candy, could be consumed over and over again. And movies—every epic, every saccharine love story, even the blundering cheap Ed Wood-type grade-C sci-fi movies that are now the staple of jokes on U.S. television.

There in Chile I made myself into much more of an all-American kid than any child back in the States. As if the still unacknowledged tug of Spanish and this new country had sparked an even more violent counterattachment to the United States. As if I had fervently to display my fealty, set to rest any suspicion that I might, in fact, be in danger of losing that connection.

The connection, however, was in no danger of losing me. Everywhere I turned, America was abundantly present, particularly in the music young Chileans were starting to listen to. My newly recovered Spanish might let me understand the lyrics of the bolero and the tango and the *ranchero*, but I continued to despise these Latin-American songs, thought—along with my pro-Yankee cohorts from the fortress of the Grange with whom I gabbed in English at school and at home—that they showed the taste of the dark-skinned lower classes, *las sirvientas*, the old farts. In our rooms and at our dances the radio was invariably plugged into one of the stations that, more and more as the decade wore on, played only American records, at first Frank Sinatra and the Ames Brothers and Nat King Cole. But soon enough, just in time, the first defiant beats of Elvis and Bill Haley and Connie Francis, just in time for a body rebelling into adolescence, just in time for a body aching for a rhythm that could express the uncertain promise and turmoil of sex.

If I was able to tune in that easily to all these manifestations of American culture, it was because they did not need to be imported by my father, they did not arrive every three months in a shipment. They were invading Chile as fast as they were invading the rest of the world, the preamble of a a global culture which allowed any kid anywhere to sing and dance the same tunes being blared out halfway across the planet.

Years later, during the Allende revolution, I was to deplore and denounce that expansion of the United States media industry as a threat to the national ethos and sensibility, but back in the fifties I was its beneficiary. If I could lap up so many American movies, it was because the locally owned film-distribution companies were being taken over by Hollywood affiliates and the national cinematographic

industry that had flourished during the Second World War was being squeezed into irrelevancy by the U.S. monopolies. I didn't issue a
call to resistance at the time. Chilean girls with budding breasts and
wannabe-English accents were swooning over those songs, and I'd
have been out of my mind to discourage or interrupt any crooner
who was urging those blessed creatures to dance cheek-to-cheek, get
a bit closer, a little bit closer. So in the battle for the survival of the
fittest, I jacked up my one asset, my mastery of English. Though it
wasn't Shakespeare empowering me, but Fats Domino.

With everybody around me facing North in awe, I didn't hesitate
to deploy an aura of modernity, pressed my advantage as an up-to-
date walking encyclopedia of colloquial, ultra-hip Americana. Even
so, infatuated as I was by U.S. popular culture, during my high
school years I also became increasingly aware that my adopted country was responsible for the misery of Latin America and, specifically,
of Chile.

In New York I had heard, of course, about U.S. imperialism. My
parents had never lost an occasion to point out to their Yankee-
loving son that his America the Beautiful had thrived by being America the Ugly south of the border, but that ugliness only became
screamingly apparent once we had moved to the continent which
the United States treated as its back yard. Just one example: in 1954,
the very year I left the States, Guatemala had been invaded by a
U.S.-trained force (supported by U.S. Air Force bombardment) because its democratically elected President, Jacobo Arbenz, had dared
to try to nationalize some of the land belonging to the United Fruit
Company. One year later, the exiled Arbenz himself came to dinner
at our house in Santiago. His pain and the pain of his country were
the direct result of what my country had done there, in Central
America. I could go on and on with hundreds of examples, but none
was to impress me more than one single incident that brought home
to me, a few years after we moved to Santiago, the crude reality of
how an empire works.

Down the street from our house there lived a bespectacled, crew-cut American boy, Bernie, whose father was a high executive with one of the U.S. copper companies that owned and ran the Chilean mines. He wasn't exactly a friend, but more of a buddy, two boys far from their country who lived on the same street: we'd exchange comics, listen to records, discuss the latest trades in the American League back home, fantasize about "broads," eat his mother's brownies, compete to blow the largest chewing-gum bubbles.

One day—a few months before Bernie was to return to the States—he opened a closet in his room and showed me, hidden underneath a mound of clothes, an enormous glass jar. It was filled with Chilean pesos, all of them copper.

"What do you think?" he asked.

I didn't know what to think. What was it for?

"These guys are so, so stupid," Bernie said, pointing in the direction of the street, of Santiago, of Chile, of Latin America. "You know what I'm going to do with these coins? I'm going to melt them, turn them into five bars of copper, sell them. I'm going to get ten times the price. They're Indians, these guys, they like to get fucked."

I was shocked. I had heard insensitive remarks about Chile before and I would hear them again: from classmates at the Grange, in their houses, and at the Prince of Wales Country Club, where my dazzling English conned the Chilean guards at the gate into admitting me even if I was not a member. But none of those bigoted off-the-cuff remarks stuck in my gut like Bernie's get-rich-quick scheme, perhaps because none was so egregious, none so blatant and direct. In fact, I have found myself hesitating whether to consign this episode here, because, grotesque to the point of inverisimilitude, it was almost too perfect a metaphor of greed and empire: an American teenager hoarding those coins like a third-rate Scrooge McDuck, repeating on a minor scale what his father was doing in a major way, both of them bent on screwing the country out of its metal.

Was it only Bernie's covetousness, his racism, his relish at conning the local population, his disparagement of this country that, after all, had given my family refuge and provided us with a delightful existence in the midst of such natural beauty, was it only that which made me feel sick? Or can I detect, faintly stirring in the boy I used to be, the hint of a new allegiance to Chile, a tinge of pride in being Latin American, the first time I felt that I was on the other side of the divide, us against them? If so, what had created the distance, what was really coming between Bernie and me, between the United States and me, was the impoverishment of Chile.

It was not that I discovered the existence of misery when we went to live in Chile. I cannot, literally, remember a time in my life when I was not mindful of the fact that there were many in the world less fortunate than my family. I look back and see them there, on the rim of my life, watching me as I watched them, and what I recall is my compassion, my attempt to jump into their point of view, to beggar myself into their eyes, to wonder what hunger meant, what sickness meant, what despair meant, what it meant to die before having lived. But as there were not that many really indigent people around in booming New York after the Second World War, their mysterious destiny was, in a sense, an abstraction, they became an occasion for intellectual elaboration, to be explained away into comprehensible categories, particularly by my father. Whenever I asked why those harrowing figures of destitution haunted my books or comics or films (more than my streets), my father would use that example to educate me, point out that the poor existed as a direct, and necessary, consequence of the richness of a small minority.

Once we were in Chile, however, poverty ceased to be an abstraction. It was there the day we arrived, in the tired backs of the longshoremen on the docks as our ship creaked against its moorings; it was there in the weatherbeaten shacks clustered like flies on Valparaiso's hills; it was there in the bare feet of peasants laboring on fields that did not belong to them, scarcely raising their bronze faces as our car whizzed by on the road to Santiago; it was there in the endless shantytowns of the capital, the urban sprawl of cardboard-and-tin hovels among the weeds and the stray dogs; it was there in the army of derelicts of all ages that crisscrossed the avenues of the city, sleeping under the bridges of the Mapocho and blanketing the steps of the churches as if they were crippled birds.

"You'll get used to that," a UN colleague of my father's said to me, in English, when he heard me expressing amazement at such widespread misery. "As there's not very much that you can do about it, anyway."

He was more right than wrong in his rather flippant assessment. Even if I could not avoid being intermittently embarrassed whenever a human being in distress came limping through my life, I was basically walled away from the poor of Chile in every possible way: I was young, I lived in a well-to-do neighborhood, and I attended a school which trained the elite that would govern this country and its wealth.

I did make one attempt to intervene in the quagmire of Chilean poverty. I must have been around fourteen and spoke enough Spanish to engage people outside my house in ordinary conversation, and one day when I was returning from the dentist's I had taken pity on a street urchin who was singing boleros on the bus. His voice was as cracked as his blistered feet. He was covered with scabs, his hair a shock of black sticky strands, his shirt torn. He couldn't have been more than six years old. I gave him a coin, asked him a question, he saw a friendly light in my eyes and, perhaps encouraged by my strange accent, he began to tell his story: how it was better to live on the streets than risk the beatings of a father who might or might not be around; how the *pacos* (the Chilean police) had picked him up one day and threatened to put him in an institution but he had fooled them and escaped; how once in a while he made his way home to his mother, who was always sweet to him and had taught him his repertory of lovelorn *canciones*. As he talked, our bus began to enter the *barrio alto*, where I lived, and as we passed the façades of opulent estates behind which the upper classes lived in outrageous luxury, that little boy's condition became all the more pathetic, so that, when we reached my bus stop in a somewhat more modest part of the area, I impulsively invited him to come home with me for a hot meal. Our house was far from being a mansion; just a large, comfortable residence, but seen through his eyes, it took on the magnificence of a palace.

We had two servants—one who cooked and one who cleaned and served at table—and neither was delighted to see the seedy guest I had brought home. But my parents weren't around, so I was the boss. The kid chattered away while he ate, and then my mother came home and, after joining us for a moment, went off to rummage in the attic for some old clothes for the kid. I escorted my young friend to the door and told him that I hoped to see him again.

The very next day the doorbell rang and there he was. Again I invited him in for a good meal, but this time my mother didn't make an appearance with clothes or a welcoming smile, nor, when I said goodbye, did I suggest that we set up another meeting, suspecting that he would be back, anyway. I wasn't surprised when, twenty-four hours later, he turned up with two other waifs. This time I hesitated, but what was I to do? Turn them away? They marched into the kitchen and I sat them down in front of the cook and she frowned and extricated some leftovers from the fridge and warmed them, grumbling under her breath, and then the doorbell rang again and the maid went off to see who it was and came back and announced noncommittally, *"Buscan."* Somebody had come to see me.

Outside our gate stood the mother (at least she said she was) of my singing friend with a baby in her arms and a ragged older girl clinging to her dress. She asked if I had any work for her, for the girl. I told her to wait and went upstairs to my own mother, who took charge of the situation. She walked out to speak to the woman, gave her some money, informed her that unfortunately we had no work, and added that the boy and his friends would be out very soon.

Half an hour later, when all the intruders had left, my mother sat me down, complimented me on my good heart and told me firmly that this could not go on. This was not the way to solve the problems of Chile's perpetual underdevelopment. One beggar had begat two more and now others were clamoring at the door and this was incremental, there were too many indigent people out there and too few homes like ours that even cared. We would be overrun and unable to lead a normal life. I could, of course, if I was so inclined, sell my records and my books and my candy bars—but not my clothes! she added hastily—and turn them into cash for my afflicted chums. My mother warned me that within a few days the supply would be gone and I would be back exactly where I was now: they would still be as poor as ever and I would be as fed and clothed and housed as ever, the line dividing us would not have disappeared. Someday perhaps, I would be able to do something about that line and that poverty, just as my father had tried, but now was not the time and this was not the way.

The next afternoon I watched as the maid went out to the gate when my singing urchin came around again, with the same two pals, and with a couple of older kids hovering in the background. I watched from behind the curtains in a room filled with art books, a room where my mother played the piano to songs I sang in English, a room with an enormous reproduction of a Siqueiros painting show-ing Latin America as a centaur in agony, half beast, half man, always divided, I watched the maid tell the kid that I wasn't home, and he looked straight at where I was hiding behind the curtains and then up toward the second story of our house, where my room was. I watched from that house filled with books that analyzed inequality and surplus value and economic underdevelopment and the philos-ophy of justice and the rights of indigenous peoples. I watched the boy turn away, and the next day he came one last time and I forced myself to contemplate his defeat and my defeat all over again, and that was it. After that, he never rang the bell again. He understood what had happened, the limits of my compassion, he came no more, and whatever guilt I felt was insufficient to make me interrupt the life I had led up until then. I continued my estranged existence in Chile almost as if nothing had happened. But I had learned some-thing: the truth of who we were, the boy and I, the cards we had been dealt. I lived here, in a safe, happy house, the foreign, bilingual son of a diplomat going to the most exclusive school in Chile, and that child had nothing but his throat and his songs of adult love and betrayal to ward off death. I watched him wander off under the splendid trees of Santiago and the mountains that years later would urge me not to leave this country, and his tribulation and abandonment were made all the starker by the contrast they offered to the breathtakingly beautiful surroundings in which they festered, that land which had more than enough resources to feed him a million times over and could not even guarantee him, and so many others like him, one meal a day.

If I ended up transitorily trapped in the prophecy of my father's UN colleague, unable to intervene in the age-old injustice of Chile, I would not be left there for very long. All around me, thousands of other inhabitants of Chile were ready to take more decisive action.

Two hundred years before I arrived on the shores of that country and wondered how so much bounty could produce so much suffering, a Chilean named José Cos de Iribari had asked a similar question even before independence had been gained from Spain: How is it possible that, "in the midst of the lavishness and splendor of [Latin American] nature," most of the population was "groaning under the yoke of poverty, misery and the vices which are their inevitable consequences"? And now, after that question, repeated by each generation of Chileans (and Latin Americans in the rest of the continent), had received no satisfactory answer, a left-wing movement of intellectuals and workers and peasants that had been forming during most of the century was gaining strength. Since colonial times, the same ruling classes, and their allies abroad, had kept a stranglehold on the country's economy and, most of the time, on its government as well, and the result had been social injustice, educational and technological stagnation, a scandalous disparity between the means and lifestyle of a small oligarchy and those of the vast impoverished nation, a productive system geared to the exigencies of the foreign marketplace rather than the needs of the citizens themselves. The left proclaimed that it was time to institute real reforms amd wrest control of Chile's wealth from foreign corporations and a handful of greedy families. It was time for a different class to take power. It was time, they said, for a revolution.

It must have been around then, in 1956, that I first heard the name of Salvador Allende, a socialist doctor who had been the youngest Minister in the 1938 Popular Front government of Pedro Aguirre Cerda and who had, from that post, instituted the first social security and national health care system in Chile. He was now a senator and he had been instrumental in formulating a program that was supposed to solve the country's structural problems. Nationalize the copper, nitrate, carbon, iron mines, expropriate the main industries and banks, divide up the large haciendas among the peasants that worked the land. And this overturning of privilege was to be accomplished democratically, through the electoral process. It was a program virtually identical to the one Allende set in motion when he did win the Presidency in 1970 and which he came within a hair's breadth of implementing in 1958, when he lost the elections by thirty thousand votes to the right-wing candidate, Jorge Alessandri.

As a red-diaper baby, I was, of course, destined to be an Allendista. It never occurred to me that it might be otherwise. If my political education had been limited in the States by the caution that had to be exercised in the McCarthy era, in Chile there were no such restraints. My left-wing parents gloried in the company of like-minded friends. The table that could not receive the beggars of Santiago dined and wined the Chilean and Latin American elite dedicated to the cause of ridding the continent of beggars, from the future President of Argentina, Arturo Frondizi, to the future President of Guyana, Cheddi Jagan. Plus a number of North American lefties, Huberman, Sweezy, the *Monthly Review* crowd. The air was thick with debate about socialism, democracy, liberation, and the future of revolutionary change on the Soviet model, particularly once the Twentieth Congress of the U.S.S.R. had admitted the monstruous crimes of Stalin, an admission which was immediately followed by the brutal suppression of the Hungarian revolt. This had put my hard-line father on the defensive in the ongoing discussion with my mother, who in the late 1940s, tongue firmly in cheek, had already announced that she was forming a party called the SRCLCP—the Slightly Reformed Conservation Life Communist Party. Membership, she acknowledged, was limited for the time being to one person. Herself. But it would grow, she had prognosticated, and now the explosion of defections from Soviet Communism by a host of former true believers around the world, along with news of repression and unhappiness in the Eastern Bloc countries, was proving her right. My mother had also come out, early on, against the use of violence and the death penalty. If in the years to come, under the influence of Allende and his followers, I would identify increasingly with my mother's position and become critical of my father's, at that point in my development it was all speculative. Oh yes, I skimmed and scanned some Marxist texts, I parroted my parents and their cronies in discussions I held with the affluent parents of my friends from the Grange who tolerated this charmingly eccentric leftist who adored James Dean, this atheist with mystical tendencies, this Jacobin with the most exquisite manners and the gentlest of dispositions, this advocate of the Chilean unwashed and uneducated who wrote entangled and hermetic stories in English. They had an easy way of deflating all my elaborate arguments: Wasn't I going back to the United States? Didn't I consider myself American?

They were right.

I was unable to confront them because I was unable to confront myself, the life I had made for myself in Chile, my urge to travel back to the very place on the planet that was responsible in great measure, I thought, for the suffering that surrounded me. I could never engage that suffering while I dreamed of returning to the Promised Land of New York.

My future was elsewhere, and as the date of my graduation from the Grange approached, I continued to make plans to leave Chile, sending applications to several American universities. Just in case, I also interviewed for a job with an American company that was looking to hire young representatives willing to travel through Latin America selling books and magazines in English, with the promise that a year later they would be sent to the States for further training. The job was mine if I wanted it, an executive called up to tell me, and then Columbia University let me know that I had been admitted, with a scholarship, as a freshman.

For several feverish days, I could hardly contain myself. I was going back! Finally!

My parents watched this frenzy apprehensively, allowed the fever to subside, and then gingerly ventured a suggestion: perhaps it would be better to postpone this trip, wait until I was a bit older. At seventeen, after all, I was too young, at least by Latin American standards, to be leaving home. They told me to mull it over, instead of rashly throwing away the enchanted existence I led in this country, a spacious house with a mesmerizing garden and adoring parents and servants who took care of my every need and loyal friends and a record collection and all my books and a motorcycle and . . .

I went out for a long walk by myself.

I loved then, and still love now, the Santiago evenings in the summertime. Even now that smog has ruined the Central Valley, now that too many cars befoul the air and the trees have been cut down to make way for ugly blocks of buildings and infested avenues, even now that we have mercilessly dirtied what was once a magical landscape, even now there still remains that sense of wonder and gratitude when the sun begins to go down. To be alive at the moment when a breeze descends from the mountains and you breathe deeply, not only with the lungs, but through the skin itself, as if the earth were calming you down, is to know a measure of forgiveness. It is only a lull in the dark, but whenever I stand under the Andes of Santiago and feel that sudden gust of air that seems to come from the very gates of Paradise and pushes back the dry mad heat of the day, when I look up and the mountains are all on fire from the setting sun, the Andes are turning orange and then red and the sky behind them has grown purple and it darkens and the night is held in abeyance, I am certain that this is the condition we were made for, this peace. It is all an illusion, it cannot last, this interlude of twilight when we seem to be blessed, when we seem to have refound our lost path, and yet for a while it is true, the body, the breeze, that quiet moment suspended between light and darkness that you never want to end.

I feel it now and I felt it then, breathing in the gift from the Andes and desiring somehow to be buried here someday, to have my ashes scattered in this place someday.

And that is where and when I asked myself, under those mountains, if this country had not become, in some way I had not anticipated, my home. That is where I decided, far from New York and far from Buenos Aires, a different future for my life.

But what about my literature? What about my English?

My decision not to return to the States would not have been conceivable if I had not come to the conclusion, during my high school years, that I could continue to write my fiction in the English language even if I was far from the States.

This divorce, the extrication of the English in which I wrote from the nation where I had learned it, had come gradually and was as much a product of my reading habits as it was of my own existential experience. During my first years in Santiago, I used my writing according to my plans back in New York: obdurately to get myself home, following in the footsteps of so many exiles through history, nostalgically traveling through words to the country I could not inhabit, and doing so, not surprisingly, in genres which were themselves typically North American. I churned out endless adventure stories, modeled on the Hardy Boys and their imitators, and wrote dozens of half-hour comic radio skits set in a mythical American landscape.

When I was about fifteen, my writing abruptly matured. Again, a sickness intervened, a dangerous strain of hepatitis. If consulted, my old friend Thomas Mann, who believed in the symbiosis of illness and creativity, death and artistic exploration, internal decomposition and the external order we impose on the page, might have explained my sudden turn by this brush with mortality. Whatever the cause, during my two-month convalescence, I wrote a delirious sci-fi four-hundred-page utopian epic, marrying for the first time politics and fantasy in my writing; but also setting my characters far from the United States, a decisive turn away from realism.

And when I went back to school and resumed my normal activities, I discovered that writing—creating an alternative vision—could influence the way one lives one's life. My day became split in two: I still adhered, of course, to the cheerful world of Doris Day and Rock Hudson, who presided over my diurnal, apparently normal everyday existence, my colonialized personality; while at nighttime and on weekends I would write stories that got increasingly darker and more daring and more intimate, privately drifting further and further away from childhood and its hunger for simplicity, optimism, and easy solutions.

It was an evolutionary leap that had been percolating for some time, anticipated by the literature, from the States itself, that I had started to read. As I moved from the Hardy Boys to Hemingway, from Tom Swift to Steinbeck, from Nancy Drew to Kerouac and the Beats, from Woody Woodpecker to John Hersey and Howard Fast, I found myself able to contact in my writing an ambiguity and a turbulence that had not till then been allowed expression. Or maybe it was the other way around: I was able to understand those disturbing books, absorb *The Great Gatsby*, for instance, because in my own life I was starting to live, however faintly, the same discovery those American authors were dragging their characters through: that the American dream might be, after all, a nightmare. This intellectual and emotional growth was also nourished by an avid plundering of the British classics, Shakespeare, Dickens, Sterne, Milton, Hardy, Donne, Austen, and then an expansion into French authors (also in English), Stendhal and Zola and Romain Rolland, and, in my last year at the Grange, the existentialists Sartre, Camus, and Beauvoir, and the brooding, tormented Russians, and I can remember the day

I plucked the *Buddenbrooks* saga from my parents' bookshelf, the pages that had been waiting in the back of my head ever since I had exchanged those brief words with my mentor-in-exile on the steamer to Europe; and at last, one wondrous night, I encountered Kafka's *Metamorphosis* and Joseph K. and I knew that literature could be a prayer and a pickax, a way out of the frozen world in which we find ourselves trapped, our only protest against death and loneliness.

So that by the time I took my walk under those Chilean mountains, I had already come to the conclusion that my writing did not need to be based in any community other than the community of like-minded individuals, the *humanitas* of select spirits; I really believed that I could live in Chile indefinitely and at the same time write fiction in English, without my identity eroding or being put to the test.

How could I have anticipated there, that evening, as the sun set magnificently on Santiago de Chile, that what awaited me, less than a decade into the future, was the moment in Berkeley when I would swear never to use English again? How could I have known that history was about to interfere drastically in my life once more?

Something was heading toward me and the country I had chosen as my refuge. With my schizophrenic, adulterous existence, writing in English and speaking in Spanish, singing American songs at sunrise and being lullabied into sleep by the Chilean mountains in the evening, crazy about Conrad and crazy about Cervantes, suspended vulnerably between two nations and two languages, I was totally unable to recognize what was bearing down on me, on us, the man-made future about to envelop my world and change it forever.

The revolution was coming to Latin America.

The continent I had been born to and now lived in, the continent I had finally decided not to flee, was about to explode in the sixties.

PART TWO

SOUTH

AND

NORTH

NINE

A Chapter Dealing with the
Discovery of Death, Sometime
in September 1973,
in Santiago de Chile

I t is the morning of September 14, and for the first time since the coup, I am alone.

I've said goodbye to Alberto, received the information from our Party contact that Angélica is waiting for me at a café uptown, and that is how I find myself walking up Avenida Eleodoro Yáñez, alone for the first time with my loss, with no need to pretend that I can deal with this sorrow without another human being to help keep my desolation at bay. I am alone with the extraordinary evil and violence that is being visited on this country, and as I walk I can feel hope being sucked out of me as if I were bleeding it. I can feel all the rage of Chile filling me and there is nothing inside me or outside to counter that despair, not even tears. I can't find a tear inside me to cry for my dead President and my dying land and my dry heart: I am hollow, adrift, someone who does not know who he is or what to do with his life.

It is then, when I am most lost, midway through my life, just past the age of thirty-one, that I see that man.

In truth, he sees me first.

He sees me as I cross a street, he reads my face as I cross the street, he understands everything I am feeling as I cross the street, and as I turn to him momentarily, for a split second that no camera could capture, no spy could register, at that instant when his person passes mine in mid-street, that man, a Chilean worker, bronzed, short, muscular, determined, dignified, that man I have never before seen and would probably not recognize today, that man closes and opens his left eye and then he is gone, he vanishes as if he had never existed.

He winked at me. Just that. No more than that. But that wink said it all. It said to me: *No es para tanto, compañero.* Things are not that bad, *compañero.* It said: *Vamos a salir adelante.* We'll find a way out. It said: *No está tan solo como piensa.* You're not as alone as you think.

He saw me there in the pit of my sorrow and offered no more than his encouragement, proof that I was not really alone, that he was there even if we never saw each other again, that we could communicate even if the soldiers patrolled the streets and there seemed no place of refuge and they were beginning to torture prisoners a few blocks away, forecasting with the closing and opening of his eye how we would start rebuilding the country that had been stolen from us, bit by bit, wink by wink, under their very guns and boots. But, above all, it said to me that I was recognized, that I belonged, that he spoke my language, and that language was not Spanish and of course not English but the unspoken language of solidarity, the gesture of one man who had not lost hope toward another who was on the verge of losing it. It was a welcome, I thought, a wink of complicity that told me I had ceased to be a stranger and had finally become a *compañero*.

Compañero. A word for which there is no adequate English equivalent, because soul mate, buddy, friend, comrade, even companion, do not contain, like an echo, the Spanish word for bread—*pan*—and it is that *pan* which speaks most profoundly in *compañero* of two people who break bread, of that other who is a brother even if you have never met him, of that trust.

Many months later, I will see this encounter more as a *despedida*, a farewell; I will fantasize that he was giving me a goodbye present, because he could tell that I was already leaving, that I could not remain; he was giving me that wink to remember and cherish in the long years ahead, when the despair I felt on that street in Santiago on September 14 of 1973 would seem like nothing compared to the abyss of distance and guilt and horror that exile would bring as I watched my country, from afar, being defiled and my friends being slaughtered and men such as this remote *compañero* of mine being humiliated day after day after day. That would be the time when that wink would return to me, remind me that he was counting on me as I had counted on him the day of my despair. But that was not how I understood our encounter then, not that it will keep me warm in the winter of my exile, but that I belong here, that nothing will make me leave this Chile which, now more than ever, has become my home.

Nobody agrees with me. Angélica offers the news that my mother has had two threatening phone calls, a male voice on the other side relishing her fright, her son-of-a-cunt Marxist bastard is going to get it now, if you see him, lady, say goodbye because you won't ever see him again, your *conchatumadre* Jew-boy traitor, so it does not exactly look like a brilliant idea to try to go home to my parents. And certainly not to our own house, where Angélica has started to burn papers, from posters of Che Guevara to minutes of Party meetings to innumerable political documents, up in smoke, joining the smoke that casts a suspicious pall over the whole of Santiago, where it is much too warm this spring to have all those chimneys ablaze, thousands of proud men and women turning to ashes and air the words of the Allende revolution. From the conflagration she has begun to rescue my manuscripts, and I do not ask her why, I do not want her to tell me that this is a step toward leaving the country, a step toward admitting that we will never more sleep in our little bungalow, that I will never again sit down to write in my study.

I ask her something else. Where am I to go, then?

Angélica has also been trying to set up a meeting with Abel, my superior in the Party structure, to try to get some sort of decision about what we should do. Meanwhile, she has arranged that I spend a couple of nights, though no more, at the apartment of a friend—let's call her Catalina—who has strongly right-wing parents and has only recently become an Allendista sympathizer and whom no one would ever suspect of harboring a fugitive.

"Is there any good news?" I ask.

"Yes," Angélica says. "Well, maybe. It's crazy, but you got a phone call from the Cultural Institute of Nuñoa, to remind you that you're on the jury for the 1973 literary prizes and could you please send in your list of candidates, so that you can vote on the winners at next week's meeting."

So life does go on. I clutch at this straw like a lunatic drowning. The organizers of the literary prize don't think I'm dangerous, they're calling me as if nothing has happened. Maybe this is the sign I'm looking for, maybe they'll leave me alone. But I don't say this to Angélica. She would reply that it could be a trap, who knows if on the other side of the line there is a military officer and what he wants is for me to show up. Instead, I ask: "What did you tell them?"

And Angélica: "I told them you were at the beach, writing a new novel, and that you'd get back to them." She pauses. "It's what I've told Rodrigo as well."

"And he believed you?"

"Not really. He thinks you're dead."

"He thinks I'm dead?"

"He doesn't say so, but that's what he thinks."

"I'll call him."

"I don't think you should, just now. The Party contact suggested that you not call home at all, that I tell anybody who calls that I don't know where you are, that we've . . . split."

That night, at our friend Catalina's apartment, my hostess switches on the television and one of the news items is the burning of books in the center of Santiago. Forty years after Hitler came to power, forty years after his Nazi followers lit fires to consume the degenerate texts that corrupted the German youth, Chilean soldiers are relighting those flames and torching books all over again. And suddenly the camera zooms in—and there it is, my own book, hated by every right-wing person in Chile, *Para leer al Pato Donald. How to Read Donald Duck.* There it is, publicly being consumed by the Inquisitorial flames—and perhaps I have finally made the *Guinness Book of World Records,* the first author in history to have watched his own work burnt live on TV. I look up at Catalina and she averts her eyes and we both think: If they are doing this to the book, what will they do to the hands that wrote the book, and what are they doing right now to the eyes all over Chile that read that book, and what will they do to her body if they find my body here.

Two days later, Angélica comes for me and we are on our way to a diplomat's house, a Paraguayan lawyer who works for the UN. On our way, we stop to see another friend, Angel Parra, one of Chile's foremost singers, the son of the greatest folklore artist of Latin America, the long-deceased Violeta Parra. I had called Angel two days before to urge him to seek asylum. He wasn't in, but his wife, Marta, had come to the phone and told me that Angel refused to leave Chile. Now she comes to the door to greet us in a state of shock. *"Por Dios,"* she whispers, *"ándate,* go away, get away, quick. They just came for him, *se llevaron al Angel,* half an hour ago, the soldiers just burst in and took him. I've got to find someone who can save him, who can intercede before they . . ." She turned to me: "Ariel, you've got to get out. You've got to get out before the embassies all fill up." The advice I had wanted to give her husband, which he had not wanted to listen to, which I now don't want to listen to as I keep running. And two days later, at the house of our diplomat friend, I hold my first conversation with foreign journalists that he has gathered so they can be briefed by somebody who can speak English, who can tell them what the resistance intends to do, and I analyze the political situation with a security I am far from feeling ("They think this is Indonesia, people being massacred as in Djakarta; they will find this is another Vietnam," is one of my unprophetic phrases) and I end up learning more from them than they learn from me, confirming the death of the singer Victor Jara, another friend, in the six-thousand-person-capacity Estadio Chile, confirming that the military has decided to establish a bigger detention center at the Estadio Nacional, which holds sixty thousand. Yet I ignore the signs, I begin to feel invulnerable and detached, as if the unlikely combination of luck and design that saved my life—a colleague who casually switches places, my name crossed off a list, a cartoon character who kept me from my appointment with death—will somehow continue to repeat itself forever. I run and I run and Angélica tells me that, absurd as it may seem, she has been able to collect my salary at the university, and I smile and point to this as proof that I will be able to go back to work, but she also tells me that she's going to meet Abel soon and will have news for me and that the news may not be good, and the next day I have to leave the Paraguayan lawyer's house; last night the soldiers raided the residence of another UN employee. I run like a fugitive in a B-movie so I will not have to accept what is happening to me and my unrecognizable country, running until finally I have to listen to the news that Angélica cannot help but bring me, there in the café of the Plaza Nuñoa, the cups of coffee clinking nearby, the orders from the *mozo* for the *lomito con palta*, eyes smarting from the cigarette smoke, shifting to the door to see if someone will come in and nail me, running from the words Angélica now passes on to me: Abel has met with her, the resistance has decided that I am to leave the country, seek refuge in an embassy. I am to go into exile.

"I'm not leaving."

"What do you mean? It's been decided."

"Tell Abel I want to see him. Tell him I want a second opinion."

A second opinion. As if you were sick, as if a different doctor would come up with a different diagnosis, as if you had been coopted by the Junta's language, their medical prognosis of the country as a body that needs to be operated on, the cancerous growth cut out so that it can live, as if somebody's second opinion would decide that no, you are not a cancer, you do not need to be extirpated, you do not need to leave Chile.

Angélica agrees. It is hazardous for her, for Abel, for me, but she agrees. She knows I am making believe I have a choice, she knows I cannot survive much longer on the run like this, she knows I will eventually acquiesce to my destiny; but she also knows that in the years ahead I need to be able to tell myself—and others, just as I am telling my readers right now—that I was forced out, tell myself that I am not a coward.

Angélica makes one last try. "You're not immortal, you know," she says.

There is nothing I can answer.

Two days later, however, I will discover how mortal I am. I find myself here, in this car being driven to my next safe house by a woman I have never met. She is part of an informal network that has sprung up all over the country, people who are risking their lives to protect those in danger. I will not be told her name—better not to know anything about her—but years later, when I am writing *Death and the Maiden*, I will have my protagonist, Paulina, do something similar in the months after the coup, though I can only hope that the woman who came to my rescue back then was never caught, that she never went through Paulina's experience of torture and rape.

This woman whose name I never wanted to know tells me that her son, who is studying at the Catholic University, has a classmate, let's call him Esteban, a freshman studying psychology. Esteban is the perfect collaborator for the resistance, a committed Allendista who is not suspected by the authorities at his university or his neighborhood of harboring sympathies for the left, because an illness has forced him, during the last year, to stay away from politics. Esteban's father, a textile worker I believe he was, has offered his house for the few days it will take to set up my scheduled meeting with Abel to determine whether I must leave Chile.

"So we shouldn't expect any trouble?" I ask the woman.

"Nothing much," comes the casual answer.

I begin to feel tension mounting in my body as we head for the industrial belt of Santiago, and the tension jumps another notch when my driver turns off the main road and winds along a half-finished street that flanks working-class developments. I become acutely aware of my body. My green eyes, my Woody-Allen-like glasses, my six foot two, my Jewish nose, my blond hair, my overly white skin, my every gesture, make me conspicuous here. The car stops in front of a modest one-story house. As I get out, I can feel eyes on me, somebody watching. Some boys are setting up a soccer match a bit farther down the street. One of them kicks the rag ball hard, too hard, and it lands near me. I look at it, go over, kick it back, then kick myself mentally, wondering if this has not called attention to my presence, though to ignore the ball would have been even more eye-catching. An old woman materializes on the threshold of the house next door, looks at the car, at me, at my smartly dressed driver. The old woman doesn't say a word, just remains there like a drab spiteful statue of stone watching Esteban, who has come out to greet us warmly, watching me say goodbye to my driver with a quick peck on the cheek, watching me disappear into Esteban's house: in this neighborhood, there are no secrets.

I am soon put at my ease by the family's sense of humor, their simple courage, as if disasters like this coup happen to them all the time. We sit down to a quick meal, and when it grows darker, Esteban escorts me to the back of the house, a small walled-in yard, most of it taken up by a vegetable patch and a wooden shack. When he became the first member of this working-class family to make it to the university, Esteban's father built him this private space so he could study. There is a narrow bed, a table that doubles as a desk, and books lining one of the walls. A heavily curtained window looks out on the yard.

Esteban hands me a flashlight, asks me not to switch on the lights, if possible, during the night. And to be very quiet during daytime hours.

"If the military come," he says, "it'll probably be at night. They were here last week, but I don't think they'll be back. If they do come, we'll try to stall them. You escape over this wall."

He begins to draw a map. The house, the street, a gas station nearby, a church, I can trust the priest, but the best way to get there is not this way but that way, because there is a fascist who lives in this house, two roads down. The gas station has a pay phone, but it might be risky to use it after curfew. "At any rate," he repeats, "you can trust the priest. And if everything is all right here, you can always come back."

Then he asks if I have understood, and I nod, and he goes out, leaving me in the darkening dusk.

I have not understood a word he said. I stare at the map in disbelief. I can make no sense of the diagram. While he talked, while he pointed and drew arrows and told me to trust the priest and what street to use and what street to avoid, the only thing I did understand, quite starkly, was that I was doomed.

Every night since the coup, there has been some justification, however lame, for sleeping in a house other than my own. I could invent a hundred reasons. But here? What was I doing here? In the shack of a textile worker, lost in a marginal neighborhood of Santiago?

In this shack, finally, the fear that has eluded me these ten days spills into my guts, a fear that has always been missing from my life. Real, stomach-sickening, mind-crawling fear that screams at me to get the hell out of this place before it's too late. What has happened to those who are being killed can happen to me, not in my imagination, to the naked body of Claudio Gimeno being approached by an officer, but in reality, to my own body.

I am marooned here this evening, in this shack, as the shadows in the yard tell me that curfew has arrived. I am more vulnerable than my hosts. If a military commander happens to raid this *población* tonight, if my extraordinary luck runs out, the very things that would help me survive in my own surroundings—my physical appearance, my contacts, the class I was born into, my very language—are liabilities here. I would be punished precisely for having stepped outside the boundaries and privileges that had been set up for me, precisely because I have abjured them.

And that may be why, next to the fear, perhaps within it, neither dissolving nor dissembling it, I feel bizarrely, wildly successful: this is the way ordinary people in the country I now call my own have always lived, day in, day out, what most of the population of this planet experience as their daily horizon. With no father to turn to, no international connections, no second language to shelter them, no white skin to make their enemies think twice before attacking them. With no grand words to ward off death. The violence of misery, the violence of sickness, the violence of malnutrition, the violence of ignorance, and, if they dared to rebel against this condition, the violence of the police and the Army—this was something they could not avoid, this was their life.

Isn't this exactly what I have wanted since the far-off days in the sixties when I first envisaged the possibility of a revolution? What I have been impossibly looking for all these years: to fuse, no matter how briefly, with the working class of Chile, to have gone so deep into it that I could share its fate?

And now the distance that had haunted me all my life, the loneliness, was gone. My relationship with the poor and the humiliated was no longer reversible, no longer dependent, at least for the moment, on my choice. My life was now a lottery, out of my hands, and it was strangely comforting not to be able to escape or keep on running, a strange solace in the knowledge that finally, when the moment of truth had come, my body had been loyal to my dream of a world without suffering, that I was willing to risk the consequences of being a rebel against injustice. The revolution had brought me to this shack, to this possible ending, and there, alone with my death, I feel complete and whole and real as I had never felt before and would never feel afterwards.

I am at home.

I have no nightmares that night. I fall asleep and wake once in a while and listen to the faraway barking of dogs and the sporadic gunfire, wonder if a truck's engine will disturb the silence, if the shouts of soldiers will crack open the dawn, ask how it can be that daylight takes so long to come. But the fear is no longer there. I am ready to face the next day and what it brings and the next one and the conversation in which I will tell my contact Abel that nothing can make me leave this country that I can now really say is mine.

But that is not how it will turn out.

A different revelation awaits me the next day.

In that shack, with the daylight, I begin to explore the wall of books that belong to Esteban and discover there—along with my own book on Donald Duck—hundreds of other volumes, most of them the cheap editions brought out by Quimantú, the State Publishing House, sold at newsstands, gobbled up by millions of Chileans. In two and a half years, more books have been produced and distributed than in all the previous hundred and sixty years of Chilean history. I have been part of this extraordinary cultural crusade. Twice a week, as an advisor to Quimantú, I have helped to select the literary, philosophical, historical texts that have then made their way into the hands of the public. I knew, of course, that the books were being bought. The statistics said so. And I had often encountered, during the Allende years, hundreds of workers and students and housewives and even, in one case, a young peasant, all of whom had been reading our collection, Dostoevsky and Cortázar and Aeschylus and Latin American short stories and Bolívar and Balzac.

But to find these books here, in this shack, and to find one of my own books among them, to run into them now, in the midst of defeat, this was different. I had cast my words into reality like bottles into an unknown sea, and if it was true that my words, that books, could not protect me from death or torture, neither could it be denied that those books were here, being read, and tomorrow they would still be here, and what had been read and thought and nursed inside could not be erased so easily. Angélica had told me, at our last meeting, that one day Rodrigo had begun to sing, as they walked to the bus, the hymn of the Unidad Popular, *"Venceremos, venceremos, la miseria sabremos vencer."* We shall overcome, we shall find a way of ending misery. She had told him to stop, never to sing that song again, and he had refused: *Esas canciones me gustan,* I like those songs. She then crouched down next to him, and taking him firmly by the shoulders, she forced up his chin so he had to look her in the eye and she proceeded to tell our six-year-old son that if he ever sang that song or any of the other songs we used to sing in the streets, the soldiers would come and shoot his daddy. Did he understand? Rodrigo had not responded for a few seconds. Angélica waited. Then he had said: "But if I sing them in my head, nobody will know." He was anticipating there, in front of his heartbroken mother, what I was to discover a few days later in this book-filled shack. This was how the resistance would grow, this was the way the past would endure: the words and deeds we had fed to the world yesterday would not, could not, easily be eradicated from this earth.

And yet, if the books revealed to me that my life had a meaning which did not begin and end in my own self but reached beyond it, into the community, these same books were reminders that it was not possible to hide who I really was: an intellectual, a man who writes, someone who gives words and stories to others. The books were telling me that I could not make believe that my past did not exist. My books—those I wrote and those that I helped to publish— could remain in this shack. I could not, without endangering the lives of those who had offered me refuge. Maybe I will, after all, be forced to leave my country.

And so, the next day, I am confused, full of conflicting desires and signals when I ring the doorbell of the apartment where Abel is supposed to meet me, and Abel opens the door and I step inside.

It is an unassuming middle-class flat, nothing special about it, except that the blinds are down. Abel seems at home here, blends in. Who loaned him this place? Relatives? Friends? Sympathizers? It's better not to know. Better not to observe any details. Forget everything about this apartment, just as I've already forgotten, hope I've forgotten, its location. What you don't know can't be extracted from you. That's what a dictatorship does: it turns us into instant amnesiacs, forces us to glide through life as if blindfolded, impossibly also demanding the opposite—to survive, you have to be attentive, carefully register everything, a tiny particular can mean the difference between life and death. As I sit down in the armchair that Abel indicates, I can't help catching a glimpse of a portrait in the living room, I cannot disregard that striking naval officer in full uniform glaring from the wall behind Abel—like a teenager told to avert his eyes when the full-bodied woman he is about to make love to starts to undress for the first time, I am drawn to what has been forbidden, wondering if this means that the resistance has people inside the Navy, if this is the house of an admiral, and before I can go on searching for signs in the living room which might confirm or deny this conjecture, I cut into my own train of thought, as far as I can remember I try to concentrate on Abel, on this meeting with Abel I have been fearing.

"I hope you realize," Abel starts off, "that you are putting us both in jeopardy by asking for this meeting."

I realize it. I am sorry, I say, but I couldn't accept the Party's order to seek asylum in an embassy. That's why I asked for a second opinion.

"Well, the second opinion is that you should get the hell out of here before it's too late. And the third opinion will be the same, and the fourth one, and all the opinions in the universe. Look at you. For God's sake, look at yourself in a mirror. Where would we hide you? And what use would you be to us in hiding, anyway? Do you really think you're needed here?"

"Yes," I say.

"No," Abel says. "You're the one who needs to be here. You're the one who needs to stay here to write the great novel of the Chilean Revolution. That's why you want to stay, isn't it?"

How to explain to Abel in ten minutes the story of my drifting ancestors who have fled for two thousand years, how to tell him that it's time to stop, enough is enough, how to explain that I repudiated Spanish and Latin America in a Manhattan hospital at the age when most children are learning the difference between saying God and saying dog, that history forced me to come here, to this continent that bewitched me, that a man winked at me on the street, that my books were there in that shack, that I have wandered the earth and that I cannot leave now? How to tell him this when the country is being ravaged, when the President is dead, when Abel looks at his watch and we both notice there are three hours left till curfew, three hours till the sun sets on Santiago de Chile and then the soldiers own the uncontested city, policing it with their jeeps and their dogs and their machine guns, the rest of the people listening, trapped inside their houses, listening to the faraway shots, listening to the patrols getting nearer and nearer, listening for the sound of brakes and men in boots and shouted orders, listening to the sound passing by and not stopping, not this time, not this time, somewhere in this city a man like me listens to his neighbor being raided, listens to the cries, listens to his own heartbeat of relief, the horrible joy of knowing that it is somebody else being taken away, how to make him empathize with my tragedy if he is the one who is going to stay and I am the one who is going away, if he is right that I want to remain because—among ten thousand other reasons—I can't stand the idea of being shut out of this country and excluded from witnessing and transmitting its story through my words, that I cannot miss this chance to become totally, definitively, forever Chilean by writing myself into the country and the country into myself?

Abel presses his advantage. "That's where you're needed, out there," he says. "Think of what we need, not what you need."

He is right, of course. There is no argument against the cool logic of his words. I belong to the people of Chile, not because I can share their death, but because I can contribute to their fight against death.

Abel must see the pain in my eyes as I reach my decision. He must see something beaten and old in my eyes, because now he speaks to me as if he could read my thoughts, as if he knows the story of this life I have never told him.

He embraces me, he says goodbye, he whispers in my ear: *"Vive por todos nosotros."*

Live for us all.

And then, as he hugs me, his voice lowers one more notch, grows so soft that I hardly know if he said it or if I imagined his words: "If you really love Chile . . ."

If I really love Chile . . . I will be able to survive exile, I will be able to continue identifying ever more deeply with this country even if my journey has been interrupted, even if the sources that have nurtured me are far and the language is far and the people and the struggle and the grapes and the seaside, all far, far away, it is as if all this, right now, is already unreal, Abel's knowing smile and droopy eyelids and his hug and this apartment with its absurd portrait of an admiral, it is already receding into memory, all this is already a dreamscape, words in my mind to remember when things get tough and distant, mere memories that I will not be able to hold in my hands or listen to, whispered softly in my ears, Abel's words of wisdom and solidarity that cannot save me, because nothing can save me from what is going to happen now that I must face a fear deeper than death, the fear that I will never again return to this land I have come to love.

TEN

A Chapter Dealing with the Discovery of Life and Language During the Years 1960 to 1964 in Santiago de Chile

Where are you from?

It was a question that since the age of two and a half, and until I was eighteen, I had always answered, spontaneously, invariably: I was from America, I was American.

That response had been there, on the tip of my tongue, my first day of class at the Universidad de Chile in March of 1960—a response that stayed there, that I did not let roll off into the politically effervescent air of a Latin America headed for a showdown with the United States.

Where are you from?

Who asked me that, with its implied query: Who are you? I can't remember the face, only my momentary bewilderment, the fact that I did not dare to admit that I was from the United States. Perhaps it was Claudio Gimeno himself. I did, after all, lay eyes on him that day for the first time, although it would be too bizarre, perhaps too suitably literary and symmetrical, that the man who saved me for this life of exile which has ended up here in the United States should have been the first person in the world to hear me deny my North American origins. I press myself harder to recall that moment and it seems that it was just after Historia de América, the first class on my schedule, where our radical Panamanian mulatto professor had gone about dissecting the term America itself, how the United States had appropriated that word and denied it to the South, much in the way, he said, that the same United States had stolen a great part of Mexico and occupied Nicaragua and now sat on the narrow strip of the Canal refusing to return it to the people of Panama. Once lost, he said, it was difficult to get territory back, but establishing an alternative history was a start, even if his forced exile from his own country proved that such an intellectual enterprise was not without risks. But it was essential that Americans south of the Rio Bravo think of themselves differently, in freedom and with sovereignty, because from that thinking, from that territory of the imagination, history could be altered. Just look at José Martí, who died in 1895, before his dream of Cuba's independence could materialize, before his words of warning against the United States proved prophetic: the most powerful nation in the hemisphere had entered the war against Spain (and Teddy Roosevelt never charged up that hill—it was all a fraud, a trumped-up photo) and then kept Puerto Rico as a colony and occupied Cuba for years and invaded it whenever it was felt that "those people," in General Shafter's memorable phrase, "who were no more fit for self-government than gun-powder is for hell," deserved to be taught a lesson. But because of Martí and his words, Fidel Castro had staged his first insurrection in 1953 and taken the Moncada and, when captured, had turned his trial into an indictment of the Batista dictatorship and declared that he had rebelled so that one hundred years after his birth the ideas of Martí would not die. And now Cuba was standing up to Eisenhower, was getting rid of the gambling casinos and the whorehouses and taking back the sugar plantations run by U.S. corporations. And that was possible because Martí had thought of Cuba as part of *nuestra América*, our America, as opposed to their America.

As he spoke, he asked for opinions and we gave them, each of us, and then it was my turn. I don't remember exactly what I said but I do remember the way I said it, the slight smidgen of a gringo accent that still crept into my voice like slime out of a swamp, I can remember becoming aware of how foreign I must look to my new classmates, my hair, my height, my eyes, my skin, my gestures, all revealing that I was from somewhere else, I can remember how all those other students from *la otra América* turned to me with interest, they were already preparing that question, where are you from? a question I would try to circumvent in the years to come, working strenuously at my Chilean accent and my Chilean slang and my Chilean trivia. But for now I was going to have to face that curiosity as soon as the class was over and my answer would have to take into account that millions of people around the world were rebelling against a colonial and post-colonial order upheld by the United States, that one year before I had stepped into the classroom, Fidel had entered Havana with his band of guerrillas and that right then and there the first U.S. advisors were arriving in Vietnam, I was going to step out of that classroom at the exact intersection in history when the country where I was receiving my university education was being shaken by riots and strikes and protest marches aimed at the conservative government and its American sponsors, I was going to have to answer the question about my identity in a world whose walls were being painted with that famous formula: "Yankee, go home."

¿De dónde eres? Where are you from?

Somebody whose face and name I can't recollect asked me that question as soon as class was over. I should have answered: I don't know. I should have answered: All my life I thought I was a Yankee but now I'm not so sure, I wanted to be one so badly that I went to the extreme of changing my name to Edward. So your name's Edward? *¿Te llamas Edward?* Where are you from? I should have answered: You want to know the truth? I'm still attracted to the United States and who knows if I won't end up there, I may hate its politics but I love its jazz and its movies and its people and the language they gave me, which is still the language I use to make sense of the world. You want to know the truth? I've been flirting with Spanish recently, but I don't feel it deep inside me, I don't imagine myself writing anything intimate or relevant in the language you people speak. I should have answered: I don't have a country, I don't have a community, I don't have a cause. Goddamn it, I don't even have a girlfriend who might begin to anchor me to a place. I should have answered: I'm alone on this planet and I don't know where I belong.

Instead, quite simply, I said: "*Soy de Argentina,*" I'm Argentinian. I fell back on that accidental birthplace I barely knew and did not particularly care for, because I had nothing else to cleave to but the remote moment when I had fallen into nothingness and found parents and a country and a language waiting. It was a convenient way of not having to examine my own confusion, admit that my fluid life was in transition, suspended between a country to the North that was drifting away from me and this country here in the South I was not yet ready to commit to permanently. It was a way of giving myself time to figure out who I really was.

A decade later, I knew the answer.

Ten and a half years later, to be exact, on the night of September 4, 1970, I was standing on Santiago's main avenue, the Alameda, all around me the delirious dancing throngs of my compatriots celebrating our victory in the Presidential elections, and up there was Salvador Allende on the small balcony of the Student Federation building, Allende presiding over the birth of a new nation at two o'clock in the morning.

"Entraré a La Moneda," Allende told us that night, *"y conmigo entrará el pueblo. Seré el Compañero Presidente."* That was his promise to the outcasts of Chile: he would enter La Moneda and the people would enter with him. He would be no ordinary President. "I am going to be," he said, "your *Compañero Presidente.*" I was there when Allende swore his loyalty to us, his equality, his fraternity, he would not betray us. And I called back from the deepest lungs of my *compañero* soul, I called to him as if I were on a desert island and he had come to rescue me, I began to chant, *Compañero, compañero*— the echo of thousands of others who were calling to him, the words came out of my mouth as if they had been waiting forever to find that night, that place, this moment in history, *Compañero, compañero,* calling to him until there was nothing in the world but that tribal sound filling the streets which were ours forever, which we claimed as our birthright, until all the voices were one voice, we would enter La Moneda with him, the Palace of the Presidents of Chile, *Compañero Presidente.*

I called to him and it was no longer my call: in that sea of words, my word had become theirs.

We had baptized Salvador Allende.

Although, in truth, I was the one who was being baptized. I now fully knew—or at least so I told myself—the answer to that question I had evaded at the start of the sixties. I knew where I was from and, more crucially, I knew that to formulate the question in this manner was wrong, I knew, standing there in the multitude, that what matters is to know where you are going. Where was I from? I had just cast the first vote of my life and it had been for Salvador Allende. Where was I from? I was from Chile and this ocean of people stretching for blocks was my community, and by my side, holding my hand, was my Chilean wife. And the language in which I was imagining the future was the same language in which I was writing it. I had banished English from my life in order to become the privileged guardian of this Spanish I was chanting like a mantra and in which I would soon begin to tell, I was sure, the epic story that was unfolding before my eyes. And a few miles away, at home, our three-year-old Chilean son was sleeping, and he would not have to live the dislocations of his father and his grandparents. I had sworn he would be the first of his family in many generations to be born and grow up and have children of his own under the same Southern constellation of stars. I had sworn it when he was born in February of 1967 as if I were the one being born instead of him, and hammered home my point by giving him a name that symbolized my commitment to Spanish and Latin America, Rodrigo, the name of El Cid, the first Iberian hero, and Fidel, because Fidel had freed Cuba from the Americans. And now we were going to free Chile as well.

The road to that moment in which I felt at home inside a vast social movement bent on providing a home for everyone, that road to a revolution bent on shaking Chile to its foundations, had started for me, suitably enough, with an earthquake, yes, a literal earthquake which tore down the walls behind which I had lived in seclusion and ignorance and privilege all those years in the South.

It was a day in late June of 1960, a few months after that first question at the university about who I was had received no clear answer. I had gone with friends to a soccer match in the National Stadium, the same stadium where thirteen years later one of those friends and many of the working people I was about to meet would be imprisoned and tortured. I remember we were facing the cordillera. I remember my exact position, facing those mountains, because of what happened next. Suddenly, without warning, the seats began to tremble and a roar split the air and the whole stadium rocked back as if it were a gigantic boat, and then, incredibly, for a second, the Andes were blotted out, they simply disappeared, cut off from view by the other half of the stadium, rising. Everybody was too dazed even to panic. I held on to my wooden bench and absurdly focused on the players on the field, who were just as absurdly scrambling after a ball that was bouncing up and down haphazardly, even as they fell all over themselves like drunken madmen. And then it was over.

For us, in Santiago, that is. Because we had merely registered the aftershocks of a settling and grinding of tectonic plates that had devastated a vast region in the south of Chile. Whole towns lay in ruins, dozens had died, thousands were injured, and the survivors slept in the streets under an icy, pouring rain, afraid to return to houses that might collapse at any minute. As the earth continued to rumble in the south, the students of Chile—including Eddie Dorfman, soon to be Ariel—stopped going to class and spent the next week helping to collect items needed for the rescue operation: food, clothes, blankets, building materials, and, above all, money. By the end of the week, we had filled several rooms of our Faculty to the brim, and we promptly dispatched the supplies to the south in trucks. I had been tireless—and had been repaid for my efforts by discovering the working poor of Chile.

Though poor may not be the right word because it defines those people by what they lack, defines them as essentially suffering and deprived. And precisely what I unearthed, buried under their invisibility, was that these people were not to be pitied and certainly not to be patronized. They produced everything I consumed, everything that everybody consumed, and had nothing to show for it except the pride in their hands, the immense stories those hands encompassed, those hands that had paved every one of the multiple streets of Chile, not one of which was named for them or their ancestors. They had practically no possessions and yet they were ready to cheerfully give what they could not afford to help those faraway brothers and sisters in the south of Chile who, like them, were naked under a threatening sky. I discovered their courage and good humor not once that week, not twice, but over and over again, in hundreds of textile workers toiling at colossal looms and construction workers with faces covered with dust and bronze-faced women laboring in immaculate white uniforms under the harsh lights and sour smells of pharmaceutical laboratories and saleswomen always smiling in department stores while their legs cramped and lads nursing hungry mustaches behind grocery counters and impoverished peasants tilling arid plots whose eyes met mine without flinching and the clean inhabitants of dirty shantytowns and tenements, and everywhere I found—what did I find? One word? One word to describe what I saw in them? Hope. If I had to choose one word, that would be it. *Esperanza.*

I had by then read some books, meditated on some theories about revolution. I had mused over phrases about knowing the world by changing it and the proletariat being the gravediggers of the established order and the need to swim in the water of the masses, but they had all been words on a piece of paper. Workers of the world unite, Marx and Engels had urged at the end of the *Communist Manifesto*, and I was all for uniting every poor person in sight but I had never really met a worker, I had never understood until now that those ideas could become grounded, made territorial, visible, in real human beings, in a class that had *residencia en la tierra*, residence on this earth. A few blocks from where I lived in my enclave of privilege and rhetorical indignation, there existed a fierce historical agent that could make my free-floating desire for a better and more beautiful world come true, take that hope out of the dubious promise of dry texts and into reality. These workers were hidden from view, tucked away in the red belt of Santiago or in the fields or in the factories or in the bars, yes, hidden from view, but if they ever came into view, if they ever forced their bodies onto the horizon, if they ever took over the world they had built with those bodies, they would forge a society that deserved to be called human.

They were going to accomplish this epic task whether I joined them or not; but if I did, if I took up their challenge to redefine the world with the same tenacity and fearlessness with which they were ready to redefine themselves, if I could join my homeless body to their homeless lives, I could help to change not only an unjust world but my own self as well. I could imagine my life, not in terms of individual self-fulfillment, where I would disappear when I died, but in terms of service to humanity, where death does not really exist. In them, I finally found the brotherhood I had first conjectured as a child, that brotherhood I had needed back in the forties to quell the lonely darkness and which now in the sixties challenged my tenuous, confused bilingual persona to anchor itself to their cause.

It was a challenge which, at that time, back in 1960, I was not entirely ready to meet. I was not prepared to take the next logical and drastic step that derived from that overpowering vision—to join a revolutionary organization.

The earthquake had only shattered the walls that segregated me from the workers, leaving intact all the barriers I had accumulated since I was born, barriers of race and class and language and interests and life-style, and these would not really crumble—and crumble partly, at that—until an earthquake that was not nature's but social, the earthquake of the Allende revolution, transformed my existence. It was only when the workers finally came out of their neighborhoods and threatened to take over the state itself and from that state re-organize the whole of society, it was only when they crossed the boundary separating our lives, that I understood that I could not remain on the sidelines anymore, that I could no longer merely be a left-wing intellectual but had to become a militant.

But back then in 1960, at that point in my life, and for the next ten years, it was unthinkable that I devote my whole life to the oppressed. How could I, if I didn't even know who I was, what life I would be devoting? How to merge the certainty that I wanted, above all things in the world, to be a writer with the needs of these people I hardly had visited, no matter how I might admire their tenacity? And how to submit my fragile identity with its well of secrets to the scrutiny of an organization that couldn't care less about individual problems, that would have frowned on such dilemmas as petit-bourgeois deviations? Worse still, such a submission to Party discipline would wrest from me the independence I required to con-front the contradictions of my existence: I wanted to serve the poor but lived in a big house with two maids and drove my father's gar-gantuan diplomatic car, which, of course, I shamefully hid from my new comrades at the university; and vocal as I might be in support of the Latin American resistance, I kept doggedly writing my most personal work in English, the language of the "thieving Yankee" responsible for the country's underdevelopment. My very Edwardly name was a reminder that I was a mock-Chilean who did not belong in this country, let alone with the workers and their cause.

And the change in my name became, in fact, the first step, the easiest symbolic step, toward a deeper and more difficult shift in my total identity as I set out to become somebody else, almost an ironic echo of the mind-set of those European immigrants to the United States whose country I was now trying to distance from my life. In the months that followed, almost imperceptibly, I adopted Ariel—which happened to be my neglected middle name and had been on my passport since my birth.

When my father chose Lenin as the model to mark my future, my mother, given the second choice, had timidly decided on Ariel because, she said, she loved the character in Shakespeare's *The Tempest*, the spirit of air and goodness and magic, a way to balance her husband's extremely terrestrial and overtly political nomination. Not that I ever gave a second thought to the girlish and delicate Ariel when I was looking to replace the detested Vlady. But now in the university, uncomfortable with the Edward which had served me so well at the Grange, I discovered that an inordinate number of young Latin American men my age—several of them studying at my Faculty—had also been called Ariel by their parents, a collective baptism that had its origin in an essay, the most influential in the history of the continent, written by the Uruguayan José Enrique Rodó in 1900. For most members of my mother's generation, his book, *Ariel*, had been a touchstone in their evolution as they dealt with the enigma of why their Latin America had fallen so far behind the United States. Rodó identified Latin America with the figure of Prospero's idealistic helper, in contrast to the crass materialism of a Caliban dedicated to profit, positivism, utilitarian to a fault, worshipping the "fervent pursuit of well-being that has no object beyond itself." My mother had answered Rodó's call to the youth of the continent to defend this spiritually superior America of the South from the soulless Northern

Titan by giving her son a name that suggested that someday Latin America would be truly worthy of the Europe that had given it (and her) birth.

I took a liking to Ariel. Even though my sympathies were with the colonized and despised Caliban of *The Tempest* who is taught the language of his master only so that he might learn to curse; even if Ariel, in anti-colonial interpretations in vogue during the sixties, was seen as the elite servant of the invader Prospero, the native criollo who had bowed to power and decided to mimic the civilization of Europe; even so, the name my mother had given me was, nevertheless, recognized by vast numbers of Latin Americans as a symbol of opposition to the United States. For me, it became a way of defining my own growing disaffection with the land whose extreme materialism I had cherished and coveted, while at the same time subtly asserting my affiliation with the language that continued to be my constant companion and best friend, the English that had been elevated to its supreme pinnacle in the works of Shakespeare. And there you have me, bearing a biblical name that was made famous in Europe in the first work in the modern era that tried to come to grips with the tensions arising out of the colonization of the New World, a character who then had been appropriated by an Uruguayan writer and bequeathed to an Argentine mother as a way of defining a wayward gringo son who had finally come back to the Latin America she loved. There I was, a young man born in Buenos Aires and brought up in New York and on his way to becoming Chilean, an amalgam of the Latino and the Anglo. I ate up that name and gave it the meaning that I so desired. I was Caliban the savage, cannibilizing Ariel, the Hebrew Lion of God, for my own purposes.

My use of the verb *cannibalize* to describe the process by which I created my new identity is not accidental, not merely a pun on Shakespeare's character. Cannibalize: a term coined by Brazilian modernists at the beginning of the century to articulate how the New World should react to the European (and later North American) forms it was importing from abroad, how it could thrive only by eating them up, chewing them through, digesting, transforming, transubstantiating them, creating a new compound. That theory of Latin American identity suggests that, given the impossibility of turning your back on foreign influences, you should neither submit slavishly to them nor reject them as entirely alien. The solution is to devour them, to make them your own. As Latin American literature and art have been doing since their origins, as Allende promised to do with the revolution. More than the name Ariel itself, it was the process of that naming, the process of situating myself on the border between the continent of my birth and the world outside, which signals how I became a Latin American. Because there you have, in a nutshell, in that process of redefining my identity, the way in which Latin America captured me.

I was fortunate that my pursuit of a resolution to my paradoxes, my desire for a sanctuary on this planet, coincided with a unique moment in the history of the continent where I had been born, when hope was reawakening that hundreds of years of humiliation were over, a time when Latin America was breaking from its past and struggling to rid itself of the foreign influences that had dominated its destiny for so long. There was a place for someone like me in that quest, an intoxicating invitation for a youngster on the verge of becoming an adult who could not conceive his own future with any degree of stability, who had, like the continent itself, come to a dead end in his development and could not continue telling himself that the remedy for his problems lay abroad. Instead of answering my questions, this continent sent me back more questions, all of them contradictory. Like me, Latin America was an enigma, a vibrant, sprawling, messy reality which did not itself know what it was or where it was going, entangled in the process of discovering where it had been, a continent that was more a project than an object, a series of half-formed nations trapped in a history not of their own making, trying to invent an alternative.

The United States had turned me into one of its children by

offering me comfort and safety and power during its most expansive and optimistic post-war phase. Latin America, contestatory, insurgent and rebellious, would appeal to an entirely different way of imagining myself, encouraging me to merge my personal crisis of identity with its parallel crisis, my own search with its search, my journey with its journey. Afraid though I was of the gray twilight area of fluctuating identity inside me, afraid though I might be of being set adrift again, quite soon I began to understand that this was probably what I needed, a continent as mixed up as I was, itself a combination of the foreign and the local, unable to distinguish at times where one started and the other ended. Before I knew what had hit me, I was entranced by a Latin America that called out to my own deeply divided, hybrid condition. I located in that culture my secret image, the mirror of who I really was, this mixture, this child who dreamed like so many Latin Americans of escape to the modern world and had found himself back here, in the South, *en el sur*, forced to define his confused destiny as if he were a character in a story by Borges. I had decided not to go back North. It was time to take all the simultaneous roads into Latin America I could find or perhaps it was Latin America, during that frantic decade, taking the roads into me, invading me, penetrating me, saturating my senses, filling me with people, with landscapes, with foods, with colors, with projects, a jumble of interrogations. I set out to explore the space and the people around me with a fury enhanced by the awareness of all the energy I had wasted purging my Spanish and turning my back on my Latino self.

Something similar happened in my quest for a new nationality. Except that reincarnating an identity depends on your will to belong and the willingness of people to accept that need and recognize you, whereas the transition toward becoming a citizen of Chile, dependent as it was on the acquiescence of the state and not on my own desires, turned out to be a far bumpier road. As the sixties advanced and I began to reimagine myself as a Latin American, at some intangible point—I cannot really put my finger on exactly when it happened—I stopped telling people I was from Argentina, I started to lie to them and to myself, responding that I was from Chile.

That lie came back to haunt me and almost derailed my efforts legally to become a Chilean citizen.

The occasion was Allende's campaign in 1964. I had become so involved with local politics that I had ended up being elected president of the Independent Allendista Students of the Universidad de Chile. My political activism up to then had been typical of so many of my fellow left-wing students: you live at home, you read a lot, you discuss forever, you go out once in a while to a slum to participate in some sort of vounteer community service under the auspices of the Student Federation, you plot against the Christian Democrats and try to take the university away from them, you spend a month in a *población* teaching peasants recently arrived from the countryside how to read, you march forever, you get teargassed, a nightstick grazes your ribs and then a bruise or two develop, the bruise disappears, life goes on, you are more in love with the concept of *el pueblo* than with the real people themselves.

Oh, I had tried to serve those masses who I continued to proclaim would save me and the world. Suspicious of political parties and their lumbering bureaucracies, I thought, bursting with gringo can-do-ism, that I could sidestep those fossilized structures and go directly to the poorer sectors of society, people who were, after all, paying with their taxes and their work for our education and should receive some sort of benefit from us. Sometime in 1963, with funds from my ever helpful dad, I conceived—under the pompous title of Universidad Móvil para el Trabajador (Mobile University for the Worker)—a week of conferences by a group of my most brilliant classmates to be delivered directly in the *poblaciones callampas*, the shantytowns that had sprouted all over Santiago exactly like mushrooms (*callampas*), as homeless families took over unused land and, overnight, built their tin huts and put up their Chilean flags.

I contacted the communal leaders of one of the *poblaciones* where I had done some volunteer work. I presented our program. It started with "What Is Literature?" on Monday night and went on to "What Is Chile?" and "What Is Latin America?" and "What Is History?" and "What Is the Body?" on the following nights, until we ended with "What Is the Universe?" on Saturday.

They were skeptical. With their enormous problems—no gas, no streetlights, no paved streets, no trees, no playgrounds, no water, but of course plenty of mud—the *pobladores* wondered if our educational project could really be considered a priority. My answer: How were these difficulties to be overcome if we didn't make an effort to understand who we were, the origins of who we were, if we didn't believe that knowledge might make us free. The communal leaders seemed moved—more I think by my bubbling enthusiasm than by my arguments. They looked at one another and waited in silence, and then one of them offered the ramshackle one-room building that housed the elementary school. "You care enough to take all this trouble," he said. "Let's see what happens." Later on, he accompanied me to the bus stop, and before I got on the bus, he stopped me.

"The key," he said, "is the children."

"The children?"

"If the children come, so will their parents."

We took his advice. The Sunday before the first lecture, our stalwart group of would-be instructors spent the day in the *población* handing out leaflets to the kids, telling them that tomorrow night was the Universidad Móvil's inaugural session on literature and that the price of admission to the cartoons that would be shown before the class was at least one progenitor.

The tactic worked. When I arrived with my family's old 8mm movie projector and my childhood's silent cartoons, the elementary school was packed. The kids and their parents enjoyed *Mighty Mouse* above all, just as I had when I was five and my father had brought home what had been back then, in 1947, the latest technology in home entertainment. For most of them, it was the first time they had seen a motion picture of any sort; television in Chile was not widespread then. And my conversation with them had seemingly also been successful: we had talked about sounds and rhythm and images and how they were all poets in the way they spoke every day and how the simplest story was open to as many interpretations as there were readers. At the end, I reminded everybody that tomorrow there was another talk, and many in the audience promised to return.

So I was alarmed the next day when I received a harried call from Miguel, the geography student in charge of "What Is Chile?" from the one telephone in the *población*, which, as fortune would have it, was located inside the elementary school itself.

"Oye," Miguel said, "do you hear that?"

I listened. Over the phone came the sound of dull thuds and in the distance the faint screams of infantile voices.

"Did you hear it?" he insisted.

"Yes."

My friend was very calm. "It's the kids of the *población*. They're stoning the school and threatening to burn it down unless you show *Mighty Mouse* again."

"What?"

"I think you'd better come and help me give that lesson in what Chile is."

I grabbed my dad's immense diplomatic car and incongrously arrived in it to the huzzahs of hundreds of children who demanded that I show the *Ratón Aerodinámico* not once but twice, plus a couple of other short features. Then I stood by while my friend talked to the kids—and the three lone adults, sitting in the back of the schoolroom, who had straggled in once it was clear that there was no danger from the stone throwers—about what Chile was. But I was learning more about Chile than they were, learning that it was not a matter of simply parachuting into these places, that it took many years to establish the right channels, the right methods, the right contacts, and that I had tried to leap over those years of hard work and ignore the way things were done here, among these people, and the result was that, to save our makeshift Universidad Móvil made in Chile, I had been forced to call on a flying rodent made in the imperial United States.

The rest of the week went a bit better because we returned to the original formula: first cartoons, then the lecture; but by Saturday we all agreed that the experiment so gullibly organized had not been worth the effort and that it was better not to repeat it, that this was not the best way to change the consciousness of the Chilean people. Instead of enticing our compatriots to know more about themselves and how they had come to be so deprived, we had instilled in their children a desire to be like Mighty Mouse, to adore the power of the U.S. media. Our decision to close our doors was also influenced perhaps by the fact that the 1964 Presidential elections were looming on the horizon, and if this time Allende won against Eduardo Frei, the Christian Democratic candidate, efforts such as ours would be unnecessary. It would be the government itself which would work to establish a whole new system for bringing knowledge to the workers. A whole new system? If we were victorious, a whole new world would be fashioned by us.

With power seemingly within reach, I threw myself into the campaign with an enthusiasm that had even my Marxist father daunted. I organized rallies, helped win back the student federation of our Faculty from the Christian Democrats with a sophisticated publicity strategy (the irony of my using Madison Avenue techniques to serve the revolution was lost on me). I painted walls and made up slogans and shouted myself hoarse in street demonstrations and cajoled undecided voters and registered toothless women to vote and knocked on doors Saturdays and Sundays and went down to Valparaiso to do volunteer work with Angélica and hundreds of other students up in the hills and one day I convinced the great Neruda himself to come to our Faculty to read poetry as a way of protesting the destruction of our propaganda by our rivals and in general made a nuisance of myself. I was everywhere, vociferous, exhorting, convincing, boundless in my energy and my convictions, using to the hilt the traits of a personality formed during my Yankee childhood, my exuberance and exhibitionism contrasting with the modest, over-formal, slightly meek way in which most Chileans acted. Placing at the service of the socialist revolution my obsession with responsibility and individual effort learned in America.

One day, in late August, a few days before the elections, as I was devising slogans for our Faculty for the upcoming final march of the Allende forces, I had a rude awakening. I opened one of the left-wing newspapers (*Ultima Hora*, directed by Augusto Olivares, the man who was to become my friend, and my inadvertent savior on the 11th of September of 1973) and read that Allende had demanded that a Nazi Czech exile (purportedly paid by the CIA), caught illegally intervening in Chilean politics, be immediately expelled from Chile. I showed the news to my mother and chortled: they caught the bastard, out he goes.

And then the phone rang.

My mother handed me the receiver, perplexed. "It's Jorge Ahumada," she said.

Jorge Ahumada was the dad of Queno, one of my closest pals, one of the few I had kept from my Grange days. Jorge, a friend of my father's from the UN, was now Eduardo Frei's chief economic adivisor.

"Eddie," Jorge said, using my Grange-school name, "I'm calling you from the Christian Democratic Party headquarters. I was in the middle of a meeting on economic policy and quite by chance I happened to overhear—just plain luck—that my comrades had found a way of countering the accusations against the Czech exile, by asking the government to expel a young left-wing agitator who's intervening in our internal affairs. He's from Argentina. His name's Vladimiro Dorfman. A Russian-sounding name."

He let that sink in. Then he said: "I told them that I've known you since you were a boy and I can vouch for you, and they agreed not to proceed. I gave my word that you would cease all political activity right away." There was a pause. "Are you listening?"

"Yes, Jorge."

"If they so much as take a photograph of you in a march, if they catch you in any sort of public event that has a hint of politics, the next day they'll plaster your name all over the papers and a day later I won't be able to stop the police from running you out of Chile. Do you understand?"

"I understand. And thanks. Thank you, Jorge."

I hung up.

The following days were hell. I had to withdraw from all activities, improvise substitutes, and, worse still, I had to reveal my dirty secret, that I wasn't really Chilean, that I was Argentinian, I had to see the eyes of my collaborators slant in puzzlement, I had to walk away from them, once again a stranger, left out, rootless. I was so frustrated with my inability to contribute to the upcoming victory I had worked so hard to secure that, like so many Allendistas of the time, I made a wager with a Christian Democrat friend from the neighborhood: if my candidate lost, I would cut off the fledgling scraps of what I took to be my revolutionary beard; and if Allende won, my friend Gastón would jump naked into the fountain in front of La Moneda, braying like a donkey. (He was a prudish sort of guy and must have been convinced that Frei was heading for a landslide.)

Betting my beard did nothing, however, to assuage my feeling of abandonment, which reached its peak the day the Allende forces set out on their final march. I had waited so long for the relief and reward that marching offered, the excitement of the crowd, the fraternity, the humor, the beauty of the women's legs and the unfurled, defiant banners, the intermingling of words in the air and words on the signs, the adrenaline of the collective beast. I loved to march because it was the easiest way of abjuring for a couple of hours the curse of individuality, making believe you are not different from everybody else, an almost Nirvana-like boundlessness, all those lives so sure of where they are going and sweeping me along. Or rather: on this occasion, sweeping me into the sawdust of futility. Angélica had offered to stay home with me and miss the march, but I told her to join her classmates, I wanted to go on my own to brood and blame myself. I deserved this punishment. Wasn't this seclusion, reduced to a pair of lifeless eyes, here, on the sidelines, confused with all these detached, indifferent bystanders, a truer expression of who I was than if I had been in the crowd, dancing and shouting and cavorting and pretending I was Chilean when, in truth, I had not defined this as my country, I had spent my high school years in Chile gazing nostalgically abroad instead of exploring this magnificent collective that was now surging past me on the way to a future that did not include me? Wasn't I, in effect, a foreigner? And wasn't I destined to be one forever?

I was rescued from these harsh thoughts by Taty Allende and her sister, Isabel. The daughters of Salvador Allende were marching past me like ordinary citizens and they recognized me there on the sidewalk, watching them like some sort of crucified scarecrow. They waved, I waved back, and they must have seen something desolate and forsaken in my gesture, because they rushed out of the crowd.

"Hey, Ariel," Isabel called. Thank God she didn't call me Eddie, that she saw me as a Latin American. "You waiting for somebody?"

"Join us," Taty said. *"Ven."*

I explained briefly why I couldn't, glancing nervously over my shoulder as if a horde of imperialist photographers was ready to snap me in this compromising pose, the demonic daughters of Salvador Allende pulling me into the march. I could already visualize some minor functionary inspecting the incriminating evidence with a magnifying glass, reaching out for the expulsion order. I explained why I couldn't join them.

"Hijos de puta!" Taty growled.

They started to go. Their group was a block away. I watched them leave, feeling sorrier for myself than ever. Then I saw Isabel turn, come back. "Tell you what," she said. "Come to our house tonight, after the march. There's some work that you can do that won't put you in any sort of danger."

I spent that night and the following nights working at Salvador Allende's residence till dawn. We were compiling lists of voters that needed help in getting from the district where they lived to the district where they voted. Just a group of young revolutionaries, Taty and Isabel and a couple of their friends and Angélica and I, sprawled on the living-room floor, with a gigantic map of Chile spread before us. I saw Allende himself only once during those few nights. I remember him coming in a bit past midnight, just as September 3 was turning into election day, the fourth. He watched us from the threshold, standing there weary but upright, I see him take off his glasses and rub his eyes and then he smiled at us, his daughters and their friends.

"*¿Qué tal, muchachos?*" Allende said. "How's it going, kids?"

We murmured something about how great things were and he nodded and came over and looked at the lists and then smiled again, perhaps thinking of his campaign, perhaps thinking that he had been in each of those cities and towns and villages of Chile, that he had been to every corner of this country that he was hoping to govern. Perhaps aware that he was going to lose the election. But he didn't reveal what he was thinking, just nodded one more time and then bid us good night and went off to sleep.

We stayed till dawn, preparing what we thought would be our victory.

It didn't come. Allende lost the election and I lost my beard. On the morning of September 5, 1964, I shaved it off. "I will never grow another beard," I swore, "until there is socialism in Chile."

But I swore something far more important that day as well, something that seemed more within my reach: six years from now, Allende would try again to become President of Chile, and this time nobody in the world would be able to stop me from participating. Next time, I would be a Chilean citizen. I would have a country.

My naturalization process was not as easy as I thought: it turned out that I had been in Chile all these years on my father's diplomatic visa, and in order to become a citizen I would have to apply for residency, which meant leaving the country and then coming back on a temporary basis, and even then at least five more years would have to lapse before I could ask for citizenship, and so on and so forth.

A Christian Democrat had saved me from being expelled from Chile and another Christian Democrat was to rescue me from this legal imbroglio. A friend of Angélica's mother contacted Bernardo Leighton, Frei's Minister of Police, who, without asking for anything in return, cut the bureaucratic Gordian knot and gave me my citizenship.

During the years of exile, Leighton was to be an ally and a friend. He even survived, in Rome, an assassination attempt by Pinochet's secret police working with the Italian neo-fascists. But at this point I knew him chiefly as the man we had pelted with tomatoes in a student demonstration in 1964. Yes, I had derided the man who would eventually make me a citizen, the man who would open the door of Chile to me and allow me to participate in a revolution that considered him to be its enemy, because, we proclaimed, he was a pawn of the true enemy, the United States of America, in its plan to stop the Latin American revolution.

In 1961, in answer to Fidel Castro's revolution, John F. Kennedy had launched the Alliance for Progress, a financial-aid program intended to persuade the republics south of the Rio Grande to adopt reforms that would drain the swamp of social and economic injustice. Three years later, the Alliance seemed to have fizzled pathetically, partly because the local elites were pocketing the money, but mostly because real change would have meant attacking the U.S. stranglehold on the national economies. The Christian Democrats in Chile, however, seemed determined to carry out the program, steering a middle course between Allende's revolutionary left and the reactionary conservatives of Alessandri. They embraced the Alianza para el Progreso. We jeered back at them that it was in reality the *Alianza que para el Progreso*, the Alliance that stops progress, another Yankee maneuver to keep Latin America subdued and the people divided.

By the time of the 1964 campaign, I had begun to demonize the land which I had called my home for so long, I was already blaming it for every evil that befell my newly adopted country and continent.

And yet I continued writing in English, continued to feel, through the language, a tug of loyalty toward the country where I had learned it, all the time trying to ignore the worm of an idea that would not go away, the voice whispering and twisting in my brain that said that until I severed my relationship with that primary language in which I continued to dream my future, I would never be completely Latin American.

That was to be the challenge that awaited me in the second half of the sixties.

But at least now I was not alone.

I was in love.

Not a metaphor. Not with a country. Not with a *pueblo*. Not with the syllables of a tongue created by millions of other tongues.

I was in love.

Her name, as the reader knows, was Angélica.

ELEVEN

A Chapter Dealing with the Discovery of Death Outside an Embassy in Santiago de Chile in the Year 1973

It is late in September.

You have said goodbye to me, my love, and now you are going down the stairs. Soon the sound of the door to the embassy will be heard closing, your small figure will pass to the other side of the gates, and then you will cross the street. That's where the two men come up to speak to you. The conversation hardly lasts what it takes for a cigarette to be lit by the shorter man, the one with the checked jacket. The other one looks you in the eyes and your eyes must feel distant and startled. Then they invite you to get into the car. One of them takes your arm, but he does so with discretion, almost courteously. The motor is running, humming like a well-fed cat, but the car will not move. Now you're getting in, you and the shorter man in back, and the other one in front. His strong, decisive shoulders form a contrast to his apologetic lips, to the thin impoverished wisp of a mustache. It will not be possible to see you. Only, all of a sudden, your hand which accepts a cigarette and then cups the flickering flame of the lighter. Your other hand can be seen only on one occasion, for a moment fluttering on the top of the back seat, fingers that hesitate, the glitter of a wedding ring. Then it withdraws. The man in the front, seated next to the empty driver's seat, is the one asking the questions. Because the car is parked facing the embassy, his whole body can be seen through the front window. Now, with his left hand, he turns off the engine and pockets the keys. That means they do not plan to leave right away. He will remain half hunched up against the door, one leg raised, the shoe pressing against the upholstery, fingers entwined at the knee. Once in a while, he scratches behind his sock, rubs the skin within the sock. They will not be in a hurry. Children will pass by on bikes, calling each other by the names their parents gave them years ago; the mailman will cross this spring day that seems like summer, bringing news and ads and maybe letters from lost loves; mothers will go for a morning stroll, teaching their kids how to stand on two feet, take a step or two instead of crawling. Now a bird perches itself on the warm roof of the car and, without even a trill, flies off like an arrow. Maybe, inside, you've detected that slight presence, that slighter absence, like a leaf that falls from a tree out of season, a bit too late, maybe you've understood that a pair of wings opened up and then were gone. The man extracts a small notebook from a pocket in his jacket, and then a pencil. He passes it to you. During the briefest wave of time, your hand can be seen receiving the pencil, the notebook. Then, as if you were not really there in the back seat of the car, that extension of your body disappears and nothing more can be seen. The man tosses his keys up in the air and catches them neatly. He smiles. He points a key at you and says something, it must be a question. Impossible to know what you answer. No passerby hesitates as his shoes shuffle by the car, nobody looks inside. A beggar woman stumbles down the street, a flock of ragtag kids in her wake, she approaches the car to ask for something, and then she'll back off, half understanding, or not wanting to understand. Now the car window opens and the swarthy face of the shorter man appears, the man who has been sitting next to you. He hasn't slept much, hasn't slept well: there are bags under his eyes and his features are puffy. He blinks under that implacable daylight. Then he looks toward the embassy for a moment, giving the windows the once-over to see if there is anyone watching, if there is anyone behind the half-drawn curtains trying to register and remember each movement, each gesture. He stays like that for a good while, motionless, as if he could guess what is happening behind those walls. He takes out a handkerchief and wipes it across his forehead, cleans the sweat off the rest of his face. He needs a shave, he needs to get home for a good shave. Maybe all night while he waited he's been thinking of a bathtub full of hot water. The air dances with white spores; he blinks heavy eyelids. The breeze has begun falling asleep under the spell of the day's heat. He emerges from the car quickly. A stream of sunlight slides down his body. Now he gets back into the car, into the driver's seat. He holds his hand out so the other man can give him the keys. The sound of the back door that opened and closed, the front door that opened and closed, does not disturb the quiet. It's almost like the sound of harmony, sweet metal. The car revs up, passes the house, passes the curtained windows, for an eternal white instant your petite face can be seen, the way the shoulders breathe, the dress which presses to your body like the skin of a lover. You pass like a body of lightning that will never end, like a birth that will never end, you will pass without looking toward the house, your face will pass, your eyes sinking into the abrupt horizon of the street which connects with other streets. But they will not take you away. Now the car brakes a bit farther on, under the generous shade of that tree you have come to know so well, that you have heard moaning and dancing its branches under the weight of the wind last night, it brakes half a block from the house. All that can be seen is the back of the car, and in a hollow opened by the leaves gently swaying in the rays of this spring that has quickened into summer, a blur of color that could be your hair or the neck trembling behind your hair or the stubborn flurry of your head under your hair. If it were not for the leisurely, merciless progress of the minute hand on your wristwatch, where the slow blood inside your arm finds and flows along with the mysterious blood inside your hand, if it were not for the imperceptible rotation of this planet, it might be thought that time had stagnated, that all movement is paralyzed, that silence is definitive, and that you will stay there forever, you, the men, the car, the street. No beggar will pass. The mailman will not come back again. The children will have put away their bicycles to go eat lunch. When the sun begins again to invade the top of the car, when midday has finally come to an end and the afternoon has finally begun, when once more the intolerable heat forces the driver to seek another refuge, nothing in the world will be able to stop, neither the buzzing of bees nor the cheerful yellow burst of the flowers, nothing can stop that engine from starting up again, that car from inching away from the curb, and this time it will not pause under the shade or in the sun, this time the car will go on and on and on, nothing can stop it from losing itself there, far away down the street which connects with other streets, taking you to that place from where you will never return.

This story, seemingly fictitious, really happened. It happened to us, to Angélica and to me, exactly as written here, exactly as I wrote it many years later. Except for the ending. They did not take her away, not for a day, not for a month, not for all time. But the rest is true. By the end of September I had taken temporary refuge in the residence of one of my mother's friends, the wife of the Israeli Ambassador, waiting during the next week for a chance to slip into one of the heavily guarded Latin American embassies that could guarantee me safe-conduct out of the country. And when Angélica came to visit me, to spend the night, she was detained the next morning by two secret agents of Pinochet who had been watching the house under the impression that Senator Carlos Altamirano, the fugitive head of the Socialist Party, thin and bespectacled like me, had sought refuge there. An absurd notion, given his pro-Palestinian sympathies. But Angélica managed to outwit those detectives without discussing international affairs and escaped the fate the character in the story was unable to avoid.

When many years later I came to write about the experience, I ended it differently, tragically, partly because that is the way most episodes like this one do end, but mainly, I think, because that was the only way of conveying to myself and to others the horror of what went on in my mind during the hour when the woman I loved was in the hands of men who could do anything they wanted to her, anything they wanted, and I could do nothing to stop them. That ending did not take place in reality, but it did repeat itself over and over in my imagination as I watched from a window, praying I would not have to see it over and over in my memory in the days and years to come, praying that I would not have to imagine a world without Angélica.

Discovering, after so many days obsessed with my ever increasing distance from the country, that I would rather lose Chile than lose Angélica, that I could live without Chile but I could not live without Angélica, beginning to understand that the private home I had made with her was more important and would outlast the public home I had sought to build with Chile and its people.

It was then, I think, that for the first time in my life I clearly separated my wife from the country where she had been born.

Ever since I had met her, Angélica had been confused, in my mind, with Chile. All the readings and all the trips and all the protests and all the snow on all the mountains did less to attach me to the country than this one frail human being.

There I was in early 1961, a stranger in a land that I had inhabited for seven years without finding a real gateway, whose songs and customs and people I hardly knew, no matter how much I had come to admire them, regard them as potential avenue for liberation. And then, one day, Angélica. To be quite frank, what enchanted me to begin with were her dazzling looks and fiery spirit and joy of life, the hot sexual thought of a lithe *moreno* body under her dress, that charming smile of hers that the gods of advertising couldn't have coached out of a woman if they had had a thousand years and a ton of Max Factor makeup. How much of this I identified with the exotic Chile, the exotic Latin America that I had been secretly and transgressively hungering for all these many years, is anybody's guess. I experienced love through the metaphors available to males in Latin America—and elsewhere—at the time, no matter how suspect and gendered I may consider them now, more than thirty years later: the woman as the earth, the earth goddess to be excavated, a territory to be explored by a pioneer, a land in which to root your manhood like a tree—those were the images that surged inside me as we made love, I could never entirely rid myself of the feeling that I was somehow making mine something more than an individual woman, that I was making love to a community that was inside her, that through her body and her life I was binding myself to a permanent place on this planet.

Now that I write this, I have come to understand that it was ultimately not Chile that I desired in her. What attracted me most deeply in the woman who would become my wife were qualities that transcended national origins or boundaries, things I would have treasured in her even if she had been Lithuanian or from Mars. Her fierce loyalty, her bewildering ability to see through people, her stubborn (and often exasperating) tendency to speak her mind without caring about the consequences, her almost animal loyalty, her fearlessness, her unpredictability—none of these was necessarily typical of Chile, and some of them, such as her undiplomatic directness or her rejection of compromises, could indeed even be construed as extremely un-Chilean.

And yet, if it was not Chile that finally joined us, without Chile, the Chile I imagined inside her, it is probable that our love would not have lasted. Angélica is wonderful, but she was not then and certainly is not now, in spite of her name, an angel. Without going into details (she is, after all, the first sharp reader of my works and I do want to get this past her), it should be sufficient to state that she was, well, difficult. Not that I was that easy, either. We were attracted to each other precisely because we were opposites, and if life was never boring and never will be while she is around, it was a constant clash. Given these circumstances and our immaturity, it is quite possible that we wouldn't have made it to marriage and beyond merely sustained by the dim intuition that each of us had found the long-lost half of the soul. An additional something was necessary for our love to survive those rough and desperate breakups that all young lovers flounder through, and that something, for me, frequently seemed the vast Chile that I felt Angélica contained within herself. I could feel the country bringing me back to her for more, my need for the identity she gave me fastening me to her, Chile secretly cementing us together. It is the perverse logic of love that the reverse was true for Angélica: what kept her by my side when things didn't seem to be working out was, she has told me, the very fact that I came from some other place, her intuition that I would not treat her the way Chilean males treat women, that I could be totally trusted, that I was transparent, that I was naïve: in other words, that I was a gringo. A gringo who happened to be searching frantically for a country that would be the answer to his loneliness and transience.

Angélica possessed that country within her merely by virtue of having been born here, simply because her forefathers and foremothers had made love under these mountains and intermingled their many races, their Iberian and Mediterranean and Indian and African stock, at a time when mine had never even dreamed of emigrating. She possessed this country in the nursery rhymes in Spanish she had sung when I was reciting Old Mother Hubbard, she possessed it in the peasant proverbs she had absorbed in the dusty plaza of the small countryside town in the Aconcagua Valley where she had been brought up, she possessed it in every Chilean spice, every Chilean fruit, every Chilean meal that had nurtured her. That was Chile, all of that and more. She had been accumulating every drop of experience inside herself like a reservoir. At some point early in our fumbling and fearful and expectant movements toward each other, I sensed that reservoir, sensed that I could drink from its waters, drink Chile in her waters.

How vast were those waters and how insatiable my thirst was brought home to me the first night we became *pololos*—a word with which Chileans designate boys and girls who are going steady, a word that comes from a butterfly-like insect that goes from flower to flower dizzying itself with their sweetness. We had slipped into a sort of discotheque and began timidly exploring one another, the way you do when you are under twenty and the universe has everything to teach you and an orchestra is remotely playing a bolero, *Bésame, bésame mucho, como si fuera esta noche la última vez. Kiss me, keep on kissing me, as if tonight were the last night,* and Angélica took her mouth from mine and began to sing (a bit off-key, but who cared) the words to that song of Latin American love that I had bypassed so often on the radio as I rushed to hum along with Frankie Avalon and that was followed by a tango which she also knew by heart, and inside that brain of hers, behind those freckles, was the whole repertoire of popular Latin America that I had despised, and which I now wanted to learn by heart to prove my newfound identity. It may have been that very night when I asked her if she danced *cueca,* the Chilean national dance, and she smiled mischievously and grabbed a napkin from the table and waved it in the air and hid her face behind it and suggested that she teach me some steps, that it was a matter of imagining a rooster out courting. I had to try to corral her, corner her, this was the game. She was the treasure and I was the hunter. She would hide and I would seek.

It may have been the next day, when we went down to the center of Santiago together, that I realized that Angélica had within herself a treasure she barely knew she had, a treasure that I was seeking and that she was not even trying to hide. Her presence by my side as we strolled through the center of the city I had lived in for seven years suddenly transformed me into a tourist arriving at this foreign destination for the first time. I had often passed this café, for instance, and it meant absolutely nothing to me, but for Angélica it was the place where in the forties her journalist father, after he had put the paper to bed, would meet her mother and a group of Popular Front friends and drink and discuss how to fix the world till dawn. As Angélica casually told me the story of the night her father had waited for the news of the Allied landing in Normandy, we were interrupted by a pretty young woman. She came up to us, pecked Angélica's cheek, and was introduced to me as the daughter of her "Mami Lolo," the woman who had brought Angélica up in the countryside, when she was a little girl. The two of them chatted for a while about people I did not know and places I had never been. When the young woman said goodbye and we continued on our way, Angélica sketched out the story of her nanny, who had been brought very young into the family house as a helper and later had cared for the grandchildren—who, it would turn out, was in fact the illegitimate daughter of Angélica's grandfather. "You have to come to Santa María," Angélica said, "where I was raised, and meet my Mami Lolo." Half a block later, Angélica was greeted by someone else, and so it went and so it would go. So many people and so many conversations and so many stories. Perhaps it was then that I began to understand that Angélica was a network of stories, a lineage of stories, a wellspring of stories that had made her, that she was full to the brim with people, with Chileans, who had made her. It may have been then or it may have been later, but at some point early in our relationship I realized that Angélica's connection to Chile was the opposite of mine, that it was not and never could be willed, that she could not discard it as I was in the process of discarding the United States, that it was as much part of her as her lungs or her skin. In the months and years to come, as she guided me into her life and her body, she also guided me into the mysteries of a continent that should have been mine by birthright but that I had cut myself off from, a country I had seen for years as nothing more than a stop on the road to someplace else.

And when I was faced with the loss of that country after the coup, when I finally told Abel yes, I would seek refuge in an embassy, what ultimately made that decision tolerable like a secret silhouette inside me was the promise of Angélica, the certainty that I could wander the earth forever if the woman who had taught me Chile was by my side.

Now she was in a car with those two men and I had come face-to-face with the possibility that she would not accompany me on my wanderings, that she would not be there at all. I told myself that maybe this was the cruel, the hidden reason behind my miraculous survival: death had spared me because all along it was going to take Angélica instead. Death would punish me for having refused its gift, for having stayed in this country all month. I was going to be punished for not having left immediately, for not having sent my family away—this was what I deserved for pretending that I was untouchable and immortal.

But again I was given a reprieve.

When the two men released her and she came back into the residence and we trembled against each other, when I was able to hold my love, my best friend, my companion for life, in these arms that had despaired of ever touching her again, my hand going through her hair over and over, my eyes closing and then opening to make sure that it was still true, that she was still here, I was finally ready to learn the lesson that death had sent me one more time, perhaps one last time. It was then that the coup finally caught up with me, that it descended on me as it had descended on La Moneda, exploding silently inside me like the bombs exploding all over the city, making me understand, for the first time since Allende's overthrow, the full and irreversible reality of the evil that had visited us and that would not go away. In that working-class shack, at the moment of mind-wrenching fear when I anticipated my own death, I thought

I had discovered what the Inferno is: the place where you suffer forever, from which you are not able to escape. Now I knew I had been wrong: the Inferno is the one place in the world where the person you most love suffers for all eternity while you are forced to watch, unable to intervene, responsible for her being there.

And that Inferno was here, the country I had associated with Paradise.

It was time to get the hell out of Chile.

TWELVE

A Chapter Dealing with the
Discovery of Life and Language
During the Years 1965 to 1968
in Santiago de Chile

On May 6, 1965, I celebrated my twenty-third birthday by declaring my independence from the United States of America.

It was an aggressive celebration: I stood in front of the U.S. Embassy in Santiago, under the canopy of old trees from the narrow Parque Forestal, hurling threats and insults at the American government. And not alone in my invective: thousands of demonstrators surrounded me in the streets of Santiago, while beyond our borders hundreds of thousands of other Latin Americans protested from Guadalajara to Cochabamba, united as much by our radical politics as by our common Spanish language.

My voice, trained to speak English in that exclusive Upper East

Side private-school way, honeyed with attempts to imitate Paul Anka, my voice that had assumed a pretentious British accent while reciting Keats at the Grange, was at that moment joining in the raucous and proverbial shout of the Latin American left, inspired by the Cuban revolution and its firing squads: *Al paredón, yanqui ladrón*—up against the wall, you yankee thief.

Appropriately, the police replied to these words of goodwill toward our neighbor to the North with a barrage of new repressive weapons supplied by the very Americans who were being so virulently denounced. A colossal black-and-white police van that we had never seen before had been idling its motor in front of the embassy. On its top was a strange round, funnel-like contraption which, as soon as the vehicle sprang into action, turned out to be a water cannon from which spewed a sickening red liquid. We then sampled a good dose of teargas, which burned in our lungs longer than usual. I use the word *sample* deliberately, because instead of tasting the teargas provided by the United States aid program to Chile, I should have been inside the ivy walls of that embassy sampling a rather more enticing shrimp cocktail and other delicacies which also would have come to me courtesy of the U.S. taxpayer. Indeed, at that very moment I should have been sitting down with the Cultural Attaché and other U.S. functionaries to a lunch in honor of the poet Ned O'Gorman.

I had met O'Gorman a week before when he visited the English Department at the University of Chile, where I was an assistant to several professors, teaching English and North American literature. He was a charming man, a talented poet (as far as I can remember now) and his politics seemed fine: his radical Catholic views had led him to leave a life of comfort and serve the poor in the most abandoned parishes of New York—which was more than any of us, with all our socialist convictions, had ever done. His visit to our Faculty had gone so splendidly that the embassy had invited us all to have a midday meal with him on May 6—a free banquet which we enthusiastically agreed to attend.

If I found myself hurling curses outside the embassy rather than petals of praise to O'Gorman for his metaphors or to the Cultural Attaché for his selection of wines, it was because four days before my birthday, on May 2, 1965, President Lyndon Johnson had ordered twenty-two thousand Marines (with a token one thousand OAS support troops) into the Dominican Republic to quash a popular rebellion that was meant to reinstall Juan Bosch as President. Bosch had won the election fairly a few years back but had been overthrown in a Putsch supported by Washington. Johnson was not going to allow, he said, a "Communist dictatorship" to take hold there, though, as Senator William Fulbright and public opinion later learned, there was no evidence of the pitifully weak Dominican Communists influencing the movement that supported Bosch. The U.S. government was obsessed with Cuba and the 1961 failure of the Bay of Pigs invasion, where a ragtag group of anti-Fidelista expatriates had failed to repeat the scenario that had ousted Arbenz in Guatemala in 1954. As long as the Armed Forces inside each Latino country could guarantee order (as in the 1964 coup in Brazil against President João Goulart engineered by the U.S. Embassy), the Americans would let them do the dirty work. Otherwise, the Marines themselves would make sure that no dominoes fell in Latin America. It was the beginning of the Johnson Doctrine: the President claimed the right to send his "boys" anywhere in the hemisphere if it seemed that "another Cuba" was about to materialize.

It was also the effective end of the Alliance for Progress. The carrot had been devoured by the Latin American rich and what was revealed glaringly with the invasion of Santo Domingo was the crude reality of the Big Stick that was now, as it had been for the last hundred years, America's principal way of dealing with the turbulent South, mercilessly applied not only to the Caribbean that the U.S. had always treated as its own private lake but also to those who, in faraway Chile, protested that treatment.

Nor was it an ordinary form of repression that was being exercised against us that day in 1965 in front of the embassy. Along with the new teargas and the new vehicles with their resplendent water cannons, the police put into practice unprecedented and precise crowd-control tactics. Until then, brutality by the state in Chile had always been haphazard. This was different, we sensed: systematic, planned, scientific. The first step, we realized later, much later, when it was too late, in the modernization of repression: we might be backward in our economic structure and our old-fashioned social habits, but in this one area Latin America was rushing into the future ahead of everybody else, a future we caught a quick glimpse of right there, that day.

I remember how, when our protest was quickly broken up, the crowd scattered and I grabbed Angélica's hand and we ran off across the Parque Forestal toward the habitual safety of the river. We had resorted to the same maneuver dozens of times: the police attacked, we dispersed, we regrouped, they attacked again and then we all went home. But not this time: a black-and-white police van veered wildly onto the lawn and started to chase us through the gardens. We stopped behind a hundred-year-old tree and the truck roared past us, only to brake abruptly and hurtle back. We got out of the way just as it rammed the tree. The tree shook with the impact and I could feel the template of Angélica's body quivering against mine. The truck screeched into reverse, throttled past, and turned once more to try to pin us down. Another ramming. This time, though, several burly policemen jumped out of the back of the van swinging their nightsticks—and we were on the run again. We finally reached a bridge that crossed the Mapocho and managed to find refuge, breathless and aghast, in a friend's nearby studio, cursing Johnson and his aid program.

But along with this anger directed at the Americans who had provided the training that had almost crippled us, I also felt justified in having broken all contact with the United States; indeed, I felt that my public stance had been resoundingly vindicated. My outrage at the violation by Marines of Latin American soil had not only been expressed in the streets: a few days before our protest in front of the embassy, in fact as soon as I heard of the invasion of Santo Domingo, I had furiously fired off a letter to the Cultural Attaché, which the other professors subscribed to, proclaiming that we would not sit down to lunch or to dinner or to breakfast or to tea with Ned O'Gorman or any other person brought to Chile with U.S. funds, nor would we attend any other embassy activities—until Lyndon Johnson withdrew his troops. Cultural interchange between the Americas was unthinkable while the Armed Forces of the U.S. were violating our brothers' territory and lives.

That letter, need I add, was completely ineffective. It was aimed at President Johnson and instead squarely hit poor Ned O'Gorman, who had been looking forward for years to this tour of Latin America and was now munching a solitary lunch inside the embassy grounds, hearing the anti-imperialist chants of the multitude and the thwack of stones against the walls, and the screams of Chilean would-be poets being clubbed by the police. If I mention this letter at all, it is because it marks the first time I had personally stepped forward openly to proclaim my anti-Americanism. Not that I hadn't partic-ipated in a good share of protests against U.S interventions around the world, but I had always been lost in the crowd. Now I had gone public, put myself in the limelight. I even deliriously imagined that somewhere in Langley a file was being opened at the Central Intel-ligence Agency under my name, right next to the voluminous pages filled with innocuous data about my father.

I thought I would never be able to come anywhere near United States territory again.

I was wrong. The CIA had bigger fish to fry, and as for me, that letter—for all its pledges of integrity—did not stop me, less than two years later, from applying for a one-year grant from the Univ-ersidad de Chile–University of California exchange program, nor, when I was selected, did it keep me from going into the very building I had refused to enter for lunch to submit to fingerprinting and to being photographed for a visa and thereafter to travel in 1968 with Angélica and Rodrigo to the country I had vilified, in order to engage in the very cultural interchange that I had pronounced as unconscionable.

I should have suspected that it would end up like that. After all, back in 1965, even as I stridently denounced the mere possibility of a dialogue with the States, I was in fact engaging in one, through that incendiary letter breaking relations. Instead of forcing the Cultural Attaché and the mythical CIA to translate my sovereign Spanish words, instead of establishing my Latin American cultural autonomy, I sat down at my desk and automatically reached out for the personal and intimate language I shared with the attaché and the Marines and the CIA operatives as well as Updike and Baldwin and Bellow and Flannery O'Connor and a hundred others in my library, and which I did not share with the protesters on the street.

The very fact that I felt the need to show off my linguistic fireworks to the only people who could appreciate them—even if it was to insult them and even if they were my political enemies—conveys how isolated I felt my literary language to be, my lack of a wider audience with whom to elegantly communicate in English. My parents diligently read my stories and poetry and my metaphysical plays and dutifully found them wonderful, and Angélica was also supportive. She had been majoring in English at my university when I met her (which is in itself significant, that of all the possible Chilean women, I should have fallen in love with one who was planning to make English her profession), but her language skills had not developed to the point where she could deal with my overly elaborate and hermetic texts. A couple of friends at the university read English well enough to offer faint praise and fainter criticism, but their hearts weren't in it. Too much was going on in Spanish in the world we inhabited to waste time discussing work that seemed so removed from our everyday circumstances.

It would be misleading, nevertheless, to state that English was merely my private kingdom at a time of intense public engagement in Spanish, a space of reflection and repose segregated from the uncertain daily pandemonium of a Latin America on the road to revolution. It was also a way of making a living, an advantage in the marketing of myself. At the very time when I was shouting obscenities in Spanish at the Americans who had dared to encroach on the sacred soil of Latin America, I was working on what were to be my first major works of criticism, both rooted in my knowledge of English: a thesis on Shakespeare's pastoral comedies, and a book on Harold Pinter's Theatre of the Absurd. And the fact that I could read English (and had a father willing to import all the books and magazines from abroad that I desired) plugged me into the latest developments in literature, philosophy, history, theory, criticism, years before most people in Chile heard of it—an up-to-datedness that, by the way, landed me a job at *Ercilla*, Chile's most prestigious magazine, though it undoubtedly helped that Angélica's father was the editor in chief when I was invited to contribute. My income from the puny assistantships in Spanish and Spanish-American literature that I held in the mid-sixties was supplemented by classes I taught in English poetry and American fiction in our Faculty. And I worked with students of all kinds in the practice of the English language, along with regular classes at the School of Psychology, and remedial lessons to laggard high-school truants, as well as private lessons to young widows and recalcitrant children. I might find it politically suspect that English was expanding imperially around the world, but this did not impede me from using it to keep bread on the table.

Or dance to it.

The night after dozens of my friends joined me in cursing Johnson in Spanish for his intervention in Santo Domingo, we all reconvened in my parents' house to celebrate my birthday with a wild rock 'n' roll party where all the songs that electrified our bodies were sung in the language in which I had just written that letter, the language that many of the young Latin-American macho revolutionaries were using to warm up their lady loves and convince them to spend the night together, as the Rolling Stones would soon urge, or to do it on the road, in the immortal words of Lennon and company. English was being transformed into the lingua franca of McLuhan's global village and it would not have been easy to escape it even if I had so desired.

But I didn't so desire. At a time when I was throwing everything else in my life into the frantic public caldron of Latin America and remaking it at a furious pace, keeping my receding English intact was a way of secreting some private part of my past and person away from the overly political world I inhabited, my way of recognizing that not everything can be reduced to partisan ideological conflict. Maybe I needed one unchanging island of identity that, as I transmogrified myself into a Latin American, linked me to the gringo I had once been.

If I managed to accommodate these blatant contradictions, my private English-language self and my gesticulating public Spanish-American persona, my vanguard writings in the language of Richard Nixon and my revolutionary speechifying in the language of Che Guevara, if I managed to keep both these psyches side by side in relative harmony, it was because I had discovered a strange justification for my schizoid conduct in—well, in the history of Latin America as it searched for a language with which to express its hybridity.

I knew that there was something monstrous in the way I was becoming Latin American without fully divorcing myself from the United States, the back and forth in my mind as I delved deeper into Chile, the painstaking digging of ditches in a *población* one afternoon to build a playground for poor kids and the even more painstaking quest that same evening in the luxury of my room, probing for the right adjective I recalled from some poem by Wordsworth or Dickinson. There was something monstrous and bizarre and twisted in my journey. But wasn't that also the story of Latin America, what it had baroquely permitted, admitted, submitted, remitted since its origins?

It was, in fact, in those origins that I found a key image that was to accompany me all through the sixties as I intellectually worked

out my uneasy halfway relationship with the two continents I strad-
dled.

I became fascinated with the moment in history when other ex-
plorers such as myself had come upon this land and translated it for
the first time into a Western language and for a Western gaze. The
seminal text for me had been written at the beginning of the six-
teenth century by a Spanish colonizer called Gonzalo Fernández de
Oviedo. The book was the *Sumario de la Historia Natural de las
Indias*, and in it Oviedo tried to describe the New World to his
faraway compatriots and, specifically, to the King of Spain. One of
the first attempts to transfer into words what the sword had subjugated in a place not yet called America.

The chapter that caught my eye dealt with Oviedo's struggle to
translate to his European counterparts the *tigre americano*, an inad-
equate term, he said, because the etymology of *tigre* referred to an
arrow and to speed, whereas this never before seen creature he was
attempting to transmit was slow. And Oviedo went on to compare
the New and Old World animals, reluctantly concluding that he
could not really name the American *tigre*. It escaped his linguistic
snares, he could not domesticate it, classify it, make it part of his
system: it kept slipping away from Europe, did not fit into the preexisting rational order of the universe. And Oviedo ends with a
warning: on a visit to Toledo, he had seen one of those so-called
tigres on a leash in His Majesty's gardens and it was being treated
with far more familiarity than was prudent, so that he was not surprised later when he heard that the beast had one day gone wild and
its captors had been forced to kill it. The sword intervening again,
I thought to myself as I puzzled ominously over the text more than
four hundred years later, the sword putting to rest and to death the
unsettling barbarian reality that language had failed to seize and fix
and understand Latin America, I said to myself, savaged from abroad,
resistant, unpredictable.

Though my sympathies were with the *tigre*, stolen from its home,
shipped thousands of miles away to be paraded in front of uncom-

prehending European eyes and trying to communicate, ultimately, through those eyes with the only weapon left to it, its own evasion through death of the categories in which the invader had been trying to trap it, I could also discern, stirring in me, Oviedo's fascination with the power and vibrancy of what he had witnessed and what his compatriots back in Spain could not begin to verbalize. I could see how he had been seduced by his new home and admired even its danger, how he had begun to feel, opening under his feet, an abyss of distance separating him from Europe which made him into something other, wrenchingly like the very *tigre* he wanted to net and carry off. And if he was beginning to grasp that he was an Indiano, a man of the Indies, that this was his home, then he was as much a Latin American as the elusive *tigre*. So maybe Latin America was both of them, or neither, or rather the fantastic composite that had come out of their clash, the irreconcilable tension between the nature of the New World and the linguistic and cultural drive of the Old World to capture that nature and remake it in its own paternal image, the dissonant gap between a savage reality and a supposedly civilized language that never managed totally to bag and apprehend it.

And through the centuries the pursuit of meaning continued, this world which now beckoned to me had given itself a history and a literature and a people that were in fact too vast and variegated to fit in a name. Every definition was incomplete and incoherent: Latino was a term imported from France that did not even pretend to include the multiple non-European races which were mixed into the bloodstream and the culture; Hispanic was based on language and excluded Brazil and the multiple tongues of the Antilles and, of course, the Indians; Indo-American did not even try to register the millions of enslaved blacks who called this their home; South did not include Mexico and all of Central America; and so on. But that was the real meaning of the continent, the condition for its existence, I thought, quoting Sartre and the existentialists, who were the rage at the time: it did not have an essence; it exasperatingly escaped all

definitions and furiously demanded more visions, more communication. Simultaneously colonized and rebellious, it had a history that
was never sufficiently autonomous of foreign forces to be really free
but also never so submissive and subordinate as to he blotted out,
so that the struggle itself for a story that made sense ended up being
the sole defining element, its heart.

It was this imaginary that captured me both as *tigre* and as incessant translator, that sucked me into its whirlwind. Of course the
voyages of the imagination were supplemented by an exploration of
real space: hitchhiking to Machu Picchu and working my way down
to Tierra del Fuego and smelling the burnt smoke of the sugar plantations of Tucumán and letting myself be overwhelmed by the eternal cataracts of Iguazú and above all by Chile, with its abandoned
nitrate ghost towns in the north and its emerald-green rivers dashing
against white rocks beneath the volcanoes of the south. At every turn,
it seemed, there was someone to greet me: the Indians in Lake Ti-
ticaca holding on to their Quechua language almost half a millen-
nium after the conquest, and the miners who took me down the
shaft in Curanilahue, telling me how they waited for the haunted
subterranean hiss of the *grisú* that comes when the mine is about to
collapse, and landless migrant workers who took to the road and
could not read but had learned Latin America with their hands and
their backs in a way that my many books could not begin to fathom.
I met an explosion of human beings on the move, ardent poets and
philosophers in a bar in Lima who would someday become the gurus
of the terrorist organization Sendero Luminoso and a slick black con
man in a shantytown in Montevideo who tricked me out of my
watch and a fisherman who gave me shelter on a stormy night on
the island of Chiloe and told me tales of the *imbunches* who kidnap
children and sew their eyelids and mouths and ears shut. Nothing
binds you as much to a land as to fall in love with its inhabitants.
But let me qualify that: nothing bound me to Latin America as much
as the extraordinary renaissance of literature that coincided with my
journeys and gave them a frame of reference. That space I crossed
and those people I touched were seen by me through the prism of

visions and words that existed in an intellectual adventure that had anticipated them, made them significant, captured them with a success that had eluded Oviedo as he pursued the *tigre*, the coming of age, I thought, of a continent where culture was starting to be synchronous with the social and political body.

It was a giddy time to be alive for anyone who believed as deeply as I did in the power of words, that novels and poems and stories should not be separate from life. Relevant and urgent and provocative, these cultural offerings from Latin America immediately resonated in everything I did and saw, accompanying the surge of energy and joy and doubts of millions on the move, naming the continent that I could not yet name myself, liberating the territory of the imagination as a way of paving the way for the liberation of the real space and the real inhabitants of that territory. Latin America, I felt, could solve the dilemma of the modern artist, merge the intellectual and the social, the vanguard and the masses, the heroism of the writer and the heroism of the people.

It was a time when I lived in wait for the next book, which was going to answer the questions I was grappling with, the next Cortázar or García Márquez or Vargas Llosa, Fuentes, or the verses of Parra, Gelman, Dalton, Mistral.

I was not alone in being captivated by this illusion that our literature would make us free. An elite generation of young, educated Latin Americans who were themselves at the crossroads of their identity recognized their image in that vanguard language of experimentation and socially conscious concerns, that meeting place of the metaphysical and the social, the fantastical and the documentary, a literature that, like the reality of the continent itself, jumbled together in uneasy coexistence the modern and the pre-modern and the primitive.

But could it bring together my confused dual life?

Could my writing in English make sense of this journey of identity into Latin America that was, of course, being carried out, primarily, in Spanish?

Incredibly, my delusionary answer back then was that yes, it could.

A delusion that was nourished paradoxically by the success that Latin American literature was having abroad. The outstanding talent of the "Boom" authors, combined with a smart marketing campaign, took Europe and the United States by storm in the 1960s. One part of me felt pride: we might not be able to compete with developed nations economically and we were for the moment—with the exception, we thought, of Cuba, ignoring that island's increasing dependence on the Soviet Union—politically subordinate to their whims; but that did not mean we could not outshine them culturally, establish this one area of accomplishment where we were not behind but ahead. Another part of me felt, well, I suppose envy would be the best word: my Latin American masters had elbowed their way into those prestigious foreign peaks that I aspired to, that my writing sought to reach, and they had done so using the Spanish I still refused to consider the language of my literary destiny. But instead of taking that success as proof that if I wanted to be universally recognized, Spanish was as advantageous an instrument as English, I construed the whole phenomenon quite differently. These were the facts: there existed, for the first time in the history of Latin America, a literature that could speak to its own readers while simultaneously appealing to a vast public abroad, and this literary movement asserted that in order to be Latin American you did not have to reject the international. I interpreted these facts as a green light for my bizarre experiment, the peculiar way in which I combined the native and the foreign, the national and the transcultural, the Spanish everyday experience and the English reelaboration at night. I thought that I could become the first Latin American writer to address the United States and Europe directly in English, without any need of translation.

Perhaps that was the ultimate attraction of the United States for me, the one place in the world where the boy I still had inside me whispering in English could meet on equal terms the adult breathing in Spanish, the one place where I would be able to test one against the other, measure how much, how irrevocably, if at all, I had changed.

And the one place that was willing to pay for this eccentric personal odyssey.

Nor was this merely a matter of finding my self existentially. It was a voyage that also responded to other needs, of a more material kind. Angélica and I had married tempestuously in early 1966 and a few months later she was happily pregnant—though our joy was constrained by our financial difficulties. No matter how much I worked like a madman at a plurality of jobs, I could not scramble together enough money to rent a house of our own. We ended up uneasily living with my parents. To make matters worse, my chief source of income, my job as literary critic and reviewer at *Ercilla,* dried up a few months before the baby was due. The owner of the magazine had censored an interview with Nicolás Guillén, Cuba's greatest poet (he had ripped the page from the hands of the Linotype operator, vowing that no fucking nigger Communist Cuban would be interviewed while he was paying the bills), and I had resigned. When soon afterwards the possibility of finishing a book on Latin American literature at the University of California came up, I saw that as a miraculous opportunity to solve our financial—and my cultural—dilemmas, even if it meant obeying the same historical law of the brain drain that had begun luring minds up from the South since the time my father had won his Guggenheim and that in theory I deplored. Like him, I headed for the States because there was no place else that wanted me.

Besides, I told myself, trying to wave away my discomfort at a trip that was so inconsistent with my professed beliefs, hadn't Adorno written that if you wanted to understand where the world was headed you had to visit the center of imperial power? And had not Martí himself stated that you only understood the beast from its belly, that you had to be swallowed by the Leviathan to slay it? And wasn't that Leviathan being corroded from the inside by our allies, the anti-war movement, the black liberationists, the chicanos, the thousands of Americans who sympathized with the revolution, wasn't it important to visit them?

In effect, I had stayed in touch with this contentious version of

America even as I had become more and more Latin American, I had thrilled as that America the truly beautiful flexed its muscles and spilled blood in Selma and Montgomery and forced its South to desegregate, I had watched it march on Washington with Martin Luther King, galvanize the ghettos with Malcolm X, organize the farm workers and boycott the grapes with César Chavez, I had applauded from Santiago as it spilled into the streets to stop the war in Vietnam, I followed closely the growth of a movement that questioned not only America's government but its life-style, I had shadowed from afar its intellectual contest of power and enjoyed the Beats and Arthur Penn and Janis Joplin.

And that process made me wonder if perhaps I was not that crazy all these years to persist in writing in the language that had rescued me as a child, maybe back in that country I had considered home for so long there were people—readers, by God!—who were beginning to be as politically aware as I was and also happened to speak and eat and write in English. Maybe I was not as isolated as I thought, maybe there was an audience for what I had been writing all these years, an audience that had been waiting for me with the same loyalty I had shown toward the English language. I fantasized about crossing the Bay Bridge to San Francisco and wandering into a bar not far from the City Lights bookstore to talk all night about race relations in America and about Buddhism and about Walt Whitman and about the bomb and show somebody, anybody, what I had scribbled ten thousand miles away.

And so, carrying all these conflicting reasons and desires and fears as my essential baggage, the sort of contraband you do not declare at customs, so secret that you hardly dare admit it to yourself, I boarded a plane to the United States of America with my young wife and our baby son, and twelve hours later arrived in the country of my childhood dreams.

History was ready to play one more trick on me.

Of all the years I could have chosen to try to find out how American I still was, I chose the year 1968.

And of all the places, Berkeley chose me.

Welcome home, Vlady. Or is it Eddie? Or are you really Ariel?

Whoever you are and whatever your name is, you're in for one heck of a surprise.

I had been gone for fourteen years.

THIRTEEN

A Chapter Dealing with the
Discovery of Death Inside
an Embassy in
October of 1973, in
Santiago de Chile

So here I am, when all is said and done, in this building that most of the people, peasants and workers whose lives I have sworn to join, here I am in this embassy that most of those people do not even imagine exists, here I am on this piece of territory that is legally considered Argentina, here I am, returned to the protection of the country where I was born, caught in the vicious, saving circle of my origin, here I am with no place to go but back to Buenos Aires.

I know my escape is justified, I know that there was no alternative, but I feel demeaned here, with the innumerable other refugees who have fled to this embassy, I have been stripped naked by the fear that I share with them, humiliated for all the world to see, suddenly homeless, my commitment to the revolution less important than my love of life.

It is here that I meet, face-to-face, the first torture victims of my life. During the last weeks, the rumors have reached me, they say that . . . , you know what they're doing in the Estadio, have you heard what happened to . . . but it was all hear this and hear that and hearsay. Now, a few hours after I manage to be smuggled into the embassy, they are there, these men who have been laid out on a table, stripped naked, not metaphorically as I have, but in the cold reality of a room that smells of piss and vomit and sweat, and their genitals have been connected to a clamp and a hand has pulled a switch, and they are fortunate to have escaped that room and find themselves here, shivering in the sweet October sun of Chile, shivering under a blanket, staring into nothingness, their lips twitching, trying to smile back at me, at anybody who approaches, cringing suddenly, crying out in their nights as we all try to sleep in an air thick with the breathing and the farts and the sighs of almost a thousand people laid out side by side in the great ballroom of the embassy, where only a month ago tuxedoed men leaned forward to murmur compliments to women in long, shuffling dresses, where one of the fugitives himself, Allende's Secretary of the Treasury, sipped a cocktail next to this very piano under which he now tosses and turns, trying to get some rest.

I do not have a blanket. By the time I arrived, it was too late: they had all been handed out to the over nine hundred people who had rushed here before me, and the sadistic chargé d'affaires of the embassy, a tall, flint-eyed man called Neumann, whom we all suspect of Nazi sympathies, has informed the refugees that there is no item in the budget to cover additional blankets. So a friend, known as El Gitano, shares his with me. He is a singer and for the last two years in all our gatherings we have belted out his most famous song, *"Ha llegado aquel famoso tiempo de vivir"*—It's come, that much-awaited time to start living—and now that his song has proven to be less a prophecy than a wish, he keeps me warm at night with half his blanket.

I like not having a blanket. It tells everyone that I did not dash to this embassy, it hints to those who came before me that for a few weeks I had stupidly and perhaps even courageously tried to get myself killed.

My unshielded existence is a way of warding off the guilt of having survived, a way of dealing with my decision to go into exile which will remain with me for many, many years, which will really disappear the day fourteen years from now when, with my eight-year-old son Joaquín, I am arrested at the airport in Santiago and deported, when with that violence done to me I can finally, masochistically, feel that I have paid my dues. But here in this embassy it's a way of hurting myself because the Junta hasn't hurt me enough, hasn't hurt me as it is hurting those who remain on the outside of this sanctuary.

I am not to be left in this state of blanketless distinction for long. Some days after I arrive, I am walking in the large garden enjoying the afternoon sun. I have been told to stay away from the eight-foot walls that surround us, but I cannot help it. I am fascinated by the proximity of Chile, just outside, the bustle of the city which I cannot see from here but which I can hear, the sudden singsong conversation of a child and his mother, the throttle of a *micro* changing gears, a man who sharpens knives trundling his cart there on the streets of Santiago, calling out his services.

Suddenly a bundle falls at my feet. For a moment I can't tell where it comes from, but now I see two hands grip the top of the wall— only the fingers, whitened with the effort. Somebody is trying to climb over the wall into the embassy! But now two shots ring out and—no scream, no shout, not even a grunt—just a sort of dull thud on the other side. The police have just killed the man. Why did I imagine it was a man, why have I never pictured a woman? Why did I think he had been killed and not merely wounded or simply stopped in his tracks by the shots? I am cut off from that world out there, at the mercy of my imagination.

In the bundle I find a blanket and a sleeping bag. No passport, no identification papers, nothing to let me know who has offered me these gifts. Because they are gifts. The tragedy of this victim will mean warmer nights for me—and less lonely days, because I will turn the blanket, Linus-like, into an inseparable companion. Whenever I picture myself roaming those halls where Argentine diplomats had hosted the national and international glitterati, I automatically see the blanket of the failed seeker of asylum wrapped comfortingly around my shoulders.

The real blanket that protects us, of course, is the embassy itself. The distance between security and death at this point is a trifling few feet, the negligible distance between fingers reaching out for a wall in despair and eyes that helplessly see those fingers torn from the wall, to be buried or broken, eyes that swear never to forget. Soon enough another sort of distance, another sort of helplessness, will put those eyes to the test: I know that these eyes of mine will travel far away, into the remote haven of foreign lands, the ultimate blanket and immunity that the embassy foretells.

I am already starting to learn the rules that govern the loss of a land. I am already starting to realize that my existence will be like that of all exiles who survive, like the multitude of Latin American exiles around me in the embassy, who came to Chile from their own frustrated revolutions, who have already lived the future that awaits me, all of us mercilessly defined by those who remain behind, our existence contrasted to that of those who did not or could not flee, our existence justified by the help we can bring to those who died in our stead yesterday or who risk death in our stead tomorrow. Exiles are haunted by the fingers grasping at a wall, grasping at a distance that has become immense and almost insurmountable.

That distance allowed me to bear witness to the outrage being perpetrated back home; indeed, demanded that I carry out that task. And yet, from the moment of departure, that witnessing would inevitably be indirect. Even before I depart, the embassy wall has insulated me from the person who was trying to escape. I cannot say who he was, what was his fate, how it was that he came to throw his bundle over the wall. Later, as the space grows, as miles and time

204 HEADING SOUTH, LOOKING NORTH

zones separate me from the Chile where men reach a wall and then die before they can jump over it, I will have contact only through newspaper articles, letters, cassettes, a fleeting photo, a guarded voice on the phone, stories murmured by the newest refugees or released prisoners or, eventually, friends who come to visit, everything far, lived and told by someone else. This is one of the great paradoxes of exile: the sanctuary I have found, the very sanctuary that guarantees that a voice has survived, simultaneously cuts that voice off from direct access to the land it is responsible for keeping alive, the land that demands to be transmitted to others.

But you do what you can.

And now, more than twenty years later, I tell the story of the blanket that someone I never saw sent me as if from heaven. I tell his story even if I will never know what became of him. I tell his story because it is the only way I can thank him for keeping me warm, the only way I can mourn him and keep him alive, send him this blanket of words that cannot save him from whatever happened, what already happened to him and to me so long ago.

FOURTEEN

A Chapter Dealing with the
Discovery of Life and Language
During the Years 1968 to 1970,
in Berkeley, California

I saw my first real live hippies the afternoon we arrived in Berkeley. We'd gone out, the three of us, Angélica and Rodrigo and I, into the crisp sunny breeze of the Bay Area and there, on Shattuck, in front of Oscar's Hamburgers, were two flower children. Or maybe flower adults would be a better term, because they were in their mid-twenties, about my age. But they had the proverbial flower in their hair and had, as well, all the other accoutrements that hippies were supposed to possess according to what we had gleaned from news photos and films and songs—almost a caricature, in fact. She had a long, flowing gypsy dress of the sort you buy in secondhand thrift stores and was covered with jangles and baubles, and he had ripped jeans and an open shirt like a pirate's and skin so white it could have been used in a deodorant ad, and a cascade of golden hair fell down both their backs toward feet which were shoeless. He was finishing up a song on his harmonica and she was swaying to it gently, dancing in those bare feet as if she were a spirit in a meadow, oblivious of the hard pavement of California or the nearby cries of a fat newspaper vendor hawking the *Berkeley Barb*, almost as if the nearby traffic spit-full of people hurrying to their jobs did not exist. They smelled of incense and oranges mixed in with another pungent odor I could not identify, but which would turn out to be marijuana.

We stopped in front of them, tarried there awhile, all three of us, drinking in the joy of that man and that woman at being alive, the calm pleasure they took in their bodies, serene and radiant in the midst of their idleness, greeting us, so recently arrived on these shores, making us feel that we somehow fit into this foreign afternoon and its waning sun. The girl arched her back like a wild sexual Botticelli Madonna and still without opening her eyes smiled at the harmonica player, at his soft beard and his forgiving Jesus Christ face—both of them belying the description that Ronald Reagan, Republican Governor of California, had disparagingly given of a hippie as "someone who dresses like Tarzan, has hair like Jane, and smells like Cheetah." What had probably provoked his remark was not their appearance as much as their rejection of the American dream. If they chose, they could have been one of those Bay Area couples driving a car from work, they could be managing Oscar's Hamburgers, they could be planning new outlets for those hamburgers all over the nation, they could be doing the sort of post-graduate work that I had come to do at the University of California, writing a book or listing one more essay on their résumé, but they had turned their backs on a life of affluence and worry and grind, they had rejected the suburban America of lawns and quiz shows, the get-up-and-go American freeways and the keeping-up-with-the-Joneses' washing machine. They didn't want to be imprisoned in objects or the money and the workload and the life-style these objects entailed. They had dropped out, tuned out, let it all hang out—out, out, out, they were far out, outside society and its norms, outcasts with no desire to be allowed back in or to assume responsibility in it or even think of taking political power.

And then the man took his lips off the harmonica and began to sing the words to the melody he had been playing, Bob Dylan's *Mr. Tambourine Man*, and that song I had never heard before pierced me with its melancholy twang, it reached right into me like a gentle claw and twisted at my heart, that voice called out to Mr. Tambourine man to "sing a song for me / I'm not sleepy and there is no place I'm going to." Without warning, I found myself adrift in that music, returned for a moment to the many years in my wandering life when I had been unanchored, I was the one asking Mr. Tambourine Man, I was the one who did not know where he was going, and in the midst of a deep sorrow there surged an astonishing pang of desire, I could feel the unbridled freedom of the lives of that man and that woman, that Jesus and that Madonna calling to me, asking me to hang out with them, explore with them their own quest for identity, I could feel them offering their lives and bodies like a bridge to a land I had always wanted to visit, I felt something stir deep in me and that something must have been the American part of me which I had thought I had suppressed and supplanted but which was still there, which knew who these people were and understood where they were coming from and how they had got there. For an impossible instant, something in me and in them whispered to me, invited me to join them on their quest.

Then the song died down and faded away, freeing me from its spell, and the girl opened her eyes and saw us and smiled, and suddenly I knew that under that gypsy dress she had slipped on that morning she was wearing no bra, no underwear, that she was naked under that dress.

And then she spoke to us. She cocked her head to one side like a bird, sizing us up, and queried: "Spare change?"

"What?"

"You got some spare change?"

I didn't answer right away. Oh, I understood her words, what they meant—the famous Depression era phrase, "Brother, can you spare a dime?" echoed inside me. What I found dumbfounding was that she should actually be asking us for money, that these flaxen-haired, healthy, saintly gringos, these blue-eyed beauties, should be acting like paupers. In the racist Latin America I was from, light-colored eyes and blond hair and white skin were a passport to privilege, a stamp of upper-class origin, and it was unheard-of that anybody born to such fortune should end up begging on the streets.

Our Latin American suppliants were dirty, maimed, hungry, smelly, as if they had crawled out from the Court of Miracles in *The Hunchback of Notre Dame*. They didn't wear shoes because they couldn't afford them. It was misery—and not fashion—that had tattered their clothing. The boy I had brought home for a meal and then turned my back on, that child had sung himself hoarse on a bus because he had no alternative, the Santiago streets he roamed were one more nightmare into which he had awakened at birth and from which he could not escape, just as he was unable to escape the cold and the mud and the beatings and the rapes and the homelessness. He sang boleros because they were the only way to postpone death. Not like these hippies, whose poverty was so artificial and self-imposed that they could escape it with the snap of a finger. Whereas that Chilean beggar boy, like practically every indigent person I ever saw in my country or in any part of Latin America, was trapped in his race as well as his class. He had his Indian ancestry indelibly etched on his face and his stature and his skin. You could read in those dark features how his native blood had been used to condemn him to a life of subjection, to keep him from ever leaving the ghetto of his poverty.

All of a sudden, the happiness of the two hippies that had so seduced me a few instants ago seemed an insult.

"I haven't got any," I said. "No spare change."

"That's cool," she said. And the man added: "God bless you, man."

I was about to leave, when Rodrigo half crawled, half toddled over to them and, gleefully oblivious of the cultural shock that had overcome me—and Angélica, I later found out—pointed to the harmonica and reached out for it and promptly received his first lesson in blowing in the wind. I still liked them (after all, they were cooing over my child), but I began to feel smugly superior to them, I ensconced myself in the knowledge of the remote suffering and sorrow I had witnessed and of which they had not even the faintest notion. I wanted to go up to them and shake the illusion from their eyes, force them to awaken from their dream and look at the real world, I wanted to whisper in their ears that the way to finish with oppression was not to drop out of the system but to overthrow it. Standing there, I felt redeemed and pure and intact, strengthened in the knowledge of who I was. I had left this country as a Northern Edward and was returning as a resolutely Southern Ariel and here, on the first afternoon, was proof of how thoroughly my fourteen years of absence had turned me into a Latin American, the proof I had been searching for, one of the reasons I had taken this trip back to the land of my childhood. My reaction was satisfyingly visceral, almost instinctive: those ecstatic, festive, innocent American toes wriggling with delight on these Yankee streets had been automatically put in their place by the dark vision of my destitute fellow countrymen's bare feet. I was haunted by my experience of underdevelopment, I was possessed by the memory of the penniless people back home. I told myself that I knew where I was going: I knew the answer, Mr. Tambourine Man, I was going back to a country and a continent that needed a song for its lost millions, I was going back to the reality of people who did not have the obscene luxury of being able to choose poverty like these sham hippie paupers.

I did not know, of course, that a night awaited me a few years later when we would throng the Alameda and celebrate our victory, I did not know that those Chilean streets were calling to me from the future, but that very first temptation which Berkeley put in my path revealed to me early on that the pull of Latin America and Chile would end up being far stronger than the remnants of Yankee identity still within me. My stay in Berkeley was to lash me even more tightly to the Chile I had chosen as my own, was to force me eventually to realize that in order to really go back I needed to rid myself of that last link, the English language, which still tied me to the United States.

But to tell the story this way is to miss what is most intriguing about it. The journey back home was not to be as smooth and effortless as I thought it would be that afternoon when I saw my prototype hippies and dismissed anything and everything they could teach me, celebrated how different I was from these *gringos huevones*.

Stupid gringos. Gringo assholes.

That had been my parting shot at them as I gathered Rodrigo in my arms and turned in the direction of my hotel (and, metaphorically, in the direction of faraway Chile), but before our year and a half in Berkeley was over, the brothers and sisters of these two hippies, the youth of America, would have challenged me, shaken my every belief, tested my commitment to the revolution, made me question culturally and sexually and professionally the life I was leading and profoundly altered the way I understood my relationship with the United States.

To begin with, that same day, just a few minutes later, I met a second pair of young Americans more or less my age, and they were just as contestatory as our singing and dancing hippies, but dressed a bit more conservatively and with a mission that was overtly political: to gather signatures to protest I can't remember what policy concerning Vietnam, the recruiting of students by the CIA at UC Berkeley, I think it was, but it may have been a petition to the City Council or to hippie-loving Ronald Reagan. The two anti-war activists, one white and one black, were seated behind a small table at the corner of Shattuck and University, calling out to passersby to sign their petition.

"Hey, man."

We stopped, listened attentively to what they were protesting, though Rodrigo would probably have preferred another harmonica lesson.

"So, what d'you say?"

"I'm sorry," I answered. "We can't sign."

"Why not?"

"We're from Chile."

"From where?"

"From Chile. You know, South America."

"Oh, Chile."

They both looked at me incredulously, as if I was trying to pull a con job on them, trying to slither out of my patriotic obligation to oppose the criminal war in Vietnam. They could tell I was from New York, my accent told them that, they had never met a Latino foreigner who spoke English as I did.

"You really from Chile?"

"That's right." I smothered the temptation to sneak a slight hint of a Ricky Ricardo accent into my words.

They looked at each other and then back at me.

"So—who cares where the hell you're from. You can sign anyway. This is America."

He was right. What was I afraid of? I looked at Angélica and she nodded imperceptibly and watched me sign and then she signed too and for good measure we gave them a couple of bucks for their campaign, feeling that here was a cause worth bestowing some spare change on.

As we turned to leave, the black activist raised his fist in solidarity and the white one flashed the V signal and said, "Peace now," and for the second time that afternoon I had a revelation, not only about them on that corner but about the other young Americans I had just left down the street.

This was my generation, welcoming me back home. They had been brought up on the same Amos 'n' Andy radio shows, the same

Esther Williams films, the same dirty jokes, the same idolization of Marlon Brando in *The Wild One* and James Dean in *Rebel Without a Cause*, they had undergone the same musical evolution from the sultry sounds of forties swing and fifties fox-trot to rhythm and blues and jazz and onward to rebellious sixties rock. They had been flooded with consumer goods and hundreds of brands of cereal that all tasted the same but were packaged differently, they had adored optimistic heroes who always saved the day in the same way and believed in know-how that could solve any dilemma, they had bought into the American dream as kids, just as I had, and had been forced, for reasons different from mine, to deny their native land. I had missed their rebellion because I had been exiled from New York, but the fact that my banishment had landed me smack in the middle of the national wars of liberation that were shaking the globe had allowed me, a typical American kid, to anticipate in remote Chile the way in which they would, several years later in the United States, react to the horror of what was being done, all over the world, in their name, and, in Vietnam, with their very lives.

So my anti-Americanism, far from being aberrant, had been normal, even prophetic of the shame that their America, my America, should have become the bully of the world, when those gigantic zones of humanity that lived in perennial misery were only demanding the independence—yes, and the pursuit of happiness—that my adopted country, that their homeland, had first declared was the birthright of all men during its Revolutionary War. My indignation had been born, as theirs had, from the incredible paradox that it should be the country of Jefferson that financed the tyrants, taught the police how to torture, sent Marines to keep the rich safe in their mansions and the poor wretched in their hovels. These young people in front of me were measuring the United States, as I had, by its own ideals of liberty, by the Declaration of Independence it had flourished in the face of a faraway colonial power that treated it like a disobedient and wayward child, in the same the way it was now treating Cuba and Vietnam and the Congo and Chile. We wanted it to fight along with the dispossessed of the globe as it had fought against slavery during the Civil War, we wanted it to be a force for liberation as it had been during the Good War against Nazism, we wanted it to be generous with the world as it had been generous to its immigrants, we wanted it to export its freedom and not its napalm. And when it did not live up to those ideals, we felt, I myself and these two young men and so many more of them all across the U.S.A., that our trust had been violated.

They had been stuck here, however, and I had been sent far away, and they had, in my name, kept the faith in that better America, they had set out on this march to rescue that America from the men who had betrayed what it stood for.

That first afternoon, I was given an extraordinary welcoming present: the chance to see my own destiny in those two hippies and in those two activists, briefly glimpsed one of the persons I might have been. There, but for the grace of Joe McCarthy, would go I, either playing the harmonica and dancing to Dylan without shoes, or calling out to the conscience of America to end a war which was killing people on the other side of the world who were rebelling because they really had no shoes, yes, there would go I. If I had stayed, I would have embraced one of these two forms of protest what America had become, I would have found myself in a place like Berkeley searching for my identity.

In the months to come, I was to discover that the borders between these two alternatives of rebellious America—withdrawal and engagement—were not as clear-cut as they had seemed that first afternoon, that these two versions of how to deal with the crisis of the United States crossed over and blended and intermingled with the lives of most of the men and women of my generation, precisely because what characterized most of them was their refusal to separate politics from everyday life, the personal from the political, the revolution in the state from the revolution in the culture. But I did not immediately comprehend this. The challenge that I shall call cultural, the challenge to the way I conceived and organized my life, was to take a bit longer to burrow its questions into my heart—although eventually it was to affect my convictions and probe my future with far greater persistence than the political movement that was bursting all over the United States, poised to change the course of America and the world forever.

Or so it seemed, as we were to find out that very day, that March 31 of 1968. Leaving behind both our flower-power people and our power-to-the-people people on their respective street corners, each couple trying to bag some spare change, we proceeded to use our money at a Co-op Store for something more practical: to buy some diapers (the wonder of disposable diapers!—whatever the hippies might say about the horrors of consumerism) and baby food (even if the company that manufactured it was also providing food for the troops in Vietnam), and then we gulped down a quick dinner—hot dogs. I loved hot dogs. I had spent fourteen years without greasy hot dogs and white Wonder buns and brightly colored mustard, I had eaten two hot dogs that morning for breakfast when the plane stopped briefly in Los Angeles on the way to San Francisco, had rushed to buy them while Angélica watched with sympathetic puzzlement, but that had not been enough, I required another one—quick—and then entered our hotel room and clicked on the television because I knew that Lyndon Johnson was going to make an announcement about the escalation of the war in Vietnam, Westmoreland had asked for who knows how many more troops in answer to the devastating January Tet offensive, and that was when I heard the President of the United States tell the world that he had decided not to seek reelection.

One America had kicked me out and now here was a different America with yet another gift, the news that the same Johnson who had invaded Santo Domingo and who could ignore the anti-American threats of obscure and faraway Chilean academics, had been toppled from his perch by the mutinous generation that I would have belonged to if I had remained here.

But that was not the only America that greeted me.

We had been met at the airport, in a far less metaphorical and political way, by a member of the staff of the Center for Latin American Studies, which was host to the scholars from Chile. She had driven us around Berkeley to scout out possible housing and then had dropped us off at our hotel. She said goodbye, handing me the keys to the car. It was the Center's, and they would be glad to let me use it for the weekend. I could take my time returning it.

Angélica and I were astonished and even more at the casual way in which the generous offer was made, as if this were the most natural thing in the world, that we should have a car. We didn't have one in Chile, nor an apartment, nor a bed, nor even a refrigerator to call our own. Only a society of enormous affluence and abundance could pass me the car keys just like that, only a society where a car was presumed to be practically a birthright, only such a society could entrust one's car to an unknown person, no questions asked, not even whether I had a license, not even whether I had insurance.

The next day we took the car out for a spin, decided to go shopping at a Montgomery Ward's department store. The only way there, according to the hotel clerk, was by the freeway, so I gritted my teeth and zoomed onto my first interstate, screaming like a child on his first roller coaster, Angélica holding on for dear life, both of us amazed at the mad traffic, the interforking multiple lanes, more girders and cement in a few miles of California highway than you could find in the single solitary cracked road joining Arica, our northernmost city in the far-off desert, to lush Puerto Montt, thousands of miles to the south. And then to discover in that relatively small department store so many more choices of things than in all of Santiago's shops put together, every conceivable object that we might need and many more that we didn't! And there it was, what Rodrigo required: a combination playpen and crib, a little home where he could sleep and keep his toys and which we could carry with us everywhere. Such an extraordinary device, so felicitous in its shape, so convenient in its design, carefully thought out to make our life comfortable—portable, expeditious, unavailable in Chile even if we had had the money, which, of course, we didn't.

Face-to-face with that infinite assortment of cars and blue jeans and supermarkets and brands of soup and baby clothes, face-to-face with the possibility that the simple things my family needed to live were right there, within reach of my pocket, I felt transformed, incredibly, into an adult, merely by virtue of being able to—of all things!—buy what I desired.

Our budget was restricted, of course—and yet, in the days that followed, we managed to fashion for ourselves a life with all the basics, something that America took for granted and that Chile, quite simply, could not. In the months to come, I would flirt with the hippie philosophy that detested the consumerist dream, but Angélica and I remarked that such a countercultural rebellion was conceivable only when the rebels themselves already had life's most essential goodies at their fingertips, took it as their God-given prerogative. Down with the capitalist dream, sure, but meanwhile pass the potato chips, no, not that kind, the ones over there with the honey-barbecue flavor, and while you're at it, make sure Rodrigo's snug in his stroller, which only the multimillionaires in Santiago (or the sons of diplomats!) would have in their homes. I might denounce the way in which that American cornucopia was built upon the deprivation of Third World serfs, but I was not about to deprive myself of those wonders, not after having been reduced for so many years to nibbling candy bars bite by tiny bite, not after having read about Kentucky Fried Chicken in the magazines and being able, now, to stand in front of a real Colonel Sanders and order take-out food that made life so easy and, yes, so dependable and comforting, I was not willing to forgo those small raptures during the short year and a half of my stay.

If the pseudo-ascetic rejection of mass-produced goods had only a marginal attraction for me, the way in which a wide array of young men and women around us in Berkeley were contesting the conventional, repressive, clockwork rationality of contemporary society, the way in which they echoed what millions of others around the world were proclaiming—that the system was bankrupt—the fact that they were not going to wait for somebody else to come from below or from outside to liberate them tomorrow, they intended to start right now, right here, experimenting with their own lives, that movement which insisted on personal freedom as the basis of any change in society, was to have a profound impact on my existence.

When we arrived in Berkeley, Angélica and I considered ourselves extremely revolutionary in our politics, though our lives, the way we lived and the rules we obeyed and our personal aspirations, were relatively conventional and might even be called bourgeois. In spite of our fiery proclamations of a different future, and though our families and most of our friends considered us eccentrically bohemian, the Chilean world we inhabited was staid and placid and boring, our existence had not really extricated itself from the sleepy rhythms of the past, though we were consumers of countercultural artistic products, trends and ideas and fashions and music and books and films trickling in from abroad. And now we were in Berkeley, one of the hippest places on the planet, and from here Santiago, quite frankly, looked like a provincial backwater, a timid, dull city at the farthest edge of the world where, culturally, nothing very exciting ever happened. It is one thing to hum the Sacco and Vanzetti song in Santiago as a record scratches along and quite another to sing, along with Joan Baez in person and ten thousand brothers and sisters, that very song, or for these ears to absorb the sad, hopeful voice of Pete Seeger asking us where have all the flowers gone or these legs to jolt to the Grateful Dead at the Fillmore West or these lips to smoke a joint and pass it on to Country Joe, not to mention the Fish, one, two, three, four, what are you waiting for? It is one thing to read Marcuse in a plush Chilean armchair and a quite different thing to watch his theories come alive in a multitude of young people who, one by one, enact the idea that pleasure can be revolutionary in a society that represses itself, people who, one by one, defy you to act out the same idea if you dare. This was the first time we had ever lived, either of us, away from home, the first time we were free of the constraints of family and jobs and studies and friends and timetables and the-way-things-are-done. As our new American friends invited us into their freewheeling existence with openness and generosity, we felt both truly liberated and truly scared.

Suddenly we were confronted with men and women who were

rebelling against authority in all its forms, daring to question the way everything was structured, from the family to the market to the brain to the rearing of children, asserting their right to do what they wanted with bodies that were not the property of their parents or of their bosses, asserting their right to fuck whom they wanted when they wanted and to insert into those bodies anything that would intensify their rapture and camaraderie. There was no doubt about the danger of what they were attempting but that was part of the magnetism they exerted on me, a terrifying attraction that was enhanced by the playful irreverence with which they were dancing at the edge of the cliff, of themselves, dancing right at the edge of the cliff of history, willing to risk death and self-destruction and radiantly enjoying every moment of it.

During that year and a half, we plunged into that whirlwind, but not so wildly that we were unable eventually to extract ourselves. It may have been the fact that we knew we would be returning to Latin America or that the vision of the bare feet of the millions who could not engage in our games continued to fester in me and spoil the party, or perhaps it was simply Angélica's caution and pragmatism that held me back from going further. She had been able to establish in Berkeley relationships that were much more authentic and challenging and democratic than anything she had ever found in hypocritical, repressed, middle-class Chile, but not even that enchantment made her lose her down-to-earth perspective. She suspected that you could not live permanently like this, on the edge, that our life in Berkeley was artificial and transitory and that it needed to be tested back home, that only when we returned there would we find out what was deep enough in us to survive the clash with our country, which after all was, in its customs, very conservative.

And yet there was a moment, perhaps halfway through our stay in Berkeley, when the idea occurred to both of us—almost simultaneously we looked up from whatever we were doing that day and wondered what if we stayed, what if we did not return? We're happy here, our eyes said to each other, I said to Angélica silently as I watched her blossom and dance, she said to me silently as she watched me so at home with all these gringos who knew who Mickey Mantle was.

If that idea never went beyond a formless, unexpressed hint of a possibility, it was because of two developments, one of them political and the other literary.

If I had discovered that English was still the basis for my identity, maybe, who knows, I might have tried to stay on. In Chile, Spanish had been my companion in travels and travail, the place where I met my friends and loved Angélica and figured out with my Latin American generation who the hell we were and dreamed of changing the world, while English was increasingly relegated to a private conversation I held with myself. In Berkeley, that situation was almost symmetrically reversed: the language which, against all odds and against all logic, I had kept alive in Chile flourished joyously in my everyday Berkeley life while Spanish receded to the secluded desk where I labored over my essays on the contemporary Latin American novel. All the six months it took me to complete the book in Spanish, I could feel English calling to me, promising me that the new energy infused in it by the bubbling vernacular of America would spill over into my fiction. So when I finally finished the essays and packed them off to my editor in Santiago, I sat down to work on my stories, expecting a resplendent renaissance. What stared back at me was a stilted, suffocating, stagnant prose, an excessively bookish English that inhabited some remote rudderless no-man's-land, like a coughing cancerous guest in a Samuel Beckett novel, a relative nobody dares to evict, hoping that he will eventually die on his own. There was only one way to invigorate my English and that was to lay it open to the rambunctious creativity of the language exploding in the streets, in the bedrooms, at the picnics, in the marches, in the discussions of real-life California, lay myself open to my gringo self, my American self. But, instead of that, I said to my typewriter: instead of trying to plunge deeper into English to express my Latin American experience, instead of one more monstrous artificial step, what if I . . . what if I . . . and when the decision came, abruptly, in the middle of a phrase I was writing in English, when that revelation burst into my consciousness, it was not to be denied.

All the energy that these long years had marshaled to constrict my Spanish now manifested itself in a fierce and fanatical determination to banish what had been the love of my life. Repeating more than twenty years later my childhood gesture in that hospital, reacting in Berkeley just as I had back in New York, I drastically broke off relations with the language in which I had sought refuge from solitude all my life, I embraced a tongue that would link me to the community that was imagining a different history for itself and for me, I chose to become a contiguous human being. I told myself, and anybody else who cared to listen, that I would never again write another word in English as long as I lived.

Where was I from?

Sitting at my typewriter in Berkeley, California, that day, precariously balanced between Spanish and English, for the first time perhaps fully aware of how extraordinarily bicultural I was, I did not have the maturity—or the emotional or ideological space, probably not even the vocabulary—to answer that I was a hybrid, part Yankee, part Chilean, a pinch of Jew, a mestizo in search of a center. I was unable to look directly in the face the divergent mystery of who I was, the abyss of being bilingual and binational at a time when everything demanded that we be univocal and immaculate. All around the world, people were dying for their right to bread, housing, dignity, they were dying for the right someday to afford the luxury of asking themselves that sort of question. This was the sixties of extreme nationalism, the all-or-nothing, the either-or sixties. It was not a time for shades of difference, for complexity, for soul-searching about the enigma of heterogeneous identity. You were one thing or you were another, you had to be on this side or on that side of the conflict for the soul and wealth of the world, and the mental maneuvers whereby I had disassociated my love for English from my everyday existence and political options had finally become inoperable. I was not willing to be a young man in between, not knowing his own name, adrift in a world torn by the two Americas inside and outside him. I was not even willing, at that point, to ask myself how the two languages differed, how each of them might complement or oppose each other, the subtle way in which English made me one kind of writer, one kind of person, and Spanish somebody else. The rival languages had been kept separate throughout my life, and now that I was switching again, that is where, more than ever, I wanted them to remain, exiled from one another, supposedly belonging to unconnected and compartamentalized universes, as if the very act of comparing them would force me to accept that I was indeed irremediably dual, that there was a tainted middle ground that they both shared and from whence each language would examine and touch the other, demand to know what changed when I said *se me fue la micro* instead of "I missed the bus," the fact that in Spanish the bus was leaving me blamelessly behind, had gone off on its own, whereas in English . . . But I did not want to know, I did not want to think. I was not ready to look too closely at the way I spoke and wrote the Spanish I was embracing then with such unilateral ferocity, for fear, I suppose, that I would discover the subterranean, contaminated influence of English persisting, flooding my consciousness, judging every word as if it were remote and foreign. But there may be more to my automatic decision not to probe how those languages affected me, because even now, in fact, even now that I swim merrily in them both, the mere attempt to establish where one ends and the other begins and how they overlap causes me acute discomfort, as if I were transgressing a taboo, getting too close to the mysterious center that unifies me in spite of language.

Then it was even more imperative to stay away from any comparisons. I needed to be whole, intact, seamless; that is the way, I told myself, you go into war and survive. That, I told myself, *es lo que mi pueblo necesita*—what my people need from me.

This political realization was the second link holding me to Chile, and it was helped along by my coming to understand, one night in late October of 1968, why the U.S. revolution was doomed to failure, a night when the real limitations of the New Left movement were revealed to me.

Early that morning, I had found myself approaching a picket line that stretched in front of University Hall, where a wonderful class I was attending on late Shakespearean tragedy was supposed to meet. I can't for the life of me remember the occasion for the boycott of classes called by student activists—it was something related to the Free Speech Movement or a Third World Studies Program—but I do remember that I hesitated at the picket line, fully aware that if I honored the strike I could not go to that Shakespeare class I so immensely enjoyed, aware that back in provincial Chile I would regret the loss of that intellectual space of free discussion, and aware also that I would have to quit the karate lessons scheduled for later that day, which I was taking as an exercise in meditation and self-discipline.

My role in the American protest movement had until then been that of spectator, not varying fundamentally since the moment I watched Lyndon Johnson announce on TV that he was not running for reelection. I had cheered then and kept right on cheering later, participating circuitously, encouraging the political action with occasional sideline cries, taking mental notes or filming with my super-8 camera. I grieved over the death of Martin Luther King and repudiated the repression in France and in Prague and in Mexico and the police brutality that greeted so many protests in the United States, but I had been extra-careful to stay out of the way of the security forces.

This seemed to be my fate. In Chile, I had been Argentinian; here, I was Chilean; always the danger of deportation, my foreign passport weighing down on me. So I looked on while heads were broken, sit-ins were disrupted, and damsels in distress were dragged off by the "pigs" (as I uneasily called them, not sure if such linguistic dehumanization, rather than truly describing the enemy, did not end up numbing our own minds). My participation was always surreptitious and oblique, my enthusiasm inevitably dampened by my awareness of the pain that some of the protesters were enduring. It had been easy in the remote safety of Chile to feel good every time I read about a baby-boomer burning his draft card, but here in Berkeley those cards belonged to friends, here in Berkeley those friends were agonizing over a moral quandary that had no easy solution. One decided at the last moment to accept the draft rather than risk jail; another was desperately trying to get into a post-graduate study program he wasn't interested in and couldn't afford; and another one, whom I had met at a march (I loved marching!) came knocking at our apartment one midnight, trying to scramble together some money to help him get to Canada. History was being made right here, right now, and my contribution was to join my voice faintly to the chorus, add one more body to the human wave, fork over some spare change when it was needed.

So that picket line was the first time I was allowed to offer something—minimal, it is true—in expiation, and I virtuously stepped back and went home. When I told Angélica, she said I was a fool—an ethical one, she added, but still a fool. Nobody cared or even knew, for that matter, if I stayed away from class, and by tomorrow the campus would be opened up again anyway. Better to reserve yourself, she said, for more important struggles. But that night my wife said nothing when I told her I was going to check out an open meeting of the striking students, not to worry if I didn't come home till dawn. She understood that I needed to measure whether it had been worth flushing Shakespeare and Japanese martial arts down the toilet.

There were a couple of hundred activists loosely scattered behind a barricade close to Sather Gate, discussing how to react when, the next day, the police came to clear the campus. Should they resist with violence? Or was passive resistance called for? Or no resistance at all? Was there room for negotiation? Were the majority of the students with the movement, or had they turned against it? How to reach out to the blacks in Berkeley and Oakland and bring them into the struggle? And so it went, all night long, five, six, seven hours. Some of those who talked were pissed off because the tactics had not gone far enough, and others were equally pissed off because they had gone much too far, had ended up alienating the liberals, the unions, the professors. There were almost as many groups and factions and fragments of factions as there were people, Socialist Youth and Black Panthers and Trotskyites of different stripes and Communists and SDS representatives and many others I cannot recall, and none of them agreed on anything, except that they were all wary of coordinating their actions with one another, they all feared surrendering their individuality and all were obsessed with how to communicate their message, how to ensure that the cameras picked up what was happening.

I sat to one side, listening carefully, biting my tongue, wanting to stand up and shout at them to look at the enemy and learn that the monster they were fighting was rational and functional and organized and that, with no plan, no strategy, no clear goal, they had no chance whatsoever of winning. These activists, I thought, had fallen into a very American trap, too much in love with themselves and their own righteousness, orchestrating everything for the image it projected, confusing that image with reality, so desperate to become the first revolution to be televised that they ended up serving up photogenic moments that they no longer controlled. I wanted to tell them that fervor and moral superiority were not enough, were never enough. But it would have been useless: they were only mirroring a debate that, nationwide, was tearing the whole movement apart.

I watched them with admiration and sorrow. This was not a revolution. It might have enough strength and integrity to help end the war that the faraway Vietnamese were winning, but it was centuries away, I thought, from taking power. I was aware that my critique of this New Left movement was remarkably similar to how the old American left reacted to this astounding explosion of energy, the generation of the Lincoln Brigade who, like my father, had come of age in the thirties and had managed to survive the repressive fifties and were now confronted by this totally unexpected renewal of social unrest from a quarter they had never even conceived of as potentially revolutionary. My physical age had me sharing with my hippie and SDS and Black Power buddies a generational disgust with authority and an understanding of the role of the media in the shaping of public consciousness, but my mental age made me older, my experience of mass movements, my education by the Allendistas of Chile, made me feel almost like a grandfather to these people born when I was born.

The next day I watched them being routed by the police, I filmed them from the roof of one of the halls and anticipated how their figures would look projected on a wall in Chile. I heard them shout, "We are the people," and from my distance and my parallel desire to become one with the masses, I mourned the disaster that awaited them, I understood that it was make-believe, that they were not the people, that they were pushing themselves to excesses and rage precisely because they were not the people. I understood that they were punishing themselves for not being the heroes of this movie. They were punishing themselves for not being Vietnamese.

These innocent and fearless activists had a surplus of vehemence and ingenuity, decency and courage. What they lacked was something that they could not invent, conjure up from their imagination, no matter how they tried: through no fault of their own, they lacked a working class that could ground their revolution in reality.

As for me, I had the good fortune of coming from Chile, I had inside me the memory of the working poor of my country, I belonged to a movement that had a very different strategy for taking power.

Ever since my arrival, I had been fervent, even ecstatic, about the existence of this contestatory wave of Americans, this vindication of my own opposition to the United States, but the fact that I was growing tired of their egocentric rebellion and its exhibitionistic streak and the unbearable naïveté, meant really that I saw the need to go beyond those infantile tendencies in myself, what I called, rightly or wrongly, the American part of myself, the part that America had always stimulated in me and that, having been given free rein on this visit, practiced to excess, now was ready to submit to the discipline, the purpose, the order, that a real revolutionary movement needs in order to succeed. Listening to the American men and women of my generation ramble on during a whole long night and arrive absolutely nowhere, I felt nostalgia for the place I was lucky enough to call home and its older, more trusted and tried, methods and principles. I was, I discovered, not really American anymore.

And yet, the person who was to return to Chile and its less flamboyant but more effective form of political struggle was not the same person who had arrived in Berkeley. My willing seduction by the ideals of the New Left was obviously helped by the American zone of my existence, the fact that I could identify with its protagonists in ways that Angélica and other Chileans who were on the same exchange program could not even begin to approach; but to reduce this fascination to a mere question of identity is to misinterpret the reasons why that movement in Berkeley proved so compelling and its effects so long-lasting in spite of my misgivings.

The rebellion of enormous numbers of young people all around the world was trying to address issues and problems that the socialist revolutions of the twentieth century, in spite of taking power in myriad large and small countries, had not been able to solve. My SDS comrades had good reason to suspect organizations and hierarchies because the coherent, overly militant Leninist structures that revolutionary parties engendered in order to free humanity had ended up creating monsters in the name of purity and bureaucracies in the name of abolishing the state and repression in the name of liberty and chauvinism in the name of international solidarity.

Those revolutions, in their first phase, when they had just triumphed, had stimulated liberating artistic and sexual and life-style practices, and had ended up, just as invariably—Russia and Cuba came to mind—clamping down on those experiments. Besieged by enemies from the left and from the right, they sacrificed their quest as irrelevant or counterrevolutionary or merely wasteful, and proceeded to militarize society in order to survive. A direct result, I thought, of the circumstance that these revolutions had always come to power in the poorest, least-developed parts of the planet, and had been forced to catch up with their enemies, had to impose discipline (and the resulting solemnity) in order to modernize and capitalize and defend themselves. If power were ever to change hands in a society that was itself rich and developed, then it might be possible to destroy all forms of authority simultaneously, change the ways in which the economy produced goods, along with ways in which the body produced joy, change the human heart along with the human organization of labor.

It was this joining of the personal and the political, the social and the aesthetic, which most appealed to me and to so many members of my generation worldwide, this possibility of bringing together two strands of rebellion that had coexisted uncomfortably for centuries. That this project, toward the end of the tumultuous year of 1968, seemed destined for failure in the European and North American arenas did not invalidate the need to infuse the old revolutionary struggles with the questions and needs of the new movement. I was to be permanently affected by those libertarian and anti-authoritarian and hedonistic urges, by the need to see the revolution as a territory of freedom that could not be forever put off. The New Left also helped confirm me in my anti-Stalinism, my suspicion of bureaucracy, my almost automatic mistrust of the robotic, dogmatic Soviet-inspired practices that the working-class movement I so valued was mired in, though it would only be later that I realized that the very fragmentation and chaos of the U.S. struggle that I so deplored that night in Berkeley was the necessary precondition for a series of social and cultural battles that had been postponed or ignored by the traditional left. There was no place in the revolutionary parties of Chile, or practically every other country, for the questions that feminism and ecology were beginning to ask, no way of fitting the search for new models of sexuality and of aboriginal rights and artistic experimentation into the world as it was conceived by those traditional organizations. I brought many of these questions (though few answers) back with me to Chile. And if at that point in my life I had been forced to choose between addressing them or constructing a society that addressed the scandal of children deprived of milk and workers without jobs and women with legs bloated with veins about to pop because they had borne too many children, if I had to choose between my liberty and the old people who died in ditches with nobody to hold their hand, if it had come down to that choice, then I would have decided, reluctantly, that first came the poor and then the concerns of the more well-to-do, even if I suspected that those concerns, if not attended to, might lead the new society to an impasse which would make it unable to relieve the sorrow and misery all around us. But I returned to a revolution that did not ask me to make that choice, whose originality and wonder was precisely that it stated that it could resolve that contradiction by doing both things at the same time. I came back to a country where I could quote Chairman Mao, who couldn't make it with anyone anyhow, and go on to sing that we all lived in a yellow submarine, sing the stanzas at the top of my lungs in the gardens of the university ripe for revolution.

I brought the modern world back with me, the new United States, when I returned to Chile.

How this new America inside me interfered with my merging with a Chile still slumbering in its stuffy traditions can be best understood in the obstacles, physical and cultural, I encountered on the streets of Santiago when I started jogging.

It was a habit I had picked up among my health-conscious California friends, along with Frisbee and marijuana-spiced brownies. So, not long after we arrived back in Chile, one early morning I put on my fluorescent sneakers.

Angélica raised herself groggily from sleep. "Oh, God. You're not going to jog, are you?"

I grinned, told her to go back to sleep.

"This isn't Berkeley," she said, propping herself up on an elbow. "You're going to run into trouble."

"Las calles pertenecen al pueblo," I answered. "The streets belong to the people."

And off I went to prove my point.

Angélica was able to follow my progress through the neighborhood by the indignant barking of dogs. Neither the dogs nor their owners had ever seen such a spectacle—a lanky, long-legged gringo with glasses and blond hair trotting by their well-to-do houses, disturbing the peace. The streets were for beggars, tramps, the homeless—or placid grandmothers walking toddlers and maids primly off to purchase bread at the corner store; most certainly not for someone to run berserk in outlandish athletic gear.

That was exactly Angélica's point every time I came home from my calisthenic sessions. She was worried (and always was and still is) that I was not *ubicado*—that I was unable to place myself, put myself in the place and the moment as I should, which meant, basically, that I was always doing something outrageous by the rather rigid rules and codes she had learned to live by. Her reaction to my running, sweating, in full public view represented the typical Chilean perspective. Don't show yourself, hide any extravagance, be moderate, don't "expose" who you are. As the days went by, however, and nothing drastic occurred, she seemed to acquiesce in my democratic pounding of the streets, even going so far as to state that she had begun to enjoy following my route by the diminishing or increasing din the dogs made—knowing when I had already headed back.

One morning, if she had listened carefully, she would have heard a different sort of barking.

There was one house in particular with an exceptionally ugly mutt that always gave me a hard time, and I made a point of always passing by that residence, almost as a provocation.

That day, someone had left the gate open on purpose and as I puffed by, the dog leaped out at me, furiously sinking his teeth into my jogging pants. I tried to shake him off, but he wouldn't let go. He snarled and salivated until a man in a bathrobe appeared at the door, calling the loathsome creature off and insulting me for disturbing him, his dog, the peace, his mother, his grandmother, every-body.

As soon as his fanged pet was safely behind the gate, I countered his aspersions with some of my own. I threatened to sue him and his *quiltro*, a disparaging Chilean term for a dog, and he'd better make sure that this was the last time this happened because I would run by there tomorrow at the same time, but this time I'd be carrying a club—which further incensed him. I was the one who should be clubbed, me and my mad foreign habits. It was obscene, he shouted, I remember that word, and how fed up he said he was with foreign-inspired, hippie, Commie attitudes, next time he'd put me on a leash.

And then, all of a sudden, I realized who my adversary was: Chino Urquidi, a crooner who had become popular by peddling, in gushy oversweetened songs, a paradisiacal Chilean countryside. I had been forced to tolerate his falsified folklore on the radio, an endless series of musical postcards in which rural dwellers were faced with unre-quited love as their only problem in life. No ravenous peasants or pesticides in his songs. Or in his political speeches. He had made a run for alderman on a far-right-wing ticket and, having failed to convince the rather stuck-up conservative constituency that his mu-sical talents would serve him well in the filling of potholes, was now engaged in a virulent campaign against Allende. Although he had not yet accused the left of planning to devour the country's children (a Swiftian ploy that had been used against us in 1964), he did warn his listeners that if we won, nobody would have anything to eat at all. Maybe his cur attacked me out of hunger, its master starving it to prepare for the dire days of the socialist victory. If I hadn't been so flustered (and scared), I might have enjoyed the irony of the situation: a man who swore that the United States was the best friend Chile had in the world was offended by an American habit as or-dinary as jogging in the streets, imported by a socialist who pro-claimed that the gringos were exploiting Chile. He rejected me and my jogging shoes in the name of the old Chile he had always lived in and did not want to change; and I rejected him and his fascist hound in the name of the new Chile I hoped to build, to fill with the freedom I had experienced on the glorious streets of Berkeley.

The irony would get even more elaborate, and less funny, when Allende won the elections half a year later: then Chino's conservative life-style and property would be protected by the Yankee country that had taught me as a child to respect the rights of others and stand up for the oppressed. What a travesty. Chino and his anti-democratic allies were going to be coddled, sustained, and rescued by the country that called itself the greatest democracy in the world, that had itself been born out of a rebellion against a foreign power.

To be fair, this suppression of our democratic revolution was facilitated by the East–West conflict. It is true that we were on an entirely different road to socialism than the totalitarian states that ruled half the globe, but they were our allies—without their aid, we had no alternative to the West—and we ended up identified with the behavior of the Soviet Union and the countries it had pressed into a Stalinist, bureaucratic version of socialism. We ended up satanized and imprisoned by proxy in the parameters of the war the two nuclear giants were playing out in the Third World. Just like the Czechs in 1968, we were not given the breathing space we needed to survive by the superpower under whose sphere of influence we fell.

Not that at the time I was worried about this sort of breathing space. Bent on claiming my territorial right to breath and space, the next day I stubbornly jogged by Chino Urquidi's house again and, noting that the dog was chained and the gate locked, decided never to venture near the place on my morning rounds. That was not to be our last encounter, however.

The night Allende won the election, that September 4 of 1970 that I have described as the moment when I realized I had finally come out of my exile, I met Urquidi again.

With a group of Allendista friends, we had gone up to the *barrio alto*, the wealthiest neighborhood of Santiago, to honk our horns at the shuttered windows of our defeated adversaries, to confiscate for one night the streets that had belonged to them and their families forever.

All of a sudden, we saw in the middle of one of Santiago's broadest avenues some thirty to forty people gathered in a circle, apparently celebrating *la victoria*. Or were they holding some sort of soap-box discussion at three in the morning? We got out of our cars to join the fun, and there he was, Chino Urquidi in person, holding forth with all those Allendistas, spouting about democracy and the need to become friends now that the election was over. Everybody around him seemed to be in complete agreement. Yes, one woman said to him, that's it, Chino, let's sing the national anthem, let's all sing together of a new Chile. And the owner of the dog that had assaulted me put the very hand that had opened that gate, he put it on his fascist heart, and opened the very mouth that had denied me the peaceful streets of Santiago and had insulted Allende day after day on the radio, that very crooner started to sing the *Puro Chile*, the *Star-Spangled Banner* of Chile.

He did not get far. Before the others could join in, I jumped like a lunatic into the circle, and pointing a finger in his direction, I addressed all the comrades who were getting ready to join the chorus. "Are you crazy?" I said. "Have you lost your sense of history? *No les da vergüenza?* Aren't you ashamed of yourselves?"

The crowd quieted down and Chino's voice warbled a few more notes before grinding to a halt.

"This man," I continued, and of course my political indignation was inflamed and fanned by my personal vendetta against his mutt, "hates us, has spent the last years attacking everything we believe in. Look at him, he's the enemy. The people who pay him and love him are behind those windows"—and I gestured toward the mansions where, in effect, the owners of Chile were at that moment conspiring to destroy us and our liberation movement, were planning the currency scare which the very next day emptied half the banks in the country—"wondering how to kill us. He smiles now, sings now, but tomorrow he'll be singing for them, preparing our death. Don't go near him, don't even speak to him. Just pray that he leaves Chile and never comes back. *Que no vuelva nunca más.*"

I was met by a round of applause and the militants formed a circle of hands and left Chino Urquidi out of it, I had the immense satisfaction of watching him forlornly watch us dance without him.

Should I have forgiven Chino his past, his dog, his ferocious assaults? Did I make one of those mistakes which, symbolically at least, represent what went wrong with our revolution, our incapacity to reach out to those we disagreed with and build a coalition that was strong and ample enough to really conquer power?

Given that all too soon, just a few days later, that pseudo-folk crooner was back on the airwaves spewing hateful words against us, my assessment of who he was turned out to be prophetic. Though I have always wondered if it was not precisely my sectarian exclusion of his peace offering which set him off on the wrong path, whether similar scenes were not occurring at that very moment all over the country and someone like me was saying to someone like him: We don't need you. I am not sure how many of those others who were rejected as they offered reconciliation and brotherhood that night might, indeed, have been potential allies that we disdained out of misplaced pride, the belief that we could in a few quick years transform centuries of Chilean history without their help.

I certainly did not stop to think about such strategic matters that night of victory, how to tell when to accept the hand of friendship thrust toward us by an adversary and when to revile it as I had just done.

I did not stop to wonder about such dilemmas. Unnecessarily infuriated as I might be against Chino because of our misencounter in front of his house on a Santiago dawn, I was absolutely right about what was happening inside those mansions, the conspiracy that was on its way to denying Allende the Presidency and the people their freedom.

Chino and his cronies were out to kill us.

And I do not mean this metaphorically.

A month and a half later, at the end of October 1970, I switched on the radio and heard the news that General René Schneider had been murdered by an ultra-right-wing commando financed and masterminded by the Central Intelligence Agency, part of wundermensch Kissinger's destabilization plan. As commander in chief of the Chilean Army, Schneider had rejected offers from the conservatives and from the U.S. government to stage a preemptive coup against the triumphant Allende.

The response of the Allende forces was total mobilization, all militants on maximum alert, *todos a defender la revolución,* everyone at the ready to defend the revolution. But not me. I was floating again, useless, empty, rhetorical; for one last time I was adrift, with nowhere to go. So much love of the people, so many inflammatory fists in the face of the Chino Urquidis of Chile, so many incessant revelations about the foundational and transgressive power of the people. And none of it had meant a fundamental change in the way I organized my life.

I could hesitate no longer.

I picked up the phone and called my friend Antonio Skármeta (readers might recognize him as the writer whose novel inspired the prize-winning film *Il Postino*). He had been trying to convince me for months to join the MAPU, a party which had split off from the Christian Democrats and which purportedly combined the discipline of the Communists (without their dogmatic Stalinism) and the freedom of the socialists (without their chaotic factionalism), a young movement that was somewhere between the Old and the New Left, just about where I felt myself to be. Besides, I liked the name: it was an acronym for the Movimiento de Acción Popular Unitaria and also the Mapuche Indian word for *land.* Another way of making myself appear more authentic and indigenous than I could ever really be.

I told Antonio: *Aquí estoy. Espero órdenes.* Here I am, awaiting orders. A soldier of *la revolución.*

Thinking to myself with melodramatic seriousness: ready to die, so death will not rule over us.

Antonio told me to wait for instructions. And as I hung up the phone, the same phone on which I had heard Jorge Ahumada six years before tell me that I could under no circumstance participate in Chilean politics, I knew that I had crossed into a dimension from which there was no return, that I had conquered the fear of changing myself and was finally ready for the jubilant adventure of changing the world.

It is true that at that point I did not, and would not until the coup, really comprehend what death meant. But I did understand that a war is carried on with soldiers. Soldier: *miles, militis* in Latin, the origin of militant, a soldier of the revolution, somebody who defines his life not by the cultivation of the self but by the willingness to give that self up for the common good.

Where are you from?

More than half a century before, my grandparents had crossed the ocean in search of a land of equality and justice where their children could live in peace. Those children, my parents, had been forced into exile and the link had been broken. And now, after a lifetime of vacillation, I was finally ready to reconnect to that dream of my immigrant ancestors, make this place my home, fight for it.

Strange that it should be the America of the North which I had just severed ties with that would thwart my decision to return to the America of the South which my grandparents had chosen as their New World. Strange that at the very moment when I was reinventing myself as a pioneer for whom what matters is the future and not the accident of birth or landscape, on the other side of the hemisphere Richard Nixon, the President of a land settled by pioneers, a man whose power derived, as Allende's did, from the free votes of his people, was meeting with his security advisors and with the heads of ITT, planning the death of the Chilean democratic revolution.

Many years before, as an aide to Senator Joseph McCarthy, Nixon had been instrumental in my family's flight from the United States. Now he would cause me to lose the country we had escaped to, he would cause me to lose my country for a second time.

But not before we put up one hell of a fight.

FIFTEEN

A Chapter Dealing with the
Discovery of Death Inside
and Outside an Embassy in
Santiago de Chile in
Early November of 1973

The woman from the United Nations clears her throat, barely throws a glance at me sitting across from her at a resplendent antique table in the Argentine Embassy, and proceeds to read from the UN statute of 1951. A refugee, she drones, is any person who, "owing to well-found fear of being persecuted for reasons of race, nationality, membership of a particular group or political opinion, is outside the country of his nationality and is unable or, owing to such fear, is unwilling to avail himself of the protection of that country."

She looks up briefly. "Is that understood?"

I nod, saying nothing. What is there to understand?

"What I'm asking"—she enunciates each word in Spanish as if explaining something to a baby, just today she had read the same paragraph to others in this embassy, she has made a career out of reading it out loud—"what I need to know is if you intend to avail yourself of refugee status."

Again, a split second to decide. Not who I am, but who I intend to be. Undoubtedly I was that person, I had that fear, the country that did not want to give me a passport or a safe-conduct was Chile. The woman from the UN dryly delineates the advantages of being a refugee: training and job placement, language courses in the country of asylum, preferred housing, free medical attention, social security, no need to renew visa approval each year from the local immigration authorities. Well?

I hear myself saying no, I see the surprise in the woman as her head startles upward and, for the first time, she looks at me as if I were somebody different, somebody distinct, somebody real.

Perhaps that is why I have refused to be classified as a refugee: so that people like her, so people in the outside world, will recognize me as an individual and not part of the helpless masses that flood the newsreels and the TV screens and appear in photos in far too many books and newspapers, overwhelmed by forces outside their control that they do not seem to comprehend. Inside me, milling around inside, are the Jews during and after Hitler, the Palestinians that those Jews displaced, the endless straggling lines from Pakistan and Biafra and Southeast Asia moving across frontiers and rivers and time, holding on to their suffering as if it were their only identity, their sole weapon. When the woman from the UN had said the word *refugee*, that is what came to mind: the camps in which people without a country stagnate amid the filth and the flies.

I knew, of course, that Chilean refugees would not be sent to camps. But having just denied myself history as heroism by seeking asylum in this embassy, I was now being offered a future in history as a victim. Now that I had escaped the physical danger of death, this was the more permanent face of our defeat: to have one's life decided by other people. The humiliation of those long weeks in the embassy had marked me: we did not trust these functionaries who reigned over us and yet we depended on them for our food, our safety, our contact with the outside world. They could resell part of that food, and did, they could delay our departure, and did, they could block messages from our relatives and did; they did, they could, and we could not and did not dare to complain. Understand: I was living in utter destitution in that embassy, as if I had just crossed a border to escape a famine.

Yes, that definition of refugee might fit me perfectly; but I did not fit snugly into its image, the self it suggested I was to become. It is true that my existence had been swept up in a historic catastrophe which differed only in degree from those that had uprooted and would continue to dislocate millions of others in this miserable century of ours; yes, but I had the means, no matter how slight, to rescue a certain control—or was it the illusion of control?—over my existence, over my self-image.

"I'm not a refugee," I said to the woman, aware of the hundreds like me waiting their turn in the next room, right there, behind me, waiting to be accepted by Holland or Ireland or the Soviet Union or . . . anywhere. I blurted out: "I'm an exile."

The term had no legal significance, no international or technical meaning, no guarantees, no protection.

I chose it automatically because I wanted to see my emigration as part of another tradition—a more literary one, perhaps. There was something Byronic, defiant and challenging, about being an exile, something vastly more romantic and Promethean than the fate embodied in that recently coined word *refugee* that the twentieth century had been forced to officialize as a result of so much mass murder and wandering. I was, of course, just as much a victim, just as doomed, as the blurred constellation of anonymous beings who had preceded me, but by rejecting the passive term and opting for the more active, sophisticated, elegant one, I was projecting my odyssey as something that originated in myself and not in the historical forces seething outside my grasp. Instead of formulating my future in terms of what I was seeking, refuge, I conceived myself as ex-cluded, ex-pelled, ex-iled, as if I had absolute freedom to choose which of the many countries of the world my free person would wander. Not for me to be a speck in the dust of history, a statistic in a yearbook: I was going off into the wilderness like a rebellious, solitary, persecuted angel.

I could already sense what lay ahead, years of pleading, jobs offered to me out of pity, customs officials ripping through my bags, I was anticipating that the list of friends tortured back in Santiago would grow while the space to defend them in the newspapers would shrink into indifference, I was sensing many more defeats before me, and I chose to salvage the one thing that could guarantee me safe passage through the desert I was facing: that I was my own person, that I would rise up, that I did not need any help from anybody to survive. I had spent so much energy demolishing and denouncing the myth of individualism in books and articles and here I was, clutching on to it as the one element of stability in a world that was disintegrating. It did not dawn on me then that, having taken pride in my proximity to the poor, having found peace when I might have been killed just like them in that shack in that working-class neighborhood, I had, nevertheless, at the first opportunity, set my egalitarian convictions aside, refusing to be classified with my homeless brothers and sisters abroad. I had chosen instinctively to exploit my difference, thank-fully reached out for the first jetsam that washed up from my per-sonality, tried to set myself mentally apart from the multitudes I had sworn to fuse with forever.

The death which had brought me so close to them was already beginning to drive a wedge between us, whispering that in order to avoid its grasp, I would start to float away.

It is not something I am aware of at the time.

On the contrary. In the embassy, every day, I renew my pledge to serve the Chile of the workers that is being assailed by forces considerably more dangerous than my self-doubts and equivocations.

No, not the obvious repression of the military, but a more perverse sort of peril that I begin to brood about at that time. At the end of my UN interview, as I am about to get up from the table, I am approached by another UN official, who surreptitiously slips me a note. It is from Angélica, the first direct communication I have had from her in weeks. She writes that, before leaving Chile with Rodrigo and my parents to wait for me in Argentina, she will try to pass in front of the embassy to say goodbye.

To say goodbye, in a manner of speaking.

Relatives of those of us confined in the embassy have discovered that they can be sighted by their loved ones if they take a *paseo*, a stroll, on the sidewalk across the street from the building that shelters us, and these sightings constitute one of the ways to pass the time during the endless days, hundreds of us honeycombed like bees at the window watching for hours to catch a faraway glimpse of a friend, a member of the family, even an acquaintance fleeting by. I say we and us, but I had not joined the exercise: it was too depressing to scrutinize the country I had lost.

Now I join the other refugees in the hope of spotting Angélica and I'm finally rewarded by a brief flash of her presence, with Rodrigo ambling along in tow. He does not look toward the window. I pray that he might, but he has not been told by his mother that his father is behind those walls which the police and the Pinochet spies guard; no sign must be given that those who walk out there are related to the castaways who watch from in here. The relatives never stop, never acknowledge who they are—only a slight movement of Angélica's hips now, a smile that lightens the air in my direction, and she is gone. A few minutes later she is back again, tugging at Rodrigo, I can see that he is complaining about something, probably the fact that they are plodding back and forth along this desultory avenue; and now they are out of sight and I wait a while longer and it is clear that they will not return, that I have just said goodbye to my family for who knows how long. I cede my place at the enormous curtained windows to someone else, one who has made relative-spotting a vocation.

I try not to look out those windows again.

During the days when I stood there waiting for Angélica's brief passage, I was visited by a vision of Chile that was too painful to contemplate. Hundreds of people walk by the embassy every hour. It is impossible to know who is there as part of a ceremony that secretly contacts us and who is there simply in an ordinary way, going about their lives, but that is precisely the point: life out there in the city flows on as if nothing had happened. In order to survive, those who care for us and mourn for our violated nation must imitate the many who do not care at all, who mourn nothing or who have mourned their share and now want to go on with whatever life is left to them. There at the window, I have a vision of a tribe of zombies sleepwalking past the embassy, my seminal glimpse of the Chile where I myself cannot walk but where, if I were free to do so, I would also walk in the same inhibited, detached way; I have seen Chile as a country of the dead, where you have to kill yourself in order not to be killed, split yourself in two, smother whoever you have been, create an outer shell of indifference to match the other shells around you. I have seen that Chile and I wonder how long people can live this madness before the outside person you pretend to be implodes, before the mask becomes the face, before the country is corrupted and lost.

It will be brief, I say to myself, I lie to myself as I turn from the window, we will be back soon and they will remain pure under their simulated lives. I turn from that window and the vision of my child who is not even able to wave to his father, my Angélica who can do no more than smile in my direction and then disappear, I turn from that Chile because I do not want to admit that it is not only people who can die, but countries as well, I do not want to tell myself that a country can also die.

SIXTEEN

A CHAPTER DEALING WITH THE
DISCOVERY OF LIFE AND LANGUAGE
DURING THE YEARS 1970 TO 1973,
IN SANTIAGO DE CHILE

In front of me as I write, staring straight at me, is a photograph of the balcony of the palace of La Moneda in Santiago. The Chilean photographer Luis Poirot snapped it on November 4, 1970, the day Salvador Allende was inaugurated President of the Republic. In that photo, he waves a handkerchief from the balcony, greeting an unseen crowd that is gathered in the plaza below him. Behind the President is his wife, Tencha, and we can catch a glimpse of the goateed, mischievous face of José Toha, a Minister in Allende's government.

Next to that photo I have hung another one, of the same balcony, snapped by the same photographer almost three years later, a few days after the Hawker Hunters attacked the Palace on September 11, 1973. Their bombs left a black yawning gap where the balcony stood. Where the President once waved his handkerchief, there is nothing. Allende is dead, Tencha is in exile, Tohá is in prison, where he will be killed by guards some months later. And we can sense that outside the frame, below where the balcony jutted out, there is only emptiness, that only the cold, implacable solitary lens of the camera witnesses the scene. Nothing else. All too soon, I will be forced to face the black hole of that photo.

For now, I want to return to the day when that balcony was as intact as our dreams, when these eyes of mine and all the thousands of other eyes in the crowd did not have an inkling of the destruction that awaited us. There was no room for absurd premonitions: this was a turning point in history, the first peaceful, democratic revolution the world had ever known. Who could stop us? Who would dare to even try?

It was then, in the midst of that multitude of men and women I had never met and did not know, it was then, as I breathed in the air that they were breathing out, that I had an experience which I hesitate to call mystical but which was as near to a religious epiphany as I have had in my life.

Allende was making a brief speech, something about how we were now going to be the masters of our own destiny, the owners of our own land and the metals under the ground and the streets we walked through, how we would have to fight for the possession of everything in Chile, from the state to the city to the fields, how this country belonged to the people who had suffered in it, something like that, I can't remember the details, but at some point during that speech I stopped listening and let my eyes wander over the crowd, thousands and thousands of hopeful faces as far as I could see, and all of a sudden I knew what my mission was to be in the years to come. These men and women who held my destiny in their hands might be an absolute mystery to me but they were also, I realized, a mystery to themselves. The story of their lives had never been told, the words had belonged to somebody else. That was going to change. I could almost feel their stories struggling to come out, spill into that plaza, right then and there. Since their birth, those men and women had been told the limits they could not cross, the questions they could not ask. They had been told that their failure in life was deserved, that the very fact that they had not found a way out of their destitution proved that they deserved it, that they were by nature subhuman, incompetent, inferior, worthless, lazy, all their lives treated like something disposable and defective, all their lives taught to bow their heads and lower their eyes so as to survive, warned to obey or else, the doctrine of submission drilled into every nerve of their bodies, taught that the only road out of their misery was individual and solitary, each person scratching his way to the top, where, if he was lucky or ruthless enough, he could then become the exploiter of his brothers. But above all, they had been warned that any collective attempt to change their lot was doomed to failure and pain. And they had defied that warning, they were about to break out of the script dreamt for them, they were about to start telling their own lives in their own way after having lived endlessly under the shadow of somebody else's story. And if they could do it, so could I, so could I, and then it was as if I had stepped out of that space and inhabited some other zone where I could watch myself and the multitude as well, suddenly all the voices went silent and in the silence I felt reality begin to crack open, literally, under my feet, as if a real, physical crack had opened in the very architecture of the universe, and that was when, peering into the crack that my own life had become, immensely vulnerable and open, I felt life quicken and accelerate, I felt the giddiness of those few great moments in your existence when you know that everything is possible, that anything is possible. I felt as if I were the first man on earth and this was the first day in history and the world was about to begin in all its beauty and that all it would take to give birth to that beauty which was just within our reach was to dare to invent it, dare to name it, and I believed for one transparent moment that I could merge with *el pueblo*, I believed that their story and my story could be told simultaneously, I believed that a time would come when no distance would separate us, when our stories would be the same story.

It was a magnificent vision and I kept it inside me all during the Chilean revolution, it was so intense that even now, more than twenty-five years later, I am able to commune with it. Even though, as soon as the crowd dissolved and we began to celebrate the new age that was dawning, each in his own way, as soon as I was back in my middle-class house with my books and my records and my manuscripts and my obsessions and memories of a pampered existence, as soon as I returned to who I was, an intellectual educated in traditions and tastes and codes that most of the people in that plaza did not have access to, as soon as all the breaches and disparities that divided us came roaring back into my elite existence, I realized that I had given myself an impossible, utopian goal.

And yet pursue it I did, with an energy that amazed me then and that amazes me even more now. If I could not immediately fuse with the people, if their story and my story were still on separate tracks, I could, at least, help create the space that would allow their stories to emerge, work as a citizen and a militant so that the resources and education available to someone like me could become available to them. And, of course, I wasn't going to wait for that breakthrough: liberated from the foreign, English-language realm in which I had secluded myself for so long, I started to make up for the time I had wasted by letting Spanish flow out of me as if I were a river.

Everything was new and crying out to be written and I shared a glorious language with the people who were writing the text of reality itself and I wanted to put every last word of it down on paper.

I wrote essays and screenplays and poems and magazine articles and television programs and pamphlets and newspaper ads and radio jingles and political slogans and propaganda tracts and an experimental novel and cultural policy reports and political diatribes and songs and plays, all of them juxtaposed, all of them given equal attention in my life. A typical day might see me rise at dawn and frenetically type a surrealistic short story, take Rodrigo to school, teach a class at the university, burst into my office to scribble part of an essay at noon, then lunch with the producer of a quiz show for adolescents I was hosting on TV, rush off to a powdered-milk factory whose workers had called for volunteers to help load and unload trucks, run back all sweaty to the center of town to collaborate with some writers who were issuing a cultural manifesto, talk over the phone with a colleague at the university about the possibility of our Spanish Department joining forces with a trade union to launch a poetry festival, and then, as the afternoon began to wane, meet with a Party committee that was deciding what political slogan we would issue, to be painted by the brigades, and then that night, after a quick dinner with Angélica, who had been through an equally hectic schedule, and after a good-night story to my son, my wife and I would join our group of comrades to splash the walls of the city with the very message I myself had conjured up a few hours before. And then, if there was time and energy—and there was, there always was—off we'd go to somebody's house to dance and drink and celebrate the fact that we were alive.

They were the best years of my life.

Ever since I could remember, perhaps since that hospital in Manhattan, perhaps before, a vague heartache of guilt had been gnawing away at me, dripping into me like a deformed twin who whispered that I was to blame, always to blame for whatever was wrong, that I could never do enough to make things right. Those years were like a balm: day by day the revolution cleansed the slow cesspool of my shame and taught me to forgive myself. And if it had allowed me to drain my remorse, there was nothing that I thought the revolution could not do. Just as it taught us to tolerate those with whom we disagreed, it would teach me to tolerate my own dissonant voices inside. Just as it would resolve the contradictions of our misdeveloped society and modernize Chile without using force and establish social harmony without hurting anyone and purge the country of its past, so it would allow me painlessly to change into someone new, liberate me from all the quandaries that had plagued me.

If this identification of my own person with the revolution, my belief that what I imagined was real or could become so, might in retrospect be judged as a sign that I had gone slightly mad and was unable to distinguish between what was and was not possible, it was out of that same madness, my incapacity to detach my imagination from reality, my insistence that everything was simultaneously social and aesthetic, it was out of enthusiasm for a society that could be prefigured as if it were a work of art, that I wrote a book which was to transcend its moment of creation and withstand the test of time and is still read around the world, a book which, significantly, was both an extremely personal form of self-expression and, at the same time, was conceived as a very practical means of contributing to the possibility that millions of other Chileans could defeat silence.

The book in which I confused my own journey with the epic journey of discovery of the people of Chile came as an answer to a question about culture that had been vexing me for several years before Allende won the Presidency.

Our left-wing strategy to attain economic independence and achieve self-sufficiency did not take into account, I felt, that there was another sort of wealth that was dominated from abroad, equally as one-sided as the copper-mining operations that were in gringo hands. Just as we imported most of our advanced technology from abroad, just as we had never developed our own cars or our own detergents or our own electronics, we also were massively subservient to foreign films, TV series, soap operas, comics, songs, advertisements, cultural products that originated for the most part in the United States or, when they were produced nationally, were based on American models. These mass-media messages explained Chile's powerlessness as much as our lack of command over the foreign-owned telephone companies did. It was in those imported stories that our citizens learned to dream their lives in ways that eliminated confrontation, penalized rebellion, ridiculed solidarity, caricatured critical thought, and reduced all social conflicts to easily resolved psychological dilemmas.

Before 1970, my worries about this form of cultural domination had been primarily theoretical, developed in a couple of university seminars that analyzed comics and TV serials through methods borrowed from literary criticism. There was not much that could be done, beyond this critical examination, to modify those messages, which were owned and distributed by large corporations tailoring their productions to profit-making.

With Allende's victory, the situation changed drastically: what had been my speculative university elaborations were transformed into urgent questions of policy and strategy. For the first time in the history of Chile, the rebellious forces of the left had at their disposal massive-media outlets, radio, TV channels, recording studios, film companies, publishing enterprises which had previously been in private hands, churning out messages that predisposed the Chilean public to see the explosive changes besetting their lives as threatening rather than liberating.

Who was going to tell the story of Chile? Who was going to narrate us?

Those questions were going to be decided not only in the battle for information (the CIA was pouring millions into the right-wing media) but in the battle for the entertainment of Chile. We needed to create forms of massive popular art to accompany the marginal, alternative stories people were beginning to tell themselves and each other about their lives.

The problem was that hardly anybody in the government (or anywhere else, for that matter) knew how to go about making those major changes. Previous socialist experiences with the media were useless: all those violent revolutions had simply expropriated the organs of communication and turned them into humorless, boring, gray propaganda machines. A monopolistic solution that, given our commitment to freedom of expression, was impossible but also, we thought, counterproductive. Pluralism was not, for us, a mere tactic but a strategic option: the liberty of our adversaries to produce their own stories was something not merely to be tolerated but to be welcomed. The presence of messages from our enemies in the marketplace would force us to be creative rather than repressive, to compete against them with better ideas, more participatory forms of popular amusement, riskier and more transgressive stories. It was a chance to bring into the media a flood of people who worked in culture and had spent most of their lives writing and painting and singing and thinking for a reduced circle of select spirits.

Because I happened to be one of the few intellectuals in the country to have studied a wide variety of popular artistic media genres, I was asked in early 1971 to work as a consultant in a number of different enterprises which had begun to produce alternative TV dramas and comics and youth magazines and a panoply of other diversions. As soon as I started, I realized that it is easier to challenge cultural domination in university essays than to alter it in the day-to-day reality of the media. I had already written a piece on neo-colonialism as reflected in Babar the elephant, analyzing the inner workings of children's literature, but it was an entirely different matter to create a magazine for kids—or for adolescents, for that matter. Our audience had been bred on superheroes and sob stories and intrigue, but we had no clear idea why these forms of entertainment were so appealing. In fact, there were thousands of studies about the manner in which an empire controls economic resources or influences political or military decisions, but there were hardly any which probed how stories from abroad subliminally and covertly indoctrinate millions of consumers without anyone realizing what is being done.

It was the innocence with which these products presented themselves that seemed to be the key. If I could examine the hidden political agenda inscribed in one exemplary and apparently innocuous case, I might be able to denounce that cultural penetration and also take a significant step toward understanding, and therefore perhaps changing, the media messages we were importing from abroad. The victim of my attention had to be both exceedingly popular and obviously apolitical. I soon stumbled upon one of the most beloved fictional characters of the twentieth century. He inhabited a comic book made in America that sold more copies in Chile in one month than all the stories we had produced locally in our 160 years as an independent nation. He was an old friend of mine, whom I may have met in the hospital in Manhattan at two and a half or who may even have been introduced to me before that, in my native Argentina. He had delighted me and countless other children and adults with his irate, squawking, unfortunate, and ultimately benign existence: I ended up investigating Donald Duck.

For this project, I teamed up with an expert on mass communications, a Belgian sociologist named Armand Mattelart, who had settled in Chile and was an ardent supporter of the Allende experiment. Together, during a feverish ten days at the beach in mid-1971, we produced what was to be for many years my most notorious book, *How to Read Donald Duck*, a close reading of hundreds of Disney comics from a Third World perspective.

Unexpectedly, the book became an instant best-seller in Chile, denounced bitterly by the right and hailed ecstatically by many on the left (though not by the Communists, who were extremely suspicious of any book that emphasized cultural struggle as essential to the success of the revolution). The fact that it would later sell millions of copies around the world and be translated into over a dozen languages indicates that our "manual of decolonization," as John Berger later called it,* touched a raw nerve in inummerable readers. But the enduring popularity of the book cannot be solely traced, I believe, to its having been the first text to address the issue of how to confront America's culture industry as it expanded prodigiously across the globe. Its impact must also be attributed to the style of the book: wildly playful and original, lyrical and defiant, it broke out of the dry academic language, the abstruse sociological terms in which these sort of treatises were supposed to be couched. Just like Chile itself, it was full of life, and, in fact, behind its insolent style, you could hear, you can still hear if you lis-

---

*From John Berger's review of the English-language edition of a few years later.

ten closely, the Chile of the revolution marching fearlessly on the Gates of Heaven (or of Hell), you can hear Chile inspiring us to go ever further, egging us on to bite the mental and emotional hand that feeds us. *How to Read Donald Duck* can be interpreted, therefore, as one of the ways in which the nation of Chile declared its national independence of foreign influence, its desire to think for itself. But that book, and a series of other essays that I wrote by myself at that time, which were eventually to become *The Empire's Old Clothes*, can also be read as a declaration of another sort of independence.

It cannot be an accident that the first book written about U.S. cultural imperialism should have been created by a man who had himself been seduced by that country as a child, who had spent his adolescence yearning for that land and dancing to its sweet melodies, who had struggled as a young adult to make sense of the American part of his life and the English in which it was embedded. Or that I should have sought a foreigner as a partner in this venture, someone who, like me, had been so fascinated by Chile as to end up making it his home. Both of us from abroad, trying to inoculate our adopted land against the perils of what we had once adored.

As a child of seven, when I had preferred my parents to my flag, I had been able to live with the ensuing crisis of who I was by separating American politics and the transitory U.S. governments from what I understood to be the true and eternal America expressed in its popular culture, I could fear one while enjoying the other, I could be as American as apple pie (and Mickey Mouse) and yet remain a member of a family persecuted by other Americans. This insulation of U.S. popular culture from criticism had persisted in me all through the fifties and the sixties, but now, after having cut loose in Berkeley from the language in which I had, all through my life, communed with that American identity, I was ready for one more step in the process, a final one, I thought at the time: an intellectual assault on the cultural core of the boy I used to be by the political consciousness of the man I had become.

Trying to reverse completely and radically the decision I had made as a toddler in that Manhattan hospital.

Trying to do to America what America had done to my Latino origins.

So, if the book on Donald Duck can and should be seen as an answer by two left-wing intellectuals to the very concrete and collective historical dilemmas posed by a revolution, it can also be understood as the culmination of my own very personal journey into Latin America, the ritual and public purging of my last links to the United States. That is the secret origin, I believe, of the book's vitality, of the sense of danger and excitement that jumps out at the reader: I am there, seated in a chair in a Chilean beach house, banging away at the typewriter, while Armand paces up and down, and I know that with each word I am breaching a boundary, I am committing a transgression, I am breaking a taboo, I am killing the country that fathered me, I am finally daring to confront the America inside me and bring it into the light of day and burn it at the public stake. Engaging, in fact, in that most North American of ceremonies, dreaming of burying the past and starting over with a clean slate.

I am, undoubtedly, like Chile, like Latin America at the time, going too far.

In my pursuit of purity and national autonomy, in my desire for a rebellious Chile that would totally expel the American part of me with the same fury with which it was trying to eradicate American influence from the country's economy, I have exaggerated the villainy of the United States and the nobleness of Chile, I have not been true to the complexity of cultural interchange, the fact that not all mass-media products absorbed from abroad are negative and not everything we produce at home is inspiring. And I have projected my own childhood experience with America onto Chile and the Third World, assuming that because I had been so easily seduced, so willingly ravished and impregnated, millions of people in faraway lands are empty, innocent, vessels into which the Empire passively pours its song, instead of tangled, hybrid, wily creatures ready to appropriate and despoil the messages that come their way, relocate their meaning, reclaim them as their own by changing their significance.

But these are forms of resistance that I was only to learn in the years ahead. At that point I was not engaged in a dialogue with the United States, as I am now, not searching for a space inside the system from which to perturb that system. I was looking for a divorce, trying to settle accounts with an old lover.

Throughout the sixties, I had been ashamed of my previous infatuation with America, I had tried to hide it, make believe it had never existed. And now, all of a sudden, that liaison had become valuable, indispensable to free the *patria* in its hour of need. It had a meaning, it all fit into place: that is why I had gone to the States, that is why I had fallen in love with America. So that many years later I could discern and dissect the risks of that love affair, warn my new compatriots not to follow my path. So that they could reject now what I had been unable to reject back then as a child.

It is paradoxical that it should have been my penetrating and intimate knowledge of the United States that would finally allow most of my compatriots and many other people around the world to identify me as a Chilean writer, that I should have become a spokesperson for the poor of Latin America because I had spent so many years in the rich North. And what may be even more paradoxical is that the book that would moor me so successfully to the country would be one of the chief causes of my exile. My attack on Disney turned me into an object of hatred for thousands of indignant Chilean fans. Portly grandmothers frothing at the mouth tried on several occasions to run me over with their cars, and one night our bungalow in Santiago was stoned by irate mobs of children and their parents holding up placards and shouting at the top of their lungs, *"Viva el Pato Donald!"* What those defenders of the honor of Donald Duck were unable to do to me while Allende was President became more than possible as soon as the coup turned the tables and thousands of copies of the latest edition of our book on Disney were thrown into the harbor of Valparaiso. That Duck of ours couldn't breathe underwater and I wouldn't be able to either if they caught me and decided to submerge my head in shit. I could see a sarcastic captain grabbing me by the hair, lifting my head up and telling me that he had a little boy who loved Goofy and would I care to explain now, man to man, what I found so objectionable about that Disney character?

I did not anticipate anything of this sort while I was researching and writing *How to Read Donald Duck*. I simply scribbled away and relished being able to put into real literary practice the cannibalization theory of Latin American identity that I had embraced in the sixties: Disney had tried to eat me up as a child in New York, now I was eating him up as an adult in Chile, sending him his duck well roasted and his mice chopped up for good measure.

Listen to me back then in the early revolutionary seventies, listen to the arrogance in my voice. Listen to the delusion in my voice.

We were going to eat up Disney?

In my world of metaphors, in the multiple copies of our Donald Duck critique that circulated in Chile and elsewhere, perhaps. But in the real world, the corporation that bears his name has ended up by gobbling up the globe, has ended up as one of the most powerful entertainment conglomerates on this planet, and I am here alone with my memories, far from my country, remembering my dead, trying to grapple with the dilemma of how to stay loyal to that young man who stood under the balcony that day the revolution started, how to hold on to the vision he had as he looked over the plaza and witnessed the birth of a new nation.

It is a problem that has pursued me since my last day in Chile, since the day in early December when an official of the Argentine Embassy informed me that the Junta, after weeks of denying me the right to leave Chile, had finally approved my safe-conduct; tomorrow I was going to be expelled from the country, I was being allowed to travel to Argentina.

The next morning I found myself speeding down the Alameda in a police van headed for the airport with several other refugees. Outside, just outside my reach, was the bustling traffic of Santiago, people going off to work, clustering onto the *micros*, oblivious of the fact that so close to them a group of their countrymen was leaving them for who knows how many years, that in a few more hours we would not be able to breathe that air, see that cordillera. "Hold on to this memory," I said to myself with what I now recognize was excessive melodrama, exaggerated sentimentality. *"Llénate de Chile. Fill yourself with Chile."*

It was then that, on impulse, I turned to the Argentine diplomat who had come along for our protection. "Do you think you could ask them to pass by La Moneda? It's only a short detour."

It was the sort of suggestion you make to your taxi driver, not the police escort that is about to kick you out of your country, but the diplomat decided, as if it was the last request of a dying man, to do me that favor. He ordered the car to swing by La Moneda.

I had come back to that balcony as if it had been calling me. Three years before, it had represented hope, and two months ago, when I had passed by La Moneda a few days after the coup, the day when I had decided not to kill the sleeping soldier, it had overwhelmed me with a rage I was hardly able to contain.

Now, catching a fleeting glimpse of that ravaged balcony from behind the grilled crisscrossed wire of the police-van window, about to be deported, suspended between a country that was already receding and a foreign world that had not yet materialized, I knew that I was being challenged.

The emptiness of that balcony drilled itself into me as we passed through the plaza and turned the corner, and then it was gone from view, it was behind us, out of sight, but I could feel it growing inside me, its darkness threatening to engulf me in its void, to erase us all forever from the memory of Chile just as it had extirpated the presence of Allende, left nothing of that day when he had stood there defiantly, inaugurating the future. I fought back against the black hole that was sucking me into despair, I told myself that I would keep alive that other balcony, that if we could keep it fiercely alive and warm inside during the years to come, we would be able to return Chile to all its glory, we could ourselves return to the country we would resurrect.

Remaining loyal to the past would prove an almost impossible task, a task that continues to challenge me more than twenty years later, which I am still grappling with here, on the other side of the hemisphere, as I watch the two photographs of that balcony, side by side in my study in North Carolina, as they watch me, the luminous past and the threatening present.

They ask me now, as they began to ask me then, at the moment when I swore that I would not allow one to swallow the other, what is perhaps the most painful political question of my life: If that past was so luminous and promising and participatory, how is it that it became the black hole of the present? How did one balcony turn into the other? That second photo, that second balcony, its absence, interrogates our failure, interrogates our lack of vision, demands to know how we could have been so wrong that day we started our revolution, how we could have been so blind not only to the impending disaster but blind as well to the mistakes we made, which, all that time, were paving the way for that disaster.

It was not a question that would go away, it demanded a collective answer from all Chileans who had supported Allende as well as an individual answer from each of us. That black hole devouring us would not disappear by stubbornly and nostalgically reiterating and validating the past, because that past was responsible for this future we were living, and until we recognized that responsibility, our responsibility in the catastrophe, there would be no change. We could blame the CIA, the United States, the oligarchy, the military, all we wanted, but they would never have prevailed if we had been able to get the majority of Chileans behind our reforms. That had not been the case, however, and unless we now built the vast coalition that we had failed to build during the Allende years we would never rid ourselves of Pinochet; he would stay in power as long as the past continued to divide us.

How this extraordinarily complex political task was accomplished, how we created a vast front that ended up ousting the General from power and bringing back the democracy that we had not been wise and mature enough to protect is certainly not the subject of this book. But its difficulty must be at least addressed; otherwise, the true dilemma of that young man speeding toward exile in a police van cannot be understood.

Let me make this as concrete as possible, this need that inevitably awaited me to scrutinize the past for mistakes.

For the very people who should have been our allies then and were indispensable as allies against Pinochet in the years to come, for the people we had to convince to join us against Pinochet, the past that I remembered as glorious and enthralling was perceived as painful and traumatic.

No better way to illustrate this dichotomy than to focus on someone who had been unjustly hurt by the Unidad Popular, someone I recalled with regret many times in exile: Don Patricio, a friend and neighbor of ours in Santiago and the father of Rodrigo's favorite playmate. A calm, decent, quiet man, a progressive Christian-Democrat who had worked as an accountant in the government center for the distribution of flour, he had been more than willing, he told me several times over afternoon tea, to contribute to the change in Chile that Allende had inaugurated, even if he did feel himself to be in the opposition. But Don Patricio had been shunted aside, humiliated, left at his desk with no work to do for months, discriminated against merely because he was not an Allendista. I remember the day he told me, fighting back tears, that he had resigned, that he couldn't stand so much hatred. I didn't know what to say. I commiserated with him, pointed out that these were probably temporary misunderstandings, suggested that perhaps these small sacrifices were necessary for the country to be liberated. Later, back home, a stone's throw from where he was staring into space, right there next door to him, I lamely told myself, recalling his anger and frustration, that I had never done anything directly to hurt him.

But nor did I denounce the way he was being treated, recognize that it was the very way in which I was treating (and I was one of the most tolerant and empathetic of the militants!) many of my own colleagues who legitimately disagreed with me and whom I publicly excoriated and privately dismissed as traitors. I did not take the opportunity to comprehend that we were being insufficiently democratic, that we were accelerating the revolution beyond what was reasonable, that we had swept people like Don Patricio under the carpet of history, as if they didn't count, as if their dissidence was to be despised instead of valued, as if consensus were a crime. Though the fact that the other side, the Chino Urquidi side, was even more violent and sectarian and power-hungry certainly made a change in our own attitude all the more difficult.

I have written in this memoir how exuberant that experience of liberation was, how nothing could compare to the thrill of watching the poor of the earth take possession of their destiny.

It was difficult, it would take years to understand that what was so exhilarating to us was menacing to those who felt excluded from our vision of paradise. We evaporated them from meaning, we imagined them away in the future, we offered them no alternative but to join us in our pilgrimage or disappear forever, and that vision fueled, I believe, the primal fear of the men and women who opposed us. At the time, full as I was with the wonder of new voices and lives flooding into the future and inseminating it, I barely gave a thought to what they felt, people we called *momios*, mummies, because they were so conservative, prehistoric, bygone, passé, that they were, as far as we concerned, already dead. We ended up including in that definition millions of Chileans who, like Don Patricio, were on our side, who should have been with us on that journey into the new land and who, instead, came to fear for their safety and their future. We turned the Don Patricios into Chino Urquidis.

As the years of exile and defeat taught me what it means to learn abruptly that you can be entirely accidental, everything you did or believed in reduced to mistaken dust, your body spared by those in power only because they have squeezed the soul out of it, I came to understand the dread our opponents must have lived through as they saw their world collapse. But at the time I was fanatical, deaf to their affliction. I didn't really care if they were scared. The truth is that we came to enjoy their fear, the thrill that power over them and over destiny gave us. We ended up savoring the fact that for once they were on the receiving end of the shit of history instead of doling it out. We did not realize how that fear would grow until we were bloated into monsters in their minds, monsters who had to be destroyed.

It is the recognition of these mistakes and many more that the balcony at La Moneda is demanding of us, demanding of me. As the years go by, I will reluctantly, painstakingly, corner that young man and those three years he lived, I will slowly turn him into the man who writes these words, I will tell him what I have learned from this defeat, how I was one of those who inadvertently helped to bring the black hole of that balcony into being. I will tell him that he should not have trusted the state to solve all the problems of Chile or the revolution to solve all his problems. I will tell him that it was unfair to burden a whole people with his salvation. I will tell him that the desire for purity may lead to fanaticism and ethnic strife and fundamentalism. I will tell him that the poor do not need to be represented by a paternal voice, no matter how benevolent. I will tell him that if you reduce everything to politics and ideology, you end up totalizing, squeezing the mystery out of life and explaining away too easily what at times has no explanation, you end up not leaving space for your own imperfections. I will tell him he should not have turned a blind eye to human-rights violations in socialist countries out of insensitivity and political expediency. I will tell him how women were postponed in the revolution and how we did not even conceive that our attitude toward nature was one that pillaged and polluted it.

I will tell him this and much more from the retrospect of the future, everything that I think he did wrong.

But there is one thing I will not tell him, that young man I used to be. I will not tell him, I have never told that alter ego of mine in the past, that he was wrong to rebel.

Young man: you were right to rebel.

I will reach that certainty in that very police van on the way to the airport.

Next to me, being expelled along with me, is a worker whose real name I do not remember and whom I shall call Juan.

He was one of the scant handful of workers who had sought refuge in the Argentine Embassy to save his life. We had struck up a conversation several times. He had worked, he told me, in a factory that produced canned food (I think it was canned food) and when the Unidad Popular revolution had come, he and his fellows had found themselves facing a major crisis. During Allende's first year in office, the President's policies had created an economic boom: increased salaries and benefits led to skyrocketing consumption and that led, in turn, to a major increment in production. So, more goods sold and a better life for Juan and his co-workers, right? Not at all. The owner of the factory, opposed to the revolution, even if it did not threaten his property, had decided to sabotage production: he had stopped reordering machine parts, he had blocked distribution deals that were already in place, he refused to hire new workers and threatened to fire those who complained. He should have been making money in buckets and instead was secretly preparing bankruptcy proceedings, pulling his capital out of the industry, getting ready to flee the country. The workers had watched this class warfare patiently for months and, finally, when the owner had announced he was shutting down the whole operation, they had taken over the premises. It was the only way to save their jobs and keep producing the food that Chile needed. Allende's government intervened in the conflict, negotiated compensation for the owner, and put the workers in control. Juan had been elected to head the council that, for a couple of years, ran that factory, and in spite of inevitable mistakes, it had been an economically successful venture.

But it was another kind of success that stirred in Juan when he spoke to me about that time: the Chilean revolution had given him a chance to prove his dignity as a full human being, had dared to conceive through him and millions of others the pale possibility of a world where things did not have to be the way they had always been.

That is why the rulers of the world had reacted with such ferocity.

And Juan understood this and explained it to me with chilling simplicity that day as we crossed the city of Santiago on our way to exile.

"We are paying," he told me, gesturing toward the streets filled with subdued citizens and rampant military patrols, in the general direction of the factory that was at that very moment being returned to the owner, who had come back to exercise his dominion. "We are being punished. We are paying for our joy."

He understood that General Pinochet's military coup was meant to return to their previous owners the levers of economic and political power. But it was just as clear to him that the counterrevolution was conceived as an admonitory lesson for those who had surfaced from the depths of anonymity and set themselves squarely in the middle of a history which was not supposed to belong to them.

His body and the body of all our *compañeros* were, ultimately, being disciplined for an act of the imagination. Pinochet was trying to make him and millions like him admit that they had been mistaken—not so much in their tactics as in their human strategy, the very rebellion itself, the fact that they had dared to dream of an alternative to the life charted out for them since before their birth.

Pinochet was preparing the world as we know it now, more than twenty years later, where the word *revolution* has been relegated to ads for jogging shoes and greed has been proclaimed as good and profits have become the only basis to judge value and cynicism is the prevailing attitude and amnesia is vaunted and justified as the solution to all the pain of the past.

Wasn't that the ultimate message that the black hole of that balcony was sending me? Wasn't that the real blindness—not our in-capacity to see the signs of death on the wall, not our eyes shut to our own limitations and blunders, but the more virulent blindness to where the sorry planet was going? That Allende's revolution, rather than being the wave of the future, was the last gasp of a past that was dying, that the coming twenty years would confirm that we had been swimming against the tide of world history, that General Augusto Pinochet's coup was inevitable, even if we had been im-maculately blameless, even if we had not made even one of our innumerable miscalculations, because we were the dinosaurs, we were the ones buried in the past, we were the ones who wanted to resist globalization, we were the ones who wanted to base our lives on something other than neo-liberal competition and individualism, we were the ones who did not see what humanity really was and really wanted.

Isn't that what Juan was being taught?

Never to dream himself as an alternative?

And yet, no matter how many mistakes he had made, we had made, I had made, we did not deserve that balcony at La Moneda, the black hole in that balcony which threatened to engulf us all.

I was not willing then, in that van, and I am not willing now, so many years later, to tell Juan that his joy was unreal.

That was the limit of how much I was willing to change.

Don't get me wrong: I have, of course, been enormously trans-formed since the day I stood under Allende's balcony and saw myself as the channel for all the suppressed voices of the universe, and they are changes I celebrate, changes I needed to learn from history.

But I do not repent of having been that person.

Am I deluding myself one more time? Am I defending that past because I do not dare to cut myself loose, because I fear for the continuity of my identity if I let go of that period in my life when I found a home against death? Is this the last stand of my imagination as it tries to fool that death which came to visit me so early in childhood and has never left?

Perhaps.

If so, if this is one more attempt to imagine the future as it does not and cannot ever exist, so be it. This is the bedrock of who I am: a man who cannot live in this world unless he believes there is hope.

I had come to that conclusion about myself after a long journey through many countries and many languages.

It had been tested, since the coup, by death.

In the years to come, it would be tested by something far more dangerous, a reality that, like death, I had never really encountered before, even if I had filled long literary pages writing about its existence: I was going to find myself face-to-face with the undeniable reality of evil.

One more story.

In the voyages that were to come, that still awaited me, I met a woman who had been tortured in Chile.

What saved her at the worst moments, she told me, was her unending repetition of some lines by Neruda or Machado—strange, she couldn't remember the author or the lines themselves anymore—verses that contained water in them, trees, she thought, something about the wind. What matters is that she concentrated on them fiercely so she could make clear to herself over and over how different she was from the men who were making her suffer. She discovered that, inside her, beyond those hands and what they were doing to her, there was a space all her own which could remain intact. One small zone in the world that she could keep from them. Some dead poet was providing her with this shield, with this guardian angel of language. As she silently repeated those words to herself, she expected to be extinguished forever.

Who can doubt that at this very moment, in this abominable world where General Pinochet is alive and Allende is dead, there are many others just like her, anonymous, unknown people, enduring other attempts to obliterate them, suck them into the black hole of history? Perhaps they will not survive, as she did, to tell the tale. But perhaps they are also sending us messages. We cannot be sure.

We can only answer those words as if they are being transmitted.

We do know that the woman, even if there was nobody there, was hoping to be heard. Not only by herself. And what she was saying was simple. She was not willing, even if nobody was listening, even if her fate was to disappear from the face of the earth, to be treated like an object. She was not willing to let others narrate her life and her death.

While there is one person like her in this world, I will find myself defending both her right to struggle and our obligation to remember.

What more can I say?

A FINAL CHAPTER IN WHICH WE
DEAL WITH LIFE AND LANGUAGE
AND DEATH ONE MORE TIME

English made a comeback even before I left Chile.

I was still in the Argentine Embassy when the language I had sworn never again to use crept again into my life, when the America I had supposedly flushed out of my system confronted me with the future and whispered to me what it means to be at the mercy of more powerful others in a world you no longer control.

It is noon.

I am sunning myself in the garden of the embassy, my eyes closed, the blanket I inherited from the dead rolled under my head as a pillow, when I hear a gringa voice cutting through the spring Santiago air. It must be an illusion, I say to myself, there are no *norte-americanos* in this embassy, only representatives of every failed revolution in Latin America, to which ours is now added, a continent that is closing, Uruguay a year ago, Bolivia two months ago, Perón is returning to power with a right-wing agenda in Argentina, and soon there will be no place to go in Latin America, soon we Chileans will ourselves roam a foreign land living vicariously, revolutionaries without a people to swim in, we will have become these very exiles I now contemplate. All this goes through my head as I strain my ears to listen to that woman's voice with its atrocious U.S. accent and its garbled Spanish grammar, like an echo of what I must have sounded like when I arrived in Chile nineteen years before. That voice, whosoever it may be, is giving somebody orders—a gardener, a contractor, a maintenance man, she is telling him how she wants all this fixed up once these people leave.

I open my eyes, I shield them from the sun, I prop myself up on an elbow.

A middle-aged lady is standing almost immediately above me, scanning the refugee-infested garden as if she had already swept the intruders from her mind, oblivious to the screams of three Salvadoran brats playing tag, whom we have dubbed *los termitas*, the termites, because they destroy everything they touch. They have gnawed at the legs of a grand piano in the embassy ballroom, they have scratched every wall, they have flooded the bathrooms; we are sure that if they ever return to their homeland they will singlehandedly rid it of the right-wing dictatorship which afflicts El Salvador. Their shrill shouts are getting closer and I rise, slightly alarmed, clutching my blanket, hoping they won't try to steal it, but I am relieved to see them veer away. They have discerned the formidable well-dressed lady in the middle of the garden and some canny instinct has warned them to steer clear of that powerhouse as she continues to give instructions. I realize who she is. A few days ago, a new Argentine Ambassador arrived, and the rumor was that his wife would soon put in an appearance, and here she is, though none of the know-it-alls had even suggested that she might be American or that the first thing she would do was inspect the grounds to make plans on how to change the landscape ruined by the hundreds of bodies that have made this their transitory home.

Now, from a faraway corner of the garden, not far from the wall where my sleeping bag had miraculously come out of the sky, a warbling *quena* breaks into a melody. The Indian flute is out of tune, or whoever is playing it is out of practice; this is not a happy sound. Its sour disharmony interrupts the decrees of the ambassador's wife. She turns in that general direction with distaste, wrinkles her nose, turns back, mutters to herself in English: "If music be the food of love . . ."

"Play on," I suddenly pipe up, also in English. "Give me excess of it." The lady looks around, surprised, unable to apprehend who might be quoting *Twelfth Night* back at her. I press my advantage: "Though in this case," I add, "perhaps Shakespeare was right and the appetite may indeed sicken and so die."

Now she focuses her eyes on me. I see myself as she must see me, ill-shaven, clutching a smelly blanket, my hair unkempt, lanky and hungry and sad. I see her astonishment. If King Lear in person had popped out from behind the bushes, she could not have been more flabbergasted.

I stand up and hold out my hand.

She takes it, has no choice, looks at it as if it were the stump of a beggar.

"Ariel Dorfman," I say as she shakes it.

"But you're . . . You're American. What are you doing here?"

Here. As if to say among the barbarians. In this place which the Communist barbarians, the human termites, the Latin American refuse, have desecrated.

"I *am* American. Latin American. *Soy chileno.*"

We chat for a while, and there under the warm sun of Santiago I feel the winter of her discontent melting, made glorious by the sun of my conversation. I can tell that my desultory appearance has been rendered insignificant by my culture, my English chitchat. We prattle as if we were at a cocktail party in her garden, the sort she will be holding as soon as the riffraff depart. I had started the exchange on a whim, almost sarcastically, as if to upset her categorizing and show her that all these revolutionaries were not what she seemed to think, but now, as our conversation continues, I find myself liking her. I find her to be pleasant, sophisticated, also genuinely interested in trying to make life easier for her unsolicited guests. She is delighted to have someone to question. Are the children all right? (The answer is yes, they are the only sane ones here.) Is the food adequate? (The answer should be no, the man in charge of feeding us is pocketing a good part of what he should be spending, but I don't mention this. I'd rather play it safe, prefer to say, "Could be better.") Is there anything I need?

This is the question I had been waiting for. I am dying for a shower, I could swoon for a nice meal, I will go crazy if I have to spend one more day in here without being able to set foot on the streets of my city. But all that pales in comparison with what I desperately want, what every last person in this place would kill for: a phone.

But I have to be careful. It's illegal for me or any of the other refugees to contact anybody directly from the embassy. If we are caught, it could spoil our relations with the staff that cares for us. One of them has warned us that any such attempt might even lead to our expulsion from the grounds, a threat we do not take too seriously, though you never know . . .

I don't mention my need to her immediately. I figure that this is the first of several meetings and that I should wait. I am already, even before I leave Chile, receiving a crash course in exile: when you are a beggar, everybody who approaches is judged by the jingle of coins in his pockets, the glint of charity in her eyes, what they can give, what they can offer, what you can get, the world turned into a shopping list of needs.

My patience pays off.

A few days later, the ambassador's wife leads me to the forbidden elevator that takes me up to the forbidden third floor of the building and gestures generously toward a forbidden phone and then discreetly leaves me to myself.

I am able to make the calls I have been dreaming about since I came to the embassy, since I have been secluded here. To speak to Angélica, to my parents, to my friends—they breathe life and hope back into me, they guardedly give me advice and information, they transmit the country to me as they will in the seventeen years to come, bit by bit, like a puzzle of whispers that has to be reassembled in the country of my head. And in the weeks to come, I will perform a similar service for many of my fellow castaways. Through it all, my hostess never intrudes, never asks for anything, never suggests that she wants anything from me except a chance to use her English, to reminisce about our America. That's all: the chance for two expatriates to exchange memories.

That's how it happened.

That's how English started to flirt again with my mind. I could feel the ferocious tide of exile pulling at me, I could already feel the power of this repudiated language, and if its power here is so colossal, what temptations will it offer me when I venture into that outer world?

It is there, in the embassy, even before exile creates a distance from my country, even before I've left it, that I start a new stage in my journey, that I begin to concede that history may be forcing me, against my will, to become bilingual, it is in that embassy that I first explore the possibility of living in two languages, using each one for a different community. It is there that I set out on the road to this hybrid mongrel of language who writes this so many years later. It will not happen immediately: I will cling to my Spanish during my first years of wandering, as other refugees cling to the photos of parents who will die back home and never be seen again, but my other language, my despised English self, will never be far away, always waiting for me with the same tenacity as Spanish did during its years of exclusion. It will crawl back into my life by offering me, as it did in the embassy, the one service I cannot refuse: to use my mastery of its syntax and vocabulary to help free the Latin American country I now call home and speed me back to a place where I would have no more use for it.

It all begins there, at the moment when I seduce the ambassador's wife with my English in order to get to a phone. How, then, can I refuse to continue using it in the future when far more urgent situations arise, when a friend back in Chile is facing a firing squad, when the resistance is pressing for funds for a clandestine newspaper, when a journalist needs to be briefed, when a committee needs a report, when a TV producer is looking for somebody to debate the representatives of Pinochet, when *The New York Times* asks for an op-ed piece, who am I to reject the most important language in the world when I speak it like a native? And once it has reentered my life, once English has again established a foothold in my existence, who is to drive it away?

Time is on its side, history is on its side, and the years will pass and I will not be returning to my Chilean homeland so soon, until the day comes when English grows indispensable and my two languages call a truce after forty years of raging for my throat, my two languages decide to coexist. But how I became a bigamist of language, how I shared them or they shared me, how I married them both, is in the future, as I head North and look to the South where I can no longer live, the South to which I finally returned in many ways and under many guises, regaining it in spite of Pinochet, my country which, again because of a history I did not control, I was once more to lose.

So this is where this part of my life ends? Poised on the verge of a bilingual future, about to plunge into a world that will force me, in order to survive, to accept that I belong to two cultures, that I straddle a space between two cultures?

There is still something left to tell.

I still have to return to Argentina, the place of my birth, the place from which I set out on this journey in 1945, the place I would have called home if my father had not been forced to flee, back then.

That is where I head, flying over the cordillera, westward back to Argentina in early December of 1973, reversing my first voyage, when I flew eastward to Chile so many years ago on my way to the States.

My whole family was waiting for me at the Buenos Aires airport, father and mother and sister and cousins and uncle and aunt—and, of course, Angélica and Rodrigo.

So were the Argentine police.

They arrested me, interrogated me for a few hours, finally let me go. Behave, they said, be a good boy, don't give us any trouble.

I took their warning to heart.

It would have been perfect to have remained in Argentina. My wonderful parents were resettling there, I had many friends, the language was Spanish, publishing houses were interested in my work, and, most important of all, it was right next to Chile, the ideal place from which to conspire against Pinochet. But my interrogation by the police confirmed what I already knew from rumors: President Perón, just back from years of exile in Madrid, was veering strongly to the right. I could see that, in the months to come, he would acquiesce to the cleansing of his country of subversives, the very people who had fought to bring him back to power, I could see that I would be one of the victims of this massacre. I told my Argentine friends that I thought we were heading for a calamity, that this country was going to repeat the Pinochet model, but they vehemently disagreed—just as I had disagreed when foreigners had warned me during the Allende years in Santiago, my friends in Argentina answered what I had answered, that there was no danger, you don't know the country.

I wasn't going to wait for them to wake up. I could recognize death now when I saw it approaching, I was learning its lessons fast. And I knew that I had to get out of Argentina with my family before it was too late.

Of course, it's not enough to see death coming. You also have to be lucky.

I had no travel documents: the Chileans would not give me a passport, and when I tried to make use of my former nationality, get documentation from the Argentinians, they stonewalled me. The bureaucrats insisted that they could find no evidence that I had been born in Buenos Aires; the birth certificate I brought to them, they said was invalid. No matter how hard I tried, I always came up against a blind wall, an indifferent clerk, a sarcastic look. Somebody with a lot of power was blocking my application, somebody had me on his list, somebody did not want me to leave for a place where I would be safe.

It was many weeks before a powerful congressman, an old friend of my father's, was able to set up an interview with the Police Commissioner of Buenos Aires to see if he could help.

When I was ushered in, the Police Commissioner was working at his desk, signing papers. He gestured to the chair, without looking up, and kept on, paper after paper. I sat down. When he was done, his eyes came up from his desk, met my gaze. He watched me for a moment. Neither of us said a word.

"I've been told you're a writer," he said.

From my briefcase, I extracted a novel that had just been published in Argentina, that had won a major literary prize. It was called *Moros en la Costa* (*Hard Rain* in its English translation) and it had been written during a few months at the end of 1972. I had, in fact, been planning to write a different novel, in which I imagined a futuristic Latin American country governed by a dictator whom I called El Grande—who had come to power in a coup and had then turned the land into a laboratory for foreign corporations. I could not know, of course, that my mind was anticipating with icy and pessimistic precision what General Pinochet one year later would be meticulously doing to my country. And yet some part of me must have known. When, in September of 1972, I took a few months off from the university to write my fictitious tyranny of the future, I found myself unable to go on, I found myself rejecting the very notion of putting those images of horror down on paper and unloading them on the public. To invent a country governed by El Grande was to admit that we were going to lose. So I betrayed my literary vision and refused to proceed, and dismissing my apprehensions as fraudulent, meaningless, and anti-historical, I devoted the next few months to writing *Hard Rain*, in which I prophesied that we would overcome and that Chile would be free. Again, as in the case of Susana la Semilla, the only freedom that my creation managed to materialize was my own.

I used that novel to get the Chilean authorities to give me the safe-conduct they were refusing me. They had informed the attaché who was in charge of getting us all out of there as soon as possible that I could rot in that building for all they cared, that they wanted to put me on trial for subverting the youth of the country. (I could envisage the trial in mock-Perry Mason style: Is it true, Mr. Dorfman, that you accuse Donald Duck—Donald Duck?!—of being pernicious to our children?) And I might have withered in that embassy, still be there for all I know, if I had not told the ambassador's wife that my novel was scheduled to be published in Buenos Aires in a few weeks' time. She judiciously passed the information to the staff with the suggestion (which I had slipped into our conversation) that we could use this to turn up the pressure on the adamant Chileans. Let this Dorfman go to Argentina, the Argentines said to their colleagues, as reported back to me by my Lady of the Embassy. Neutralize him, she said that they said. Exiles are a dime a dozen and nobody cares a damn about them; but a prize-winning author detained in an embassy surrounded by soldiers ready to kill him commands almost heroic stature. Why promote his damn book?

They had seen the absurd logic of that argument and had let me leave Chile.

So this figment of my imagination had helped me to escape my adopted country, and now maybe it would impress this Police Commissioner enough to help me escape the country of my birth.

"If you wouldn't mind," I said, "I'd like to inscribe this novel to you."

He nodded and watched as I wrote a few devoted and hypocritical lines in the book, and received it from my hands without a smile.

"I'll read it," he promised.

I hoped not. It was the first time in my life, I think, that I prayed that someone would *not* read me. I wanted him to have it in his hands, admire it, but not open it and delve into what I was narrating. I didn't want him to read that hymn to the brilliant future of the revolution, and I didn't want him to read the signs of foreboding and violence and death that had crept into the text unawares, that belied its sunny vision of a victory that had not happened. I didn't want this man who held my fate in his hands to think I might be dangerous.

"It's a bit experimental," I said, to see if that discouraged him. He said nothing. Waited for me to exlain myself. "It's a series of book reviews," I said, "by nonexistent authors about novels that I made up. And the reality of the texts themselves interrupts the reviews."

"A bit experimental," he said.

"Yes."

"Not like your book on Donald Duck."

My heart sank. My Disney diatribe was hounding me. It was futile to try to hide who I was, make believe I was a confused Argentinian writer who happened to lurch by mistake into a political swamp on the other side of the Andes. I could tell it: this man wasn't going to help me.

And then that Police Commissioner surprised me. He carefully put my book away and turned to me and for the first time he smiled. And said the words I had been waiting to hear, which I had lost all hope of hearing.

"And what," he asked, "can I do for you?"

One week later, I had a passport. Just in time. The day I was leaving for the airport, my father informed me that the Police Commissioner who had saved my life had been relieved of his duties. Maybe he had been as blind to his future as I had been to mine.

As the plane rose up from Buenos Aires, I fought the weary certainty that history was repeating itself endlessly, that perhaps I was meant for exile. For the second time in my life I was being forced to leave the city of my birth, except that this time I was the one who was fleeing death and by my side was a son who was losing his country because of me, this time it was my wife who, like my mother, was following her husband into exile. Maybe this was the fate of my family, maybe this was a curse I couldn't escape. Twice I had made the attempt to settle down, twice I had adopted a country and a culture and a language, and both times I had found myself fleeing, I had found myself homeless in spite of all my efforts, and now it was all going to begin again, all over again. Except that this time I was no longer innocent. My first act of exile back then had been mischievously to hide my baby shoes in a hotel in Santiago. Nothing was left of that child. His adulterated older self had passed by that hotel, by the plaza that hotel overlooked, I had passed through there on my way to another exile, trapped in a police van, about to be expelled, forcing my eyes to drink in that jagged hole in the balcony of La Moneda, saying goodbye to that child I had been, to what had been left of that child inside, saying goodbye to the country that was now forbidden to me.

But not for long.

I was not going to let that sorrow destroy me. I was not going to let that hole claim me. On that plane, high above the pampas, I told myself that I would be back, I told myself that nothing could stop me from returning to my land.

I was consoling myself with one of the basic myths of the species, a story that every civilization has told itself since the beginning of history: there is a place, one place, where you truly belong, a place that is often but not always the place where you were born, and that place is akin to paradise. Paradise, a word that, originally, meant a walled-in garden, full of fruit. To lose that promised land is like dying, and to return there is to be redeemed. I swore to myself, up there above Latin America, that I would return, that I would, like the outcast son or daughter in the fairy tales, return and save the kingdom which was in grave danger, I swore that I would be back.

That was the myth of my return with which I tried to keep sane and whole on that plane that was taking me farther and farther away from my origins.

And yet I was being tempted, right then and there, at that very moment, by another myth that is just as pervasive. This story goes— and once again, all nations have told it—that to create a new society, to give a real start to anything worthwhile, one must leave the place of one's birth. One cannot grow unless one breaks out and learns and opens up to what is strange and foreign and fertile. Every founder of every new civilization has been a hero who has been expelled from his home. In this myth, salvation can only be attained through wandering.

In one myth, you find immortality by connecting with the past, with the ancestors who have died. In the other, you defeat death by creating a new dynasty somewhere else, imagining the generations yet to be born.

Which will be my story?

Look at me there, above the clouds, above a Latin America where death is spreading, poisoning the waters of the Argentine city of my birth and waiting at the gate to the Chilean city of my dreams, look at me almost twenty-nine years to the day when I set off from Buenos Aires to the United States as a child, there I am at the end of this journey into life which has also been a parallel journey into death, look at me with my two languages and my two cultures, look at me swearing to go back, look at me excited to have the world in front of me, look at me as those two myths of human existence dispute me, the myth that promised me that I would return for good, the myth that whispered that I would wander forever, there I am, unable to divine which of these two contains the ultimate truth of my life.

I don't know the answer then.

One circle in my life is ending and another circle is about to begin and the answer is not clear, as the plane goes up and up and up into the swirling blue sky of exile, as I head North again and the South begins to recede into memory, I do not know then as I do not know now if that circle will ever close.

November 1, 1996

ACKNOWLEDGMENTS

Writing is the loneliest of activities—but even in the most solitary moments, most authors are aware that we labor with others nearby nurturing our existence as well as the words themselves. If this is true of every book, it is even more so of a book which also happens to be a life.

To mention the many men and women who made both this book and this life possible would sorely test the patience of readers who by now may have had enough of the author's incessant inspirational encounters with other members of the species. I cannot end, however, without at least naming those who have been closest to me during all the long years it has taken me to complete this project.

No one will be surprised that I start with Angélica. She is my first reader, my best reader, my best friend—and my existence and my words could not have been shaped without her frank, careful, stubborn probing of the first draft, the second draft, the third one, the many versions and revisions and added paragraphs and recomposed chapters with which I would come running to her, in search of a blessing. I could never have made sense of how it was that I escaped death if I had not been protected by my Angélica, who, quite simply, kept me alive.

My extraordinary parents, Fanny and Adolfo, provided me with many of the memories and stories in this book—not to mention the life of its author. I am glad that they are still around, and very lucid, at eighty-eight and ninety, respectively, to read these pages that they have been instrumental in creating. Nor would this book have existed without the vitality and encouragement of my two sons. Rodrigo, who has became my collaborator on films and plays, offered many suggestions and was always there to help me think my way out of a dilemma, keep it simple, he would say, make it absolutely concrete, all his generous advice—even though he was the first to warn me that anybody who attempts to write his own life must surely be insane or will be before it is over. Joaquín, who was living with us while this book was crawling its way into the light, managed to keep me upbeat through the whole damn gut-wrenching process and was the first to suggest—and then continually remind me—that I would be unable to finish it if I did not play more rock music while I was working. His hints were always welcome—as was his freewheeling insomniac fellowship at four o'clock in the morning. And, of course, the newest member of our family, Melissa, Rodrigo's wife, was the merriest company I could hope for. What would I have done without her eternal dada optimism?

My editor, John Glusman, has volunteered his constant support and intelligence since I first told him in his office—sometime in 1994, I believe it was—about the frenzied project I was about to embark upon. His initial enthusiasm never flagged—and when it came to the editing process, his detailed comments and observations, invariably constructive and sensitive, were crucial in shortening, clarifying, sharpening this text, forcing me always to do better. My thanks to him for believing in this intellectual adventure and calming me down when all sorts of crises and calamities descended upon me.

Bridget Love, my agent at the Wylie Agency, who has represented me and this book with dogged loyalty and infinite forebearance, deserves more than these few words of gratitude. She stood by me, patiently, efficiently, during these years. And she did so with a great sense of humor. I am also grateful to Deborah Karl, my former agent, whose belief in me and the possibility of this book never wavered. I deeply appreciate her support during almost a decade, as I do the backing of Andrew Wylie himself, whose advice has always been crucial when needed.

Most of this volume was written during a prolonged sabbatical from my duties at Duke University, where I teach each spring semester. Without the understanding of Deans Roy Weintraub and Bill Chafe, of Provost John Strobehn, and of my dear colleagues and friends Fred Jameson, chair of the Literature Program, and Walter Mignolo, chair of Romance Studies, as well as the quiet company of Rob Sikorski and Josefina Tiryakian of International Studies, this book would have been much more difficult to conceive and write. Not to mention the invaluable help—and *amistad*—of Debbie Jakubs in the library.

Margaret Lawless, my assistant, has been central to this enterprise, as well as to so many others. She has provided material support—and resolute cheerfulness—beyond the call of duty. Day after day, she made sure I had the time to deal with this text. If I was able to concentrate and write and rewrite, it was because I knew she was there, shielding me, taking care of a multitude of problems.

Nor can I forget the hospitality of John, Cathy, and Julia Friedman, who gave Angélica and me refuge one summer in their ranch in New Mexico and discreetly never even asked to see the pages I was pounding out. Elizabeth Lira and Deena Metzger, like sisters to me, provided me with other sorts of sanctuary and advice during these years.

And all the others? My friends in Durham, in Chile, in Holland, in England, in Frankfurt, in Washington, D.C., and, yes, in New York, the ones who heard me out, who were simply smiling by my side—what can I say, except that I hope that when you have read *Heading South, Looking North,* you will feel that the *cariño,* the affection you gave me all this time, was worth it, that the book I can now give you in gratefulness and joy was, after all, worth writing.

June 1997

POSTSCRIPT

When this book was finished and in the process of being edited, my mother died.

If readers find gentleness in my words, if you find gentleness in my life, think well of her.